Advance praise for *Always Be Testing: The Complete Guide to Google™*

*I can tell you two things. The first thing is: Testing works. If you're not doing it wel[l...]
The second? Bryan Eisenberg knows what he's talking about. Time to get started, time to start testing.*
—Seth Godin, Author of *Meatball Sundae*

Always Be Testing is a very readable and practical guide to landing page testing from an experienced master practitioner. Bryan has emerged from the trenches with actionable advice and detailed testing tips that will make your cash register ring more often. Pick up a copy before your competitors do!
—Tim Ash, Author of Amazon's e-commerce bestseller *Landing Page Optimization: The Definitive Guide to Testing and Tuning for Conversions*

If you want to become an expert in website testing, this is the place to start. The book's depth and breadth are particularly impressive, from why testing matters to what and how to test. Bryan and John have combined years of experience in persuasive marketing with their deep knowledge of Google Website Optimizer to deliver actionable insights that will make rock stars out of any marketing team.
—Tom Leung, Senior Business Product Manager, Google Website Optimizer

This is the best collection of practical testing advice that is available today. If you want to get ahead in testing, then you and everyone involved in building and maintaining your website need to read it. Always Be Testing offers basic and advanced testing principles, based on years of experience, that help you optimize (with or without Google Website Optimizer) quickly and efficiently. The authors provide practical exercises to help you evaluate your site objectively, tools to help you identify what to test, and resources to expand your knowledge. This book should be required reading for anyone interested in helping online visitors achieve their goals—it easily can save you the time and expense of unproductive results that are due to common mistakes.
—Dylan Lewis, Senior Manager, Web Measurement, Intuit

By unlocking the secrets of Google Website Optimizer, Bryan Eisenberg and John Quarto-vonTivadar's clear prose combined with case studies allows any reader involved in an Internet business to go beyond the typical implementation and redefine their business goals and execution.
—Mike Smith, Senior Vice President, Forbes.com

This book provides not only valuable insight into the importance of website testing and how to undertake tests that provide meaningful data, but also strategies for dealing with website design and content elements that have a high-ranking advocate but that may be ineffective—or even counterproductive—when it comes to creating sales.
—Kurt Peters, Editor in Chief, *Internet Retailer*

Always Be Testing is the essential handbook that gets you testing and keeps you testing. In this game, the difference between Winners and Losers is that Winners take the time to figure out which of their ideas stink. Losers don't. This book is for everyone who wants to be a Winner!"
—Avinash Kaushik, Author of *Web Analytics: An Hour A Day*

Conversion is the Holy Grail for any online business. But testing for conversion—the competitive game changer—has always seemed boring, tedious, and complicated. With Always Be Testing, the job of testing your marketing is laid out in a practical fashion that anyone can grasp and do in a way that will practically guarantee your conversion success and blow away your competition. I'm a big fan of Website Optimizer, but this is the first thing I've read that really makes it seem practical and simple.

—John Jantsch, Author of *Duct Tape Marketing*

This is the 360-degree "firehose" of testing and optimization wisdom. Armed with the knowledge and wisdom in this book, you could run an A/B split between you and your competition and come out the winner. The result-oriented material in here is worth weeks of advanced marketing training.

—Sam Decker, Chief Marketing Officer, BazaarVoice

Testing has always been a bugbear, because it brings up so much data. And data is cumbersome. So we avoid intense testing. This book points out not just how to go about testing, but more importantly, what to test. And what's supercool is that you can be up and running in under 15 minutes! That, as you can imagine, is anything but cumbersome—and yes, it actually helps you get clear results instead of another mountain of data.

—Sean D'Souza, www.psychotactics.com

A: Bryan Eisenberg delivers the What, Why, and How of closing significantly more online sales. B: This is where Eisenberg's "Call to Action" philosophy gets tactical and you get better results from your website. C: Increase online sales without spending a dime or too much time. This book reveals what it takes and how to use it. D: "Keep on Testin,'" Eddie Kendricks and Robert Crumb. E: All of the above.

—Jim Sterne, Targeting.com

I have been living and breathing A/B and multivariate testing for the past few years, as illustrated in this book, and I have found that 25 years of experience in this field and best practices still fails in comparison to the feedback we get from our audience through testing. So many "best practices" mistakes can be prevented by simply putting the subject to a test and letting your audience tell you how they best interact with your product.

—Dino Bernardi, Vice President of Customer Experience, Experian Interactive

You've avoided serious testing on your website because it's expensive and hard to understand, right? Well, Google Website Optimizer has made testing free, and this book just took away your other excuse. Put this book down now, or you just might double your revenue and give your customers the website they've always wanted. Bryan and John tell you why and how to Always Be Testing. If you don't do it, your competitors will.

—Mike Moran, Coauthor of *Search Engine Marketing, Inc.*, and Author of *Do It Wrong Quickly: How the Web Changes the Old Marketing Rules*

Behind every great sales team is a marketer who understands the power of testing. Let's face it, sales teams would get no leads without a marketing team that expertly knew how to convert a visitor into a "close." Always Be Testing by Bryan Eisenberg teaches marketers just that ... how effective testing leads to a higher close rate at the very first moment of customer engagement.

—Jim Kukral, Internet Marketing Consultant, www.jimkukral.com

Always Be Testing needs to be every web managers' and marketers' mantra. Testing doesn't have to be expensive and complicated to be effective. Always Be Testing is more than a how-to guide. Bryan Eisenberg and John Quarto-vonTivadar provide a valuable, easy-to-use framework to decide what to test, how to test, and how to implement the findings. This will be one of the most dog-eared books in your library.
—Seth Romanow, Vice President and Chief Marketing Officer, Rainmaker Systems

During slow economic times, retailers of all shapes and sizes are trying to find affordable ways to bolster conversion, leapfrog the competition, and enhance the customer experience. The way to achieve this is with proper A/B and multivariate testing, and Bryan and John do a spectacular job of mapping out testing best practices that are easy to follow and implement. Bryan has been a great speaker and resource to the Shop.org community for many years, and this is just one more example of Bryan sharing his wealth of knowledge and experience. Always Be Testing—buy it, live it, love it.
—Larry Joseloff, Vice President of Content, Shop.org

Any marketer who understands the Web will keep a copy of this book on the desk at all times.
—Pinny Gniwisch, Founder EVP Marketing, www.ice.com

For years I have been telling anyone who will listen that "If you're not doing some type of testing, you're not really doing web analytics!" Well, apparently my friend Bryan Eisenberg has been listening! Always Be Testing is by far the most definitive work on the subject of website testing and optimization ever written. More importantly, Bryan, John, and Lisa manage to make this critical-but-occasionally-tedious subject palatable, using clear language and tons of helpful examples. So now instead of jumping up and down and yelling at people to "start testing," I can simply pass out copies of this great book. Thanks Bryan!
—Eric Peterson, Chief Executive Officer and Principal Consultant, Web Analytics Demystified, Inc.

Forget best practices *says Bryan Eisenberg,* every company has a different optimal strategy. *To get your suits and geeks on the same page, you need data, not intuition. Eisenberg's new book shows how to use Google Website Optimizer to get that data by refining website alternatives to optimize conversion rates. With his trademark style and humor, Eisenberg makes the complex math, like adequate sample size and statistical power sound easy. The most valuable part of the book is the second half, where he shows 30 factors to test (color, images, headlines, calls to action. . .) with over 250 alternatives to experiment with to maximize conversions.*
—Andrew B. King, Author of *Speed Up Your Site* and *Website Optimization*

A lot of "buzz" gets created around the latest powerful and sophisticated technologies/tools. Bryan Eisenberg and John Quarto-vonTivadar manage to demystify the cure-all perceptions of these tools by focusing on the often glossed-over, but truly more difficult, time-consuming, basic questions of how to form hypotheses for testing, how to come up with creative to test, and how to prioritize needle-moving activities.
—Bernardo de Albergaria, Vice President and General Manager, eCommerce, Citrix Online

This is the real deal. We've already tested Bryan's and John's ideas to optimize conversion, and they are winning ideas. This isn't pie-in-the-sky stuff. It's in-the-trenches, applicable, practical information that helps you confirm what you do know, discover what you don't know, and make more money online.
—Steve Snyder, Chief Operating Officer, CBS Interactive

Always Be Testing

Always Be Testing

THE COMPLETE GUIDE TO GOOGLE™ WEBSITE OPTIMIZER

BRYAN EISENBERG

JOHN QUARTO-voNTIVADAR

LISA T. DAVIS

Wiley Publishing, Inc.

Acquisitions Editor: WILLEM KNIBBE
Development Editor: TONI ACKLEY
Production Editor: DASSI ZEIDEL
Copy Editor: KIM WIMPSETT
Production Manager: TIM TATE
Vice President and Executive Group Publisher: RICHARD SWADLEY
Vice President and Executive Publisher: JOSEPH B. WIKERT
Vice President and Publisher: NEIL EDDE
Book Designer: CARYL GORSKA
Compositor: KATE KAMINSKI, HAPPENSTANCE TYPE-O-RAMA
Proofreader: KATHY POPE, WORD ONE
Indexer: JACK LEWIS
Cover Designers: ROB KIRBY, RYAN SNEED
Project Coordinator, Cover: MARGARET ROWLANDS

Library of Congress Cataloging-in-Publication Data

Eisenberg, Bryan.

Always be testing : the complete guide to Google website optimizer / Bryan Eisenberg, John Quarto-von Tividar.—1st ed.

p. cm.

ISBN 978-0-470-29063-7 (pbk.)

1. Internet marketing—Testing. 2. Electronic commerce. 3. Web site development. I. Quarto-von Tividar, John, 1964- II. Title.

HF5415.1265.E376 2008

658.8'72—dc22

2008022103

Dear Reader,

Thank you for choosing *Always Be Testing: The Complete Guide to Google Website Optimizer*. This book is part of a family of premium-quality Sybex books, all written by outstanding authors who combine practical experience with a gift for teaching.

Sybex was founded in 1976. More than 30 years later, we're still committed to producing consistently exceptional books. With each of our books, we're working hard to set a new standard for the industry. From the authors we work with to the paper we print on, our goal is to bring you the best books available.

I hope you see all that reflected in these pages. I'd be very interested to hear your comments and get your feedback on how we're doing. Feel free to let me know what you think about this or any other Sybex book by sending me an email at nedde@wiley.com; if you think you've found a technical error in this book, please visit http://sybex.custhelp.com. Customer feedback is critical to our efforts at Sybex.

Best regards,

Neil Edde
Vice President and Publisher
Sybex, an Imprint of Wiley

For Jeffrey Eisenberg

Your friendship, leadership, humor, and commitment made our mutual success a reality.

Acknowledgments

More than 10 years ago we began our journey to optimize websites. When all we had was imagination, our first clients believed us and let us test our theories on their websites and businesses. We are as grateful to them for allowing us to always be testing as we hope they are for the improvements. ■ To our past, present, and future clients, thank you for helping us discover why people do the things they do and for putting that knowledge to good use. ■ We couldn't succeed without the FutureNow team. We'd like to thank Jeffrey, Bill, Howard, Brian Number Two, Brian Number Three, Glen, Cinde, Esther, Jimmy, Robert, Marijayne, Karrie, Ed, Tegan, Jared, Ryan, and Jeff Number Three for all their work behind the scenes. We are indebted to our consultants who make our clients successful: Holly, Anthony, Jeff Number Two, Melissa, Peter, Dan, and Brandon. Josh, Morty, and Ron, you'll always be part of the team even if you have moved on to new endeavors. Thank you so much. ■ We'd also like to thank our friends and advisors Roy Williams, Pat Sullivan, Shmuel Gniwisch, L. Milton Woods, and Mal Watlington for your insights and encouragement. ■ An old joke goes: "How do writers feel about their editors?" The punch line is: "Like a fire hydrant feels about a dog." We beg to differ! The wonderful editorial staff at Sybex/Wiley—specifically Toni Zuccarini Ackley and Dassi Zeidel—has been amazing to work with. We've appreciated the hard work all the professional staff members have contributed. In particular, Willem Knibbe has made so much of this possible. ■ We must thank our friend and evangelist extraordinaire for Google, Avinash Kaushik, for making the introduction to Willem and for his drum-beating efforts in the wider community on behalf of the importance of testing, testing, testing. ■ We greatly appreciate working with the people at ContentRobot and especially want to thank Karen, Jackie, and Dana Rockel for their efforts on Website Optimizer's WordPress plug-in. ■ We thank Google for making Website Optimizer, a unique business tool, available to the world. There are many people from both Website Optimizer's and Google Analytics' teams who deserve to be mentioned, but we can't name everyone. However, Brett Crosby, Scott Crosby, Tom Leung, John Stona, K. Eric Vasilik, and Jon Diorio deserve special acknowledgment for their support. ■ None of our books would have been as successful if it weren't for the efforts of Mike Drew from Promote-a-Book. Our debt to him runs deep. ■ Our thanks to Dylan Lewis for introducing us to the Stinky. ■ So many others have helped make this book a reality. We apologize for not being able to include you individually, but please know you have our gratitude.

From Bryan: I would like to thank Stacey for making me complete and for her understanding when business takes me away from her and the kids. There is no greater blessing than Hannah and Sammy. They remind me to keep testing my world as I watch them explore theirs. Jeffrey is not only my brother and business partner, but also a great friend. I am eternally grateful to my mom for her support in good times and in bad.

From John: Having thanked my family in previous books, this time I would like to acknowledge my friends in the swing-dance community, none of whom have any idea just how much they really helped with this book: to John Lindo, for teaching me to dance with my heart; to Mario Robau, for teaching me to dance with my brain; and to Paula, Samantha, Keri, Laura, Kim, Michelle and John, Patrizia, Brian, and Festa, for teaching me to dance for nothing more than the love of dancing.

From Lisa: I would like to acknowledge the friends who have cheered me on and tolerated my diminished availability. I am forever indebted to Bryan, Jeffrey, and John for believing in me, allowing me to be part of the incredible FutureNow experience from the beginning, and embracing me as friend and family. Last, but never least, I am grateful beyond measure for my son, Zachary, who's been there through thick and thin, shouldered additional responsibilities while working hard to embark on his own life, and made me massive quantities of tea (the sixth food group). These are the people who have most helped me understand the true meaning of love.

About the Authors

Bryan Eisenberg   Bryan is the cofounder of FutureNow Inc. (www
.futurenowinc.com; OTCBB: FUTR.OB), an interactive marketing optimization firm.
FutureNow helps businesses generate more engagements, leads, subscriptions, and
sales by using its unique framework, Persuasion Architecture. FutureNow intelligently
uncovers improvement opportunities and creates road maps to enable your business to
integrate technology, creativity, and marketing talent to continuously improve your
marketing efforts.

He is a coauthor of *Call to Action* and *Waiting for Your Cat to Bark?*, both of which
made the best-sellers lists of the *Wall Street Journal, BusinessWeek, USA Today,* and
New York Times. He is a sought-after speaker at major business conferences worldwide,
having keynoted events for Search Engine Strategies, Shop.org, Direct Marketing Association, MarketingSherpa, E-consultancy, Webcom, and the Canadian Marketing Association. Bryan is proud that FutureNow's clients, including NBC Universal, GE, WebEx,
Overstock, and Dell, have consistently enjoyed dramatic improvement in sales using
FutureNow's Persuasion Architecture process. Bryan is also the publisher of the popular
marketing optimization blog *GrokDotCom* (www.grokdotcom.com).

John Quarto-vonTivadar   Having worked on NASA's Hubble
Space Telescope, when John says, "It's not rocket science," he does so with authority. An
inventor of Persuasion Architecture and one of the original shareholders in FutureNow,
John also spent many years trading on the floor of the Chicago Board of Trade. John
melds his business and technology background into his role as chief scientist at Future-
Now. He's a regular speaker at seminars and conferences in North America and Europe,
having written multiple books and white papers on various technology and marketing topics. His articles for *GrokDotCom* are consistently popular for their "deep dive" approach
to a topic. John's graduate work was in astrophysics, and when he needs a break from
thinking, he is a tango and competitive swing dancer.

Lisa T. Davis Lisa has been with FutureNow since the beginning, is one of the original shareholders, and fondly recalls the early days of the basement office, a crucible for the philosophies, perspectives, and practices that have informed everything since. In addition to white papers and reports, she authored *GrokDotCom* throughout its newsletter (nonblog) days and served overtly as the director of content and covertly as the chief cook and bottle-washer. She is a coauthor of *Persuasive Online Copywriting* (now out of print), *Call to Action*, and *Waiting for Your Cat to Bark?* When she's not thinking, breathing, and dreaming conversion rate marketing, she's performing early music on period instruments.

CONTENTS AT A GLANCE

Contents

Foreword

I've been in the analytics industry for more than a decade, and I'm amazed at the scope of its evolution. I've watched it grow from humble beginnings—freeware Unix scripts written by college kids; analog, odometer-style hit counters—to a fairly significant industry, complete with very powerful tools and publicly traded behemoths. By my reckoning, we are in the third wave of web analytics. The first wave started in the early days of the Web, when log analyzers designed primarily for IT teams and webmasters crunched raw web server data. The web mantra was "if you build it, they will come," and the primary purpose of web analytics was to show you if anyone did come.

In the second wave, the industry began to mature. Web analytics tools became more sophisticated, and as they did, they became more expensive. It resulted in an era of the haves vs. have-nots. Those who could afford the tools excelled online, and those who could not typically did not. The technology shifted to JavaScript-based page tags rather than log files. There was a clear focus on conversions and on successfully identifying ads that resulted in repeat sales. A relatively small number of sites had web analytics products installed, and even fewer people in the companies that owned those sites had access to the tools and the data. Web analytics tools were expensive and complex, and using them required significant expertise. Multivariate testing was generally left to the very top-tier sites whose entire businesses were focused on the Web and who could afford the resources to build their own testing platforms or hire one of the few firms in the space. Those who could afford the tools and the hard-to-find specialized knowledge needed to use them enjoyed a huge advantage.

Over the past few years, we have been seeing the shift to a third wave. It builds on the second wave and is represented by the movement away from expensive, heavy, and complex tools in favor of easier-to-use, free tools that are quickly becoming more capable than the previous generation's. It also marks the expansion of web analytics to encompass a larger tool set and conversion process. It includes offline data sources and multivariate testing solutions. This latest wave began with the introduction of Google Analytics (I may be biased here), but it is quickly becoming a larger movement. Google's free model is no longer the exception; it is increasingly the rule as both Microsoft and Yahoo enter the space with their own offerings. Perhaps the largest shift in this new model is that virtually everyone is now aware of and can afford a quality web analytics and multivariate testing platform.

Not only are we now seeing exponentially more businesses using these products than ever before, but many more people within those companies are now using these tools to drive decisions. People have heard about the promise of testing and analysis, and are learning how to implement them for the part of the business that they own. And the word is still spreading in this third wave.

The third wave values ideas over tools and creativity over specialized product expertise. With easy-to-learn, easy-to-deploy tools so readily available, the competitive advantage goes to those who can think creatively about online strategy. And so, the new online winners are marketing innovators and prolific testers.

In this new model, professional services are no longer a revenue-driving, up-sell tactic for vendors. So instead of creating overly complex tools that require a high degree of training, this new wave of vendors minimizes support costs by creating easy-to-use, friendly systems that are much more intuitive. And the trend in professional services is toward a marketplace of highly skilled third-party experts. These experts are global. They live in your city, speak your language, and accept your currency. Like professional search engine marketers and search engine optimizers, they leverage years of learning to help their clients avoid pitfalls and become competitive much more quickly than they would on their own.

The most practiced and knowledgeable of these experts are thought leaders in our industry. Some of the foremost among these are Bryan Eisenberg and John Quarto-vonTivadar of FutureNow, and I think you'll enjoy their creative insights in this book. Bryan and John think about marketing in new ways—they are the creators of the highly regarded Persuasion Architecture, after all—and they were some of the earliest consultants to use multivariate testing on the Web to improve their clients' bottom lines. I've known Bryan and John for years and shared panels with each of them at SES, eMetrics, WebmasterWorld, and other conferences. I've always enjoyed the straightforward, no-nonsense way they explain concepts, and it is no surprise that this book continues that tradition.

Ultimately, you, the reader, exemplify what is most exciting about the third wave: that the tools and processes have become much more accessible so businesses can compete not just on the size of their budgets, but by their commitment to creativity and testing. You are a few short pages away from learning how.

Brett Crosby
Group Manager, Google

Introduction

The concept of experimentation and testing is nothing new. Yet somehow, between the time we are children and the time we become fully fledged adults, we often come to overlook the excitement and value of experimenting with and testing our assumptions, following our intuition, and discovering the unknown.

As our business lives increasingly exert the need to improve our marketing efforts, this is not a time to take our assumptions and intuition for granted. Nor is this the time to place more stock in them than they may merit. Nor is this the time to cling to traditional marketing practices in an era that has turned many of them upside down.

This *is* the time to examine critically everything we do when we conduct business in the online environment. One of the best ways to realize our full potential is to roll up our sleeves, start testing, and make the commitment to "always be testing."

We've distilled 10 years of our experience helping companies optimize their websites to jump-start your testing efforts. A December 2006 JupiterResearch/ERI Executive Survey illustrated that the biggest testing challenge was demonstrating a return on investment for testing and creating test elements. This book will provide you with the framework, give you key areas to test, and show you how to set these areas up for maximum success.

In Part 1, "A Marketer's View of Testing: The Power of Optimization," we'll walk you through our process of designing your tests, show you how powerful testing can be, and teach you how to set up your tests using Google Website Optimizer.

Part 2, "What You Should Test," answers the biggest question everyone who ever thinks about testing has: What do I test? We'll examine more than 30 key factors that can impact conversion rates for websites (either retail, publishing, or lead generation) and give you more than 250 testing ideas. For each factor, we do the following:

- Explain the associated key concepts
- List specific questions you can answer about your site
- Provide resources for learning more
- Present an exercise to help you evaluate the factor in the context of your site and within the context of conversion rate marketing in general
- Suggest testing ideas
- Offer strategies for applying what you've learned to your site

Part 3, "Diving Deep for the Technically Challenged," discusses some of the challenges to online testing. We'll explore in more detail how Website Optimizer's script works, how you can run some more advanced tests, how to understand the math behind testing, and how to use Website Optimizer on a WordPress blog.

In the appendix, we also provide additional resources for your continued learning and success.

We hope this book provides you with inspiration that challenges your thinking, energizes your testing efforts, and helps you improve your conversion rate marketing.

Always Be Testing

PART I

A Marketer's View of Testing: The Power of Optimization

CHAPTER 1

Always Be Testing?

"Let's talk about something important…Only one thing counts in this life: Get them to sign on the line which is dotted…A, B, C. Always be closing…They're sitting out there waiting to buy; are you going to take it?"

—Alec Baldwin as Blake, *Glengarry Glen Ross*

Alec Baldwin came down harshly on his sales force in a film scene that still has the power to make people squirm. The Close. It's the Holy Grail of commerce. Except these days, the online arm of your business is a major nonhuman player in your sales force.

Whether you are pursuing sales, securing leads, or encouraging subscriptions, your website is out there interacting with your potential customers, trying to persuade them to take action. It's the connective tissue that binds all aspects of your marketing. In theory you can fire it, but you can't intimidate or shame it into better performance.

What you can do is test it.

A System for Closing

The book *Waiting for Your Cat to Bark?* (Thomas Nelson, 2006) discussed the state of modern marketing practice as well as the push/pull between selling and buying, and it explained a systematic method—Persuasion Architecture—that helps you improve the persuasiveness of all your marketing activities.

Persuasion Architecture includes a series of phases that allow you to create a persuasive online structure by addressing the individual needs of your audience. It offers a profoundly customer-centric way to achieve your business goals. The planning phases include performing uncovery, developing personas, wireframing, creating persuasive scenarios, storyboarding, and prototyping.

The final and ongoing phase of Persuasion Architecture involves testing, measuring, and optimizing. You'll never really know if you have the most efficient technological salesperson working for you unless you examine all the elements that make up that person's persuasive abilities.

Testing, Measuring, Optimizing

W. Edwards Deming said, "You create the system your visitor must navigate. People don't cause defects, systems do." Systems can be tested, measured, and optimized. You need to know whether the assumptions that went into creating your site meet the needs and expectations of your audience. More important, you need to know how to optimize your system so you can market more effectively.

When we say "testing, measuring, and optimizing," you may think we're repeating ourselves (redundantly!). But these are three distinct activities.

When you *test*, you compare elements on your site or in your campaigns to see which variation best persuades your visitors to complete the action you want them to take. That action might be making a purchase, generating a lead, signing up for a newsletter, or even clicking through to the next step in your selling process (or their buying process). Testing involves setting up an experiment in either an A/B (split) format or in any of the varieties of multivariate formats. Google Website Optimizer is a free testing platform that makes it a snap to perform these tests and review your results.

When you *measure*, you monitor what visitors do as they navigate your site. Using a web analytics program (Google Analytics is a free, straightforward program that logs visitor behavior), you can determine key performance indicators such as site traffic, overall conversion rate, page rejections, length of time spent on a page, and so forth. These analytics—*measurements*—help you evaluate where you have problems, which in turn helps you prioritize your testing.

When you *optimize*, you put your test results in place to improve your conversion rate. But optimizing is more than simply slotting in your "winners." Optimizing is the piece that brings you full circle. Learning is a valuable by-product of your testing efforts. As you test, you reinforce and refine the plans you developed to create your site or campaign. You grow more familiar with the nature and needs of your audience, which makes it possible for you to create more meaningful options to test so you continue improving. In optimization, we inject human insight back into the testing and optimizing process to lead it in more efficient directions.

Many marketers are starting to employ testing to evaluate the creative in their banner advertisements and pay-per-click campaigns. This is merely the tip of the iceberg. Testing provides the evidence that should guide every marketing solution; it ensures qualified traffic arrives on your site so you can begin and conclude your dialogue. For marketers, testing is at the heart of improving conversion, measuring is at the heart of holding these conversion improvements to an increasing standard, and optimization is at the heart of persuasion.

In this book, however, we look beyond testing's advertising role. We want to help you understand how to test and evaluate all the persuasive elements on your site so you can create the best closing system possible. Over the years, we have identified more than 1,100 factors that affect conversion and improve the customer's experience—these are elements that affect your ability to close. To show you what you should be testing, we will share many of these factors with you in Part II, "What You Should Test."

Overstock.com Case Study: Small Change, Big Difference

We cannot overemphasize the importance and sheer power of many of these site design elements. Sometimes an element that seems innocuous to you makes all the difference to your visitors. Testing these elements comes with such a low opportunity cost compared to the opportunity cost you lose by doing nothing. Here's an example.

Patrick Byrne, CEO of Overstock.com, asked us to evaluate Overstock.com's category landing page for DVD and VHS movies (Figure 1.1). The page wasn't converting the way Byrne hoped. The number of site visitors who abandoned this page was high.

Figure 1.1

Overstock.com movie page

Below a promotional banner with a related search (Figure 1.2), Overstock.com offered excellent categorization schemes to help site visitors quickly find what they were looking for; there were lists for Coming Soon, Top 10, New Releases, Featured Picks, and Our Buyer Suggestions.

Figure 1.2

Existing call to action for movies

We quickly found the problem on the Overstock.com page through a process we call Persuasion Architecture. This process is based on three simple questions that we'll walk you through a bit later in the book.

In spite of the helpful categories lower on the movies page, the top element—a prominent search call to action—seemed to suggest the titles were kid-oriented and that using search would find only kid-related results.

Overstock.com may have understood what it meant by this element, but clearly its site visitors did not.

We called Byrne back, and he replaced the "Kid's Titles" image with one that suggested the search was inclusive of all titles (Figure 1.3). Byrne saw an immediate 33 percent reduction in the page's abandonment rate, which translated directly to a 5 percent increase in top-line sales. For a company such as Overstock.com, this was a $2,040,000 monthly opportunity gain! Just imagine how much testing and optimization you could do with more than $2 million extra a month!

Figure 1.3

New call to action for movies

The Best Practices Issue

No vehicle without a driver may exceed 60 miles per hour. No one is allowed to ride a bicycle in a swimming pool. A person may not walk around on Sundays with an ice cream cone in his/her pocket. Slippers are not to be worn after 10 p.m. These are just a few of the hundreds of silly laws some U.S. states have on the books. It's hard to know exactly why or how laws like these came to be. They must've made sense to somebody at some time.

The Internet is no exception. It has its share of silly, though unwritten, rules that many marketers seem eager to follow. Rules make the job easier, and if you follow the rules but still don't see improvement, well, then the problem isn't with you. Or so people would like to think.

In our industry, marketers call these rules *best practices*. And there's plenty of documentation out there, more myth than fact, telling you generic best practices apply to you. They don't. If solid rules or even best practices do exist—and given the organic nature of the medium, we'd hesitate to guarantee this—they occur within a well-established company that has taken the time to understand its audience and shape its selling process to its customers' buying process. They apply only within that business. They won't necessarily work for any other business, be it a competing business or one with a completely different topology. We've seen these situations happen too many times to believe otherwise.

Every business has a different optimal strategy. Testing is the only way to discover which tactics work best for you.

Still, you needn't ignore these unwritten rules of e-commerce. Consider them a starting point when you plan, test, measure, and optimize. Consider them "best guidelines." But never think of them as inviolable sacred cows.

Your Goal Is Persuasion

Every website element has a persuasion role to fill: It must move your visitors further into your conversion process—closing in on the close. Even a lowly add-to-cart button can undermine this forward momentum. But you won't know whether that button is a culprit unless you test. Your goal is to create a system that meets the needs of your customers. And when you better serve your customers, you better serve your business. Testing allows you to hear what they have to say.

Scientific Advertising

Almost everyone buys into the theoretical value of testing. Few would argue with Claude Hopkins, author of *Scientific Advertising* (1923), when he wrote, "Almost any question can be answered cheaply, quickly and finally, by a test campaign. And that's the way to answer them—not by arguments around a table. Go to the court of last resort—buyers of your products."

Hopkins believed the only purpose of advertising was to sell something—it should be measurable and justify the results. He tested headlines, offers, and supporting content by tracking key-coded coupons and then analyzed the data so he could continually improve results and maximize the cost-effectiveness of his clients' advertising spending.

Dated though *Scientific Advertising* may be, the ideas are well suited to today's marketing environment. When Hopkins's advertising career catapulted him to fame and fortune, the Internet was far from being a glimmer in anyone's eye. But it's an undeniable player—and a powerful tool—in how you conduct business. We work in a medium where testing is incredibly easy and can yield dramatic results. "Cheaply," "quickly," and "finally" do apply!

You Can Test Cheaply

Cheap—as long as it isn't a by-product of shoddy—is one of your bottom line's best friends. And there's nothing quite so cheap as free, which is why Website Optimizer's platform should definitely become one of *your* best friends.

But there's more at stake here than just the cost of a software solution. You can invest a serious chunk of change in the design and implementation of your website. Generally, when it takes longer to do something, costs go up. The question becomes, how much time and money do you want to invest in guesswork? Over and over we've seen that sweating the small stuff in a vacuum of information comes with a heavy price tag.

Of course, inaction is far worse. Almost any form of testing is cheap when you compare it to the lost opportunity cost of doing nothing.

It's easy and inexpensive to make changes to your website. You don't have to film multiple takes to get your TV spot just right. You don't have to reprint an entire catalog edition to remove a mistake. You just run a test. You don't even have to run your test across your site using all your traffic. In many cases, simply setting up a pay-per-click ad campaign to drive traffic to a landing page is all you need.

You Can Test Quickly

Website Optimizer makes setting up and running tests a breeze. And the sheer speed at which you can generate responses online makes "quick" a far more significant qualifier than it was in Hopkins's day.

But "quick" isn't only about how long it takes to set up and run a test. "Quick" also applies to the time you need to invest to develop confidence that your data is representative and meaningful. Testing online, you needn't be constrained to temporal concerns such as a fixed buying season (say, Christmas) or the length of the buying decision process (say, how long it takes to decide on purchasing a car or a house compared to a candy bar or a pack of gum). In other words, you don't need to wait through a longer period of time if you can achieve a high degree of probability in less time.

When you can test quickly in a manner that gives you confidence in the data, you will, of course, be accomplishing your goals more cheaply—"quickly" is often an enforcer of "cheaply." In our experience, it rarely works the other way round.

You Can Achieve a Final Verdict

You test so you can be as certain as possible that the tactics you employ are helping rather than hurting your online efforts. Over time, testing reassures you that you've found better solutions, which helps you evaluate what you can do in the future.

When it comes to how your audiences interact with your site, no answer is ever completely final. The more evidence you acquire through multiple tests and multiple campaigns of testing, the greater the body of knowledge you will build to guide your decisions in the future. Furthermore, it gives you a verdict you can present to your naysayers—to dispute you, they'll need to gather their own evidence. Testing replaces conjecture and opinion with a form of proof.

Amazon.com Overview: How Final Is Final?

Few companies go about testing, measuring, and optimizing the way Amazon.com does. Jeff Bezos and his crew believe nothing is ever final and there are no sacred cows (our position exactly!).

Not many people could tell you which pieces of Amazon's current website are different from the site they saw only three months ago, but it's a certainty the site you looked at three months ago is not the same site you see today. This is largely because Bezos implements changes in ways most of us don't even notice. It's a clever strategy; consumers often react badly to change, even when the changes help them accomplish their tasks more efficiently.

Compare Amazon.com's original site at its official launch in 1995, when it mostly sold books (Figure 1.4), to its formidable presence today (Figure 1.5).

Figure 1.4

Amazon.com's original home page in 1995

It doesn't even look like the same company. And don't hold your breath; this, too, will change!

Amazon.com didn't create its current site just through major overhauls and redesigns. Marketers persistently tested small pieces of the big picture over and over again. A simple example of an area Amazon.com subjects to ongoing testing is the "ready-to-buy" or "add-to-cart" area. Let's take a look at how it evolved.

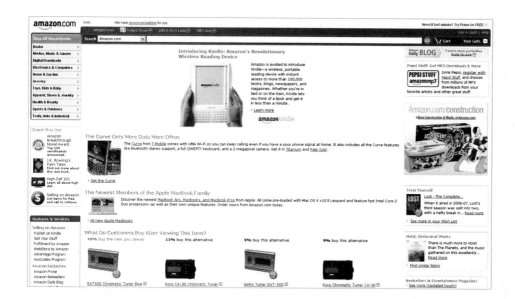

Figure 1.5

Amazon.com's home page as of February 2008

Early Days

This is what an early version of Amazon's ready-to-buy area looked like:

At the time, this add-to-cart button was unusual. It was an irregular shape that combined a rectangle "add" button with a circle cart graphic. The entire call-to-action area contained several point-of-action assurances: "You can always remove it later" and "Shopping with us is safe." And "Guaranteed" is linked to their guarantee policy.

When Amazon.com created this call-to-action area—in the early days of e-commerce—many customers feared the earth might implode if they hit the wrong button. Back then, most businesses didn't let customers edit their shopping carts. Customers were leery about entering private information and credit card numbers.

At the time, Amazon.com needed to find a way to help people feel comfortable about buying online.

The Birth of 1-Click and Wish Lists

Next, Amazon.com created its powerful 1-Click option and unveiled a new ready-to-buy area. The wording at the top of the area changed from "Buy from Amazon.com" to the more persuasive "Ready to Buy?":

Amazon.com kept the same add-to-cart button and added the 1-Click option below it. The new objective was to make sure everyone saw the bordered, stand-alone "Ready to Buy?" area with the two ways to buy. The height of the layout grew to 262 pixels.

The button point-of-action reassurances remained, but Amazon.com removed its safety and guarantee text. The 1-Click area included shipping and gift-wrap options, plus a way to edit your 1-Click settings.

Below the 1-Click area, Amazon.com also added its new Wish List feature. Notice the relative sizes of all these elements? Those will change.

Streamlining

Amazon.com's next version of its ready-to-buy area removed almost all the point-of-action assurances and reduced the size of elements within the ready-to-buy area. (We snagged this version while Amazon.com was running an A/B test.)

Amazon.com decided to test removing the assurances on the buttons. It created a single assurance—"you can always cancel later"—right below the "Ready to Buy?" header. The buttons were now condensed; this cluster of calls to action took up less space. The little notches above and below the word "or" added a nice touch.

When Amazon.com made these changes, many of our clients suddenly decided they too should remove point-of-action assurances from their add-to-cart buttons. We told them this change would hurt their conversion rates. It did.

Yet Amazon.com kept the new buttons, which begs the question, why would Amazon.com switch to buttons that don't convert as well?

The answer? Conversion isn't the only metric that matters. If you look closely, you'll notice Amazon.com made the "Ready to Buy?" area half the size of the previous version. Why? Because it was in the process of changing its business model. Very quietly, it launched its Marketplace to resell used goods. If Amazon.com didn't have to stock and ship everything, it could boost profits. Its objective now was to increase profits by showing used books higher up on the page.

There is a moral here: What works for one business doesn't necessarily work for another. Don't mimic what other businesses do if you aren't fully aware of the business issues involved.

Amazon.com 2.0

The next phase of changes showcased a major redesign of the ready-to-buy area.

The iconic add-to-cart button got a face-lift. It was the same shape and used the same colors, but now it had a 3-D effect. The "Ready to Buy?" text was removed, and to use the 1-Click option, the customer had to log in (after the user logged in, the 1-Click button appeared in this area).

The blue portion of this area included a strong promotion for Amazon.com's new A9 search engine. The Marketplace got more screen real estate, and the color of the nonbuy call-to-action buttons had been changed so they didn't draw attention away from the add-to-cart button.

Amazon.com added a wedding-registry option and removed all point-of-action copy.

Amazon.com Today

Amazon.com is no longer promoting its A9 search engine, the Marketplace area has been simplified, and there are now more secondary actions ("Add to Shopping List," "Add to Baby Registry," and "Tell a Friend"):

The current version adds a quantity pull-down menu, so you don't have to wait until checkout to change it.

The objective is to increase average order value by keeping customers engaged in the buying process. This should also lower shopping-cart abandonment by reducing the number of steps in the checkout process.

Big money, small change. Changing your call-to-action buttons doesn't guarantee higher returns on investment from your website, but it is an easy and popular test. Unwilling to accept there is ever a final, perfect version, Amazon.com continues to optimize this area (formerly known as "Ready to Buy?"), making changes based on business cycles and market circumstances.

Amazon.com has spent many years testing this area, but it has also tested countless other variables. It has tested the size and viewing options of product images, it has tested images on the left vs. the right side, and it has tested where to put product reviews. You name it, Amazon.com has tested it. And will keep testing it.

The Court of Only Resort

We call it playing by the Golden Rule: "He who has the gold rules." Online, your site visitors have the gold. You need to play the game their way.

From a more empathetic point of view, there is also that moral Golden Rule. You've probably heard it: "Do unto others as you would have them do unto you." However, this rule makes us the yardsticks against which we measure the needs of others. That's a little presumptuous, don't you think?

Not everyone wants the same things you want or wants to be treated the way you want to be treated. Yet lots of businesses still set up processes in ways they understand and in ways they find appealing. You can imagine the extent to which you limit your ability to convert when you focus only on what you want rather than what your customer wants.

We'd all do well to think about the Golden Rule differently: "Do unto others as they would like done unto them."

Online, marketers may design their equivalent of cars, but consumers do all the steering. You can apply your knowledge about your business, about your audience, about what you think will work, and about what seems to constitute "best practice" in the industry, but you will never know whether you got it right until you start test-driving with your customers.

Let your visitors design your site for you. You'll simply never build a site that's as good as the one your visitors would build for themselves. Even people with no sense of aesthetics are brilliant designers.

Through testing, you empower customers to collectively decide what works best for them. When you offer your site traffic variations of your conversion elements, they will "tell" you their reactions. Testing gives them a voice and lets you hear what they are saying.

With Website Optimizer, you don't have to guess what works and doesn't work for your site visitors. Report results quickly show you the thumbs-up and the thumbs-down (Figure 1.6).

Figure 1.6

Website Optimizer reports

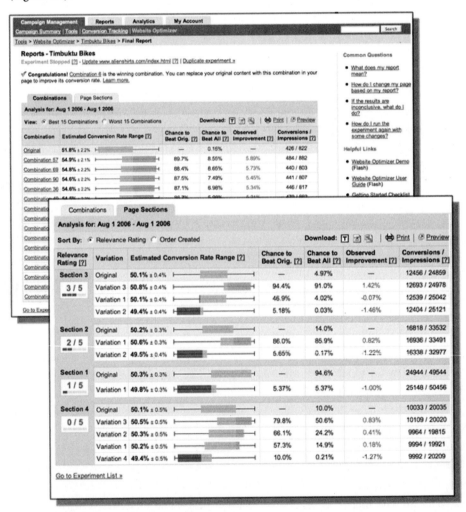

Claude Hopkins considered consumers the court of last resort. We believe consumers are the first and only meaningful court of resort—when it comes to your success, your customers are the ones you must satisfy.

Developing an Always Be Testing Culture

It verges on insanity to look at the success of a company such as Amazon.com and still hold out hope that avoiding testing will produce the results that are well within your grasp. Yet a majority of companies out there do not test. They haven't incorporated a culture of testing; they haven't even appointed an individual within their organization as the Testing and Analytics dude or dudette. They seem content to coast on their marginally above-average (or even industry-average) conversion rates.

We continually scratch our heads at this. With the quality resources available today, such as the robust and free Website Optimizer, that make testing a breeze, *why* would businesses turn up their noses at improved site performance and increased return on investment? How much profit is too much?

Intuit's Stinky

When it comes to companies that embrace a culture of testing, we have to take our hats off to Intuit. You see, Intuit has this small, cute, squishy toy skunk— the Stinky. It's an award, but it isn't given to the testing winners who achieve positive returns on investment through their testing successes. Testing *losers* earn the right to display the Stinky with pride.

Thomas Edison once quipped, "Results! Why, man, I have gotten a lot of results. I know several thousand things that won't work." When you test, you always learn something: You learn from what went right; you learn from what went wrong. Usually you learn more from the failures, but whatever the outcome, you've got a lesson. What you choose to do with it defines your TCR— your Testing Culture Rating.

The Always Be Testing culture at Intuit recasts every negative as a positive. Intuit groks testing. Intuit has an extremely high TCR.

We acknowledge there are often impediments to developing a culture of testing, but these are not insurmountable. As you'll see in multiple examples throughout this book, Amazon.com is by no means the only company to make a commitment to testing. It is by no means the only company that could sing the praises of testing's value. And it has obviously dealt successfully with the obstacles that discourage many companies from leaping wholeheartedly on the bandwagon.

Difficulty with HiPPOs

Oddly enough, marketers often have difficulties persuading higher-ups that their marketing solutions have merit. This is particularly true in companies where testing has never played any role in decision-making. In his blog, *Occam's Razor*, Avinash Kaushik describes how the highest-paid person's opinion (the HiPPO) quashes ideas because those ideas buck the traditional way of doing things. Kaushik finds this blatantly stupid but says there are two ways to earn the right to be heard: Present customer evidence and competitor evidence. He offers this idea in his "Lack Management Support or Buy-In? Embarrass Them!" blog entry:

"[Testing] is the biggest no-brainer, and the killer of most stupid ideas. It is the best way to take yourself out of the game: 'It is not my opinion that dancing monkeys, or grey text on black background, don't work. Here are data from our latest test.'

"It is hard to say no to an Executive Idea. But it is easy to say: 'Excellent idea, Mr. Executive. Why don't we split traffic and send 50% of the home page traffic to your idea and get customer feedback on a no-calls-to-action, only-video home page?'

"Testing is great because you can get the most important person's opinion: The Customer's.

"After a few times of being proven wrong even the biggest HiPPO will back off and give you all the support you need.

"And now you have no excuse to avoid testing."

—Avinash Kaushik, *Occam's Razor*, March 7, 2008

It may actually be easier to win over the HiPPO than to deal with the often less-obvious and more insidious problem within companies.

Suits and Geeks and Sandboxes

It doesn't help that many businesses suffer from Suits vs. Geeks Syndrome. (Being geeks and suits ourselves, we use the terms affectionately.) We've seen it far too many times: The online business becomes a field of battle where right-brained marketers face off against left-brained technology folks. Both have the same business objectives, but they speak very different languages. It always works to your advantage to get everyone playing nicely in the same sandbox.

Ask your favorite suit if he or she embraces the geek worldview, and you'll probably hear, "I'm so not a techno-geek! Really. I can't write one line of code. An HTML tag is a new game children play, right? I get way bored with too many details; I'm a Big Picture guy. You know, I don't even own a pocket protector. But clearly, my marketing colleagues and I need to start communicating with the techno-geeks or we won't be able to do our jobs effectively."

Geeks have an equally difficult time embracing the suit worldview. Your favorite geek will tell you, "Life is about order, analysis…precision and logical processes. Process, process, process. I just hate it when one of those opaque initiatives from MarCom lands on my desk. Suits wave their hands and create forests, but you can't have a forest without trees. I deal in trees."

It's the simplified, but classic, right-brain/left-brain issue.

The left brain is considered analytic in approach, while the right is described as holistic or global. A successive processor (left brain) prefers to learn in a step-by-step sequential format, beginning with details leading to a conceptual understanding of a skill. A simultaneous processor (right brain) prefers to learn beginning with the general concept and then going on to specifics.

Rebecca Lieb, vice president and editor-in-chief of the ClickZ Network for seven years, characterizes the problem for businesses:

"Technology is no longer at the service of marketing; it defines marketing. This places marketers on an unprecedented learning curve, requiring them to become conversant (and then some) with skills and tasks for which they are temperamentally ill-suited. On the other side of the fence, the tech folks are dealing with co-workers who cannot express their needs in the language of the realm. Programmers don't want creative briefs, value propositions, or mission statements. They need minutely detailed specs."

—Rebecca Lieb, *"Left- Versus Right-Brained Marketing,"* *The ClickZ Network,* January 18, 2002

Marketers need to understand how to present information that will help the tech staff accomplish the business goals:

- Be sensitive to the methodical nature of what you are trying to accomplish. Techies get upset when they think you are wasting their time or yanking their chains.

- Provide information in writing, not verbally. If you need to brainstorm, give them time in advance to think about what they want to say.

- Give techies the things they love: They love facts, statistics, bullet points, project-management charts, and all that stuff.

- Explain your goals as part of a process, and they'll get it faster.

- Agree on what words mean and use them carefully. Terminology is important to techies.

- Get your techies involved only after you've figured out what to do and why to do it. Then they can figure out the part they do best: how to do it. If you involve techies too early in your marketing plans, they tend to sidetrack you with the "hows."

- Trust them to handle the "hows." You'll sidetrack them if you don't get out of their way and let them get things done.

Tech folks need to understand that marketing drives visitors to your company, and sales converts them into customers. Marketing discovers the gold mine, whereas sales actually digs out the gold. Technology is a support function that helps discover and helps dig.

A distinct process is involved when people take action. This can be summarized by the acronym AIDAS. The Attention of the person is tickled, their Interest is piqued, a Desire is stimulated in their mind, and then an Action is taken—and afterward the person evaluates their Satisfaction with the process. The key here is understanding that the first three steps are emotional ones (attention, interest, desire) that are only then confirmed by the logical left brain (action). The final step (satisfaction) is a reconfirmation by this hybrid emotional-logical interaction.

When buyers buy, they basically go through a linear process:

1. Problem recognition.

2. Information search.

3. Evaluation of alternatives.

4. Purchase decision.

5. Purchase completion.

6. Was the problem solved?

Sellers, however, follow a different process:

1. Prospect for needs/desires.

2. Establish rapport.

3. Qualify the needs/desires.

4. Present to the qualified needs/desires.

5. Close on satisfying the needs/desires.

Techies must be sensitive to what is going on in people's heads and to understanding the processes that go on in the marketing and sales world. This knowledge delivers a tremendous clarity of purpose geeks can use to apply technology to support these functions. The key to converting visitors into buyers is to win their hearts. Their minds will surely follow.

The critical area for a détente between suits and geeks lies in your commitment to testing, measuring, and optimizing. When marketers understand the nature of how different forms of testing affect their ability to make decisions, they are better able to explain to the tech department what sort of data they need to collect and why they need it. When techies understand why some data is far more beneficial than other data, they are better able to implement meaningful experiments to generate the useful data.

---

*"More than simply adopting the idea that testing is good, developing a culture of testing **'means thinking as deeply about the design of experiments as it does their performance.'"***

—John Quarto-vonTivadar, *"Testing Add-To-Cart Buttons: Stuck in the Middle with You," GrokDotCom,* January 25, 2008

Intelligent testing removes opinion, guesswork, and faulty assumption from the marketing equation. It gives you truly meaningful results upon which you can act. And now, with Website Optimizer, you don't really need to secure permission to test, and you definitely don't need to justify a budget expenditure.

At the end of the day, it's not a contest between factions, be they marketers vs. executives or marketers vs. techies; everyone is participating in a joint effort to meet the business goals. One of our biggest hopes for this book is that it offers you solutions to resolving these tensions and misconceptions.

Why We Endorse (and Use) Website Optimizer

We've worked together for more than 10 years, and we've heard every excuse for not testing. Almost every one boils down to one concern: cost. But who can argue with free? Especially when free includes powerful, fast, and easy. For the first time ever, we have available to us a free platform that excels at managing the A/B and multivariate tests we use to test and optimize site performance.

Website Optimizer, which handles the testing side of your system for closing, is part of the Google suite of services. Googles' suite of products also includes Google Analytics software—an incredibly robust, free analytics package—that allows you to measure visitor behavior on your site.

Why would you choose Google as your testing platform? Besides the fact it's free?

- It's extremely easy to use. You can set up your tests (provided your creative is ready) in 5–15 minutes.

- It does not impact your search engine optimization. Content is delivered through JavaScript tags.

- It is backed and actively supported by Google with quarterly feature updates.

- It demonstrably increases conversion. Lifts of 25 percent are not uncommon, and if you apply the testing frameworks we discuss in Chapters 8 and 9 of this book, you can see even more dramatic results.

- It provides access to discussion groups, tutorials, web seminars, and Google Authorized Consultants. Like us.

- It allows you to perform both A/B and multivariate testing.

- It works with all your traffic, no matter how that traffic makes it to your site.

- Your testing and analytics information is secure, and you can keep it completely private.

You'll have to create an account with Google if you do not already have one, but you don't have to pay one thin dime to use either Website Optimizer or Google Analytics.

Why would Google make its testing platform free? It's a model similar to iTunes and Acrobat Reader: Google knows if you improve your conversion rates, you're more likely to invest in advertising campaigns, and it offers an integrated, for-a-fee solution for advertising. We call this a win-win.

We believe Website Optimizer is an amazing tool that can benefit your online marketing practice and improve your conversion rates. We'd say this even if we weren't Google Authorized Consultants! We'll run you through your first test. Then you can take all the information we present in this book and apply it to your site using Website Optimizer.

Did we mention it's free? No more excuses!

What Makes This Book the "Complete" Guide?

In this book, we will walk you through setting up a test on Website Optimizer. We will help you understand exactly what the reports tell you about the test you've run.

Google is always updating its testing program as refinements, new functionalities, and document updates are added quarterly. You will find a comprehensive list of links to Website Optimizer's knowledge base and user groups in Appendix A based on the information we have now. It's impossible to create a definitive "complete" guide when what you are writing about is constantly evolving.

The important thing to keep in mind is that Website Optimizer is a tool. It provides an interface for you to set up your tests. It crunches the numbers for you. It gives you results that compare how the things you tested performed.

It cannot do your thinking for you. It cannot plan your tests. It cannot produce the creative. It cannot interpret your results beyond demonstrating numerical significance and confidence. These tasks are up to you. If you want the tests you run on Website Optimizer to be meaningful and to provide the intelligence you need to make well-informed marketing decisions, then this is the book you need. This book provides a "framework of thinking" that marketers need to incorporate if they want to use their results productively.

You are looking for results that are going to make a difference. Website Optimizer is an excellent tool. We explain this tool and then give you everything you need to know to make it work optimally for you.

CHAPTER 2

Playing with Website Optimizer

In our experience, marketers begin their foray into testing with a measure of apprehension. It's not that they think they shouldn't be testing; it's that testing seems like such a technical activity. Marketers live and breathe solutions to marketing problems. Most don't live and breathe the scientific underpinnings of how to structure tests to gather the necessary data that will inform those solutions.

However, marketers also begin their foray into testing with a measure of excitement. The idea that testing provides solid feedback to help shape marketing tactics puts marketers in a far better position to always be closing. And that *is* thrilling!

Whether we are apprehensive or excited, we are certainly impatient to see whether things will work the way we need them to work. Many of us want to know the value of doing something up front before we'll take the time to dig deeper.

So, we'll begin by showing you how easy it is to test. There's no time like the present to help you understand that testing does not have to be rocket science or the stuff that feeds math phobias…that it is an exciting, incredibly valuable undertaking. We'll get to discussions of value and nuance later. For now, roll up your sleeves. You're going to design and run a small test.

Ten Minutes to Testing

You have any number of web analytics options from which you can choose. Some do seem like rocket science. Others are more user-friendly. Most of the quality testing platforms available are too expensive for many online businesses. The easiest tool we've discovered for straightforward A/B (split) and multivariate testing is Google Website Optimizer. It's easy to get started, and it packs the most bang for the buck in terms of insight generated vs. effort expended. Plus, it's free; Google provides free support, and using Website Optimizer doesn't obligate you to use Google's other for-a-fee services. Best of all, it takes the pain out of setting up the basic tests that will give you valuable information. It's conversion rate optimization on steroids!

To use Website Optimizer (`http://www.google.com/websiteoptimizer`), you need to have a Google account. This is the same account you use to access other Google features such as Gmail and iGoogle. (You do not have to pay for any of these services.) After you've signed up, we'll walk you through the process of performing your first test.

We've found many marketers are extremely hesitant to start testing, and not just because math isn't their strong suit. Their perfectly legitimate concerns include the following: What do I test? How am I going to get approval for testing? Who needs to be involved in this process? Will this affect my search engine optimization (SEO) rankings? The best way to get a feel for testing when you are just beginning is to start small. Set up your first tests on conversions from pay-per-click ads to a landing page or from a banner ad to a landing page. Because these situations are outside the structure of your website, testing them will not affect your SEO. And it lets you get started understanding the value of testing without rocking the corporate boat.

Choose Your Test

When you enter Website Optimizer's software, you can choose which type of experiment you want to run. You can choose the A/B Experiment ("The simplest way to start testing fast") or the Multivariate Experiment ("The most robust way to test lots of ideas"), as shown in Figure 2.1.

Figure 2.1

Choosing your experiment in Website Optimizer

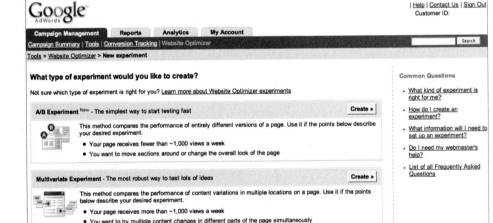

We'll walk you through a classic A/B test, which is not quite the same as the test Google calls A/B. (We'll talk about this difference later in this chapter, after you've set up your example test.) So, you won't be using Website Optimizer's A/B Experiment option here.

Click the Create button for the Multivariate Experiment option.

The Nontechnical Technical Overview

Even if you are uncomfortable with technical jargon and coding, you should understand the words Website Optimizer uses when setting up a test. That way, if you have to talk to someone who is technical, you will be able to communicate effectively. But it isn't hard to understand the limited jargon and coding—it's pretty obvious why Website Optimizer uses these testing terms. We'll explain the terms as we walk you through setting up your test.

First, you'll need to name your test (Figure 2.2); we'll call this example Headline Test.

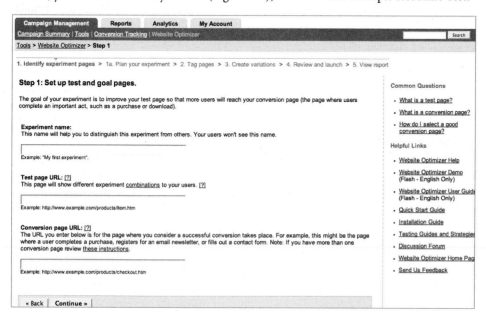

Figure 2.2

Setting up the text and goal pages in Website Optimizer

Then, identify which existing page you want to test. This is, quite simply, called the *test page*. In this experiment, we'll show how to test a home/landing page (Figure 2.3).

Figure 2.3

Test page (home/landing page)

Next, identify the page your visitor must reach to qualify as a successful conversion. This is called the *conversion page*. Some common conversion pages include your order "thank you" page, your "registration success" page, your "contact us" confirmation page, or a "begin download" page.

The conversion page (Figure 2.4) isn't necessarily the last page in your conversion process—it doesn't have to be The Official Closing of the sale. It can be any page your visitor gets to once they've taken the action you want them to take on your test page. Think in terms of microconversions and the steps in your site's buying and selling process. For this example, we'll use our "Thanks For Reaching Out" page, which is two clicks away from our test page.

Figure 2.4

Conversion page ("Thanks For Reaching Out" page)

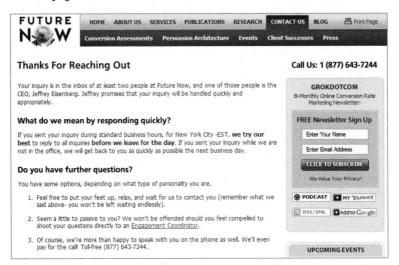

Once you have entered the web addresses for these two pages, Website Optimizer will generate little bits of JavaScript code—called *tags*—for the test page and the conversion page. All you or your technical person needs to do is copy and paste these tags into the HTML code of your pages. Google will even check (*validate*) that you've placed the tags correctly before the test will begin.

On the test page, put the control script that Website Optimizer has created for you at the top of the page (put it in the <head> element, before the <body> element of your page begins). The control script looks like this:

```
<script>
function utmx_section(){}function utmx(){}
(function(){var k='2445602570',d=document,l=d.location,c=d.cookie;function
f(n){
if(c){var i=c.indexOf(n+'=');if(i>-1){var j=c.indexOf(';',i);return
c.substring(i+n.
length+1,j<0?c.length:j)}}}var x=f('__utmx'),xx=f('__utmxx'),h=l.hash;
```

```
d.write('<sc'+'ript src="'+
'http'+(l.protocol=='https:'?'s://ssl':'://www')+'.google-analytics.com'
+'/siteopt.js?v=1&utmxkey='+k+'&utmx='+(x?x:'')+'&utmxx='+(xx?xx:'')+'&utmx
time='+new Date().valueOf()+(h?'&utmxhash='+escape(h.substr(1)):'')+
'" type="text/javascript" charset="utf-8"></sc'+'ript>')})();
</script>
```

Put the tracking script at the bottom of the test page, right before the </body> tag. The tracking script looks like this:

```
<script>
if(typeof(urchinTracker)!='function')document.write('<sc'+'ript src="'+
'http'+(document.location.protocol=='https:'?'s://ssl':'://www')+
'.google-analytics.com/urchin.js'+'"></sc'+'ript>')
</script>
<script>
_uacct = 'UA-930047-1';
urchinTracker("/2445602570/test");
</script>
```

Note how your Google Analytics user account is specified in the _uacct line, and the experiment identifier ID is specified in the urchinTracker line. Website Optimizer will generate this automatically with the correct values for you.

Put the conversion script at the bottom of the conversion page. This is the only tag you need on this page. The conversion script is almost identical to the tracking script, except it replaces the word test with goal on the urchinTracker line.

```
<script>
if(typeof(urchinTracker)!='function')document.write('<sc'+'ript src="'+
'http'+(document.location.protocol=='https:'?'s://ssl':'://www')+
'.google-analytics.com/urchin.js'+'"></sc'+'ript>')
</script>
<script>
_uacct = 'UA-930047-1';
urchinTracker("/2445602570/goal");
</script>
```

You may be wondering how Website Optimizer uses these three scripts to work its magic, or even why more than one script is needed in the first place. We'll cover a high-level overview of the why and how of the scripts later in the book. For now, just assume it all works so you can concentrate on testing.

This summarizes what you do with the scripts (Figure 2.5):

- *Test page:* Control script at the top and tracking script at the bottom
- *Conversion page*: Conversion script at the bottom

Figure 2.5

Diagram of script placement

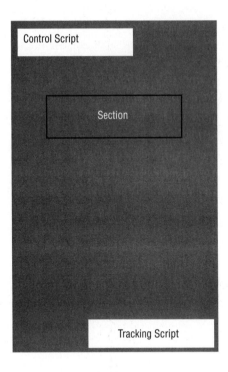

Test Page   Conversion Page

Now, look at the test page and decide what variable (Website Optimizer calls these *sections*) you want to test (Figure 2.6).

Figure 2.6

Planning your experiment in Website Optimizer

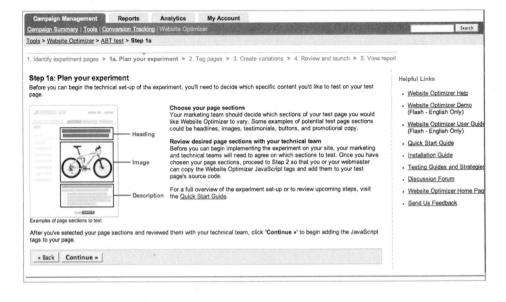

For this experiment, we'll test one section: the opening headline at the top of the page, which we know has a high impact on conversion for any site. And we will test three headlines (*variations*). We call this sort of test a classic A/B test. In our example, it's really an A/B/C test, because we are testing the conversion effectiveness of Headline A, Headline B, and Headline C against each other.

For this test, don't worry about coming up with fantastic copy; just change a few words. (See some of the headline variations we identify in Part II, "What You Should Test," of the book.)

In your code, your headline should start with an <h1> HTML tag (smaller subheaders could be <h2>, <h3>, and so on). The headline code ends with an </h1> HTML tag. Figure 2.7 shows the tagging interface.

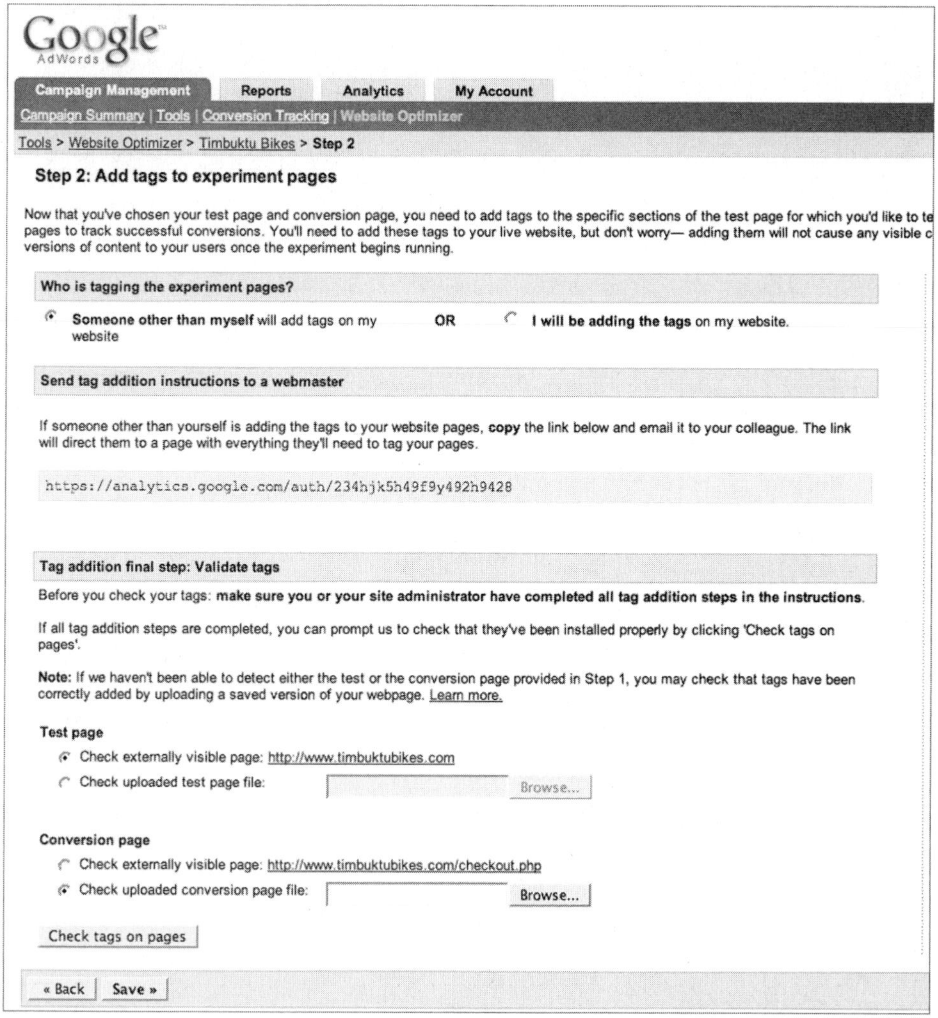

Figure 2.7

Website Optimizer's tagging interface

Once you have identified the section you are testing—in this case, the first headline—you need to place a section script (a tiny piece of code) within the headline HTML code (Figure 2.8).

Figure 2.8

**The section you
are testing appears
within the section
script tag.**

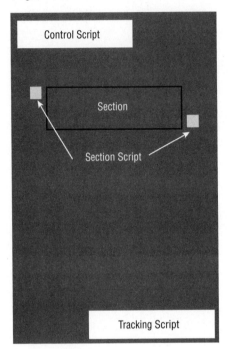

Test Page   Conversion Page

In this section script, change the name of the section in the code so you can identify it. For example:

```
<script>utmx_section("Section Name")</script>
(before content) and

</noscript>
```

The section script marks the start and end of the section you want to test; this is how Website Optimizer knows what you want to swap out when it presents the variations to your visitors.

Change (before content) and to the headline copy from your test page. If your actual headline is "Magnificent Mangoes," then Magnificent Mangoes should appear here. Also change "Section Name" to "Headline Test".

The code should now look like this on your page:

```
<h1><script>utmx_section("Headline Test")</script>
Magnificent Mangoes

</noscript></h1>
```

Make sure the </noscript> tag follows your original content in a section.

In addition to the headline you are currently using, come up with two more headlines—you'll have a total of three, such as the following:

- "Magnificent Mangoes" (your original)
- "Wild Wildebeests" (variation 1)
- "Cantankerous Corbies" (variation 2)

To get your experiment running, you'll specify these variations in the next step.

Create and Enter Variations

Website Optimizer will show you a box called the Variation Entry Form (Figure 2.9). It will be labeled "Headline Test" (the name we've given our example here), and it will show the HTML code that you put the section script around for your original headline (`<h1>Magnificent Mangoes</h1>`).

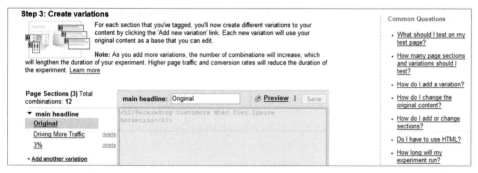

Figure 2.9

Website Optimizer's Variation Entry Form

Follow these steps to create variations on your headline:

1. On the left, you will see an Add Another Variation hyperlink. Click that.

2. A small box pops up in front of the Variation Entry Form so you can create a new variation. You just need to supply a short, descriptive name, like **Wildebeests** in our example. Click Add.

3. You will then see the code you need to edit in the Variation Entry Form with your new variation name. Between the `<h1>` and `</h1>` tags, replace `Magnificent Mangoes`

(the headline on your test page) with the copy from one of your two variations (Wild Wildebeests).

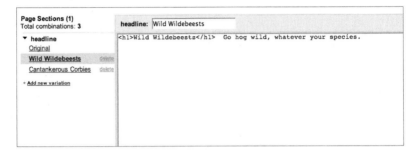

Repeat steps 1 through 3 to enter your second variation. In step 2, you would name your variation **Corbies**, and in step 3, you would place Cantankerous Corbies between the <h1> and </h1> header codes.

When you are done adding variations, click Save and Continue.

Review Test Settings and Launch

Website Optimizer summarizes the web addresses for your test page and conversion page, the names and number of variations you created, and the total number of combinations you are testing (Figure 2.10). It also lets you choose what percent of your total traffic should be exposed to the test. For now, leave it at 100 percent.

Figure 2.10

Website Optimizer's traffic selection and launch page

Step 4: Review test settings and launch

Settings and design: homepage 2	
Test page:	http://www.futurenowinc.com/index.htm
Target page:	http://www.futurenowinc.com/contactusthanks.htm
Percentage of traffic:	100% ▼
Variations:	**main headline:** 3 variations, **main image:** 4 variations, **main opening:** 1 variations
Combinations:	Total created: 12

Starting the test

When you have reviewed all the settings for your test, click the 'Launch now' button.

[« Back] [Launch now »]

Click the Launch Now button. Now the fun of testing begins! Decide how long you want the test to run and then wait for the results.

You have successfully launched your first test!

What to Do Next

How can you make sure your results are valid? Certainly it's important to be aware of "freshness" factors that can influence your conversion rates, such as seasonality, weekend vs. weekday, or even time of day. Also, it's important to run your tests for a suitable length of time. Website Optimizer includes a calculator that recommends the length of time your test should run to produce statistically meaningful results with a high confidence rating.

Remember, you do not want to beat out your current version by small percentages; you are looking for significant increases. Make sure you define what will constitute success before you start testing. You can base your criteria for success on a target number of conversions or sales or an improvement overall (*lift*), or you can measure results over the course of a predetermined time period.

The beauty of Website Optimizer is that it takes care of the math and shows you which elements or combinations of elements will work best for you.

When you are ready to move on to true multivariate testing, just add a section script before your element, and go through the same process of creating and entering variations. It really is that easy!

Headline Copy Strategies

Since we are talking about headlines, let's look at some of the ways you can vary your headlines. You can test numerous website elements. Some will have very little impact on your ability to persuade and convert your site visitors. Others will have a dramatic impact. Headlines fall in the latter category; they are an extremely important element in your conversion process. In fact, headlines should rank as one of your highest testing priorities.

Why are headlines so important? They are one of the first elements of your persuasive process with which visitors actively engage. Readers of your pages use headlines and subheadlines to understand the content on your page. Headlines help your site visitors decide whether they want to read more of your copy. *Relevant* headlines not only improve conversion rates, but they also improve organic search rankings.

Headlines also break up chunks of copy so readers can scan and skim your content. Scanning and skimming are ways your visitors self-organize the information you present. When you create engaging headlines, you encourage your visitors to read deeper into your persuasive copy.

How do you go about creating highly persuasive headlines? What sorts of aspects of headlines can you test? The following are our top-10 copy options, with examples:

- Test fractions or percentages to prove your claim:

    Nine out of ten children in sub-Saharan Africa have HIV.

    90% of the children in sub-Saharan Africa have HIV.

    9/10 of the children in sub-Saharan Africa have HIV.

- Test asking questions in the headline (make sure you directly answer the question after the headline):

    How do you make a difference in the life of a child?

Do you want to make a difference in the life of a child?

Can you make a difference in the life of a child?

Will you make a difference in the life of a child?

- Test using emotion-laden words:

    Bring comfort and solace to the life of a poverty-stricken child.

- Test different types of formatting, such as bold/italics, fonts, colors, capitalizations, sizes:

    Make a Difference in the Life of a Child.

    Make a difference in the life of a child.

    Make a difference in the life of a child.

    MAKE A DIFFERENCE IN THE LIFE OF A CHILD.

    MAKE A DIFFERENCE IN THE LIFE OF A CHILD.

- Test the number of words used in the headline:

    Make a difference in the life of a child.

    Make a difference in a child's life.

- Test using exclamation points:

    Make a difference in the life of a child.

    Make a difference in the life of a child!

- Test using text to convey the benefits vs. the features of your products or services:

    Your donations help us make a difference.

    Your donations bring medicine to the needy and support research.

    Your donations go directly to the front lines in the global war against AIDS.

- Test self-focused ("we/I") vs. customer-focused text ("you"):

    We help make a difference in the life of a child.

    You can help make a difference in the life of a child.

- Test using quotation marks in the headline (and consider the length of the headline):

    President Bush has committed to make a difference.

    President Bush has committed "to turn the tide against AIDS in the most afflicted nations."

- Test the reading level of the headline:

    Few receive pediatric antiretroviral treatment. (Flesch-Kincaid Grade Level = 12)

    Few get appropriate medical help. (Flesch-Kincaid Grade Level = 9.9)

    Few get the medicine they need. (Flesch-Kincaid Grade Level = 2.4)

Writing good headlines is an art. It takes time, practice, and patience. It also takes knowing what works best for your audience (which is not always what you think will work best for them). When you test your headlines, you'll be able to add the knowledge you acquire about your audience to your copywriting equation. And that's when your headlines will be at their persuasive best!

Want to Run a Few More Tests?

Now that you are all excited about testing, we encourage you to dig deeper into the subject by reading on. However, if you want to play around with Website Optimizer and get a good feel for testing before continuing, here are some ideas you can work with now. Part II, "What You Should Test," gives you a more comprehensive list and offers lots of graphic examples and design contexts.

Calls to action

- Prominence
- Wording
- Color
- Shape
- Size

Point-of-action assurances

- Privacy policy
- Return policy
- Third-party security verification

Fonts

- Choice of font
- Readability
- Bold/italics

Headlines

- Use fractions or percentages to prove your claim.
- Ask questions in the headline.
- Use words that evoke emotion.
- Use different types of formatting: bold/italics, fonts, colors, capitalizations, sizes.
- Use a different number of words in the headline.
- Use exclamation points.
- Use text to convey the benefits vs. the features of your products or services.

- Try self-focused ("we/I") text vs. customer-focused text ("you").
- Use quotations in the headline (and consider the length of the headline).
- Review the reading level of the headline.

Product copy

- Copy length
- Copy appeal

Product images

- Size
- Image quality
- Context of the product (If you are selling tents, are you presenting the package or an image of the constructed tent?)
- Zoom feature
- Different angles
- Image appeal

Product reviews

- Does including them help?
- Do single-score evaluations work?
- Does a multidimensional scoring system (that is, quality, support, and setup scores) work?
- Do you convert better with only positive reviews or with positive and negative reviews? (Transparency is often more persuasive.)

Contact Us pages

- Placement of Contact Us link
- Ways to specify whom they will be contacting
- Time frame for expecting a response

Forms

- Drop-down menus
- Long or short entry fields
- Appearance of Send button
- Wording of Send button

Shopping carts

- Number of steps in the checkout process
- Progress indicators
- Links back to product
- Pictures of product in the basket
- Shipping costs (when and how to present these)
- Show stock availability
- Edit shopping cart
- Error messages
- Contact information
- Alternative ways to complete checkout (telephone, fax, email)
- Registration options
- Third-party reinforcement messages
- Coupon codes
- Payment options
- Point-of-action reassurances

Multivariate Testing: Sections, Variations, and Combinations

You can think of *sections* as the elements you test on a page—elements such as headers, images, buttons, forms, and subscription areas. (We just walked you through a simple A/B test of one section.) *Variations* are different ways you can design and word these elements. (We tried three variations in our A/B test.) When you start testing more than one element on a page at the same time, you enter the world of *multivariate testing*, with its combinations of sections and variations. *Combinations* are the different ways variations across elements can be matched up.

The idea of testing multiple variables and variations, much less wrapping your mind around the concept, is daunting. But that's where the beauty of well-designed multivariate testing comes in. If you understand the concepts, your analytics package takes care of the rest.

Figure 2.11 shows a multivariate test we ran on our home/landing page header (one section) and image (another section). There are three different headlines: our original heading and two other headings (test page). There are also three different images: our original image and two other images (test page). In this example, we tested two sections with three variations each. Altogether, we tested six combinations ($2 \times 3 = 6$).

TO-MAY-TOE, TO-MAH-TO?

Website Optimizer talks about sections. It doesn't use the word *variable*, although a section is roughly the same thing. In Google's nomenclature, using a section makes sense because you "section off" your code with the tracking script. Your section can be as large or small as you want.

Recall the Amazon.com button tests we described in Chapter 1? Within a ready-to-buy area, Amazon.com included a number of different elements that affected conversion just within that area.

Website Optimizer treats that ready-to-buy area as a section. It can also treat each one of the elements in that ready-to-buy area as a section.

Thus, Google's use of the word *section* can often mean "a physical part of the page," "an element being tested," "a variable of that element being tested," or all three interchangeably. If you're using Website Optimizer, it is what it is. We prefer to use *section* to refer only to the visual location on a page where something is being tested, as in "the action center appears on the top right of the page." We prefer to call the individual pieces that can be tested *elements*, as in "an add-to-cart button is an element." These elements have *variables*, which are characteristics we can vary, such as "button color" or "button shape" or "button size." The meaning of the word *variable* has greater mathematical precision. We come at conversion from the level of the variable—from each individual piece and how it relates to other pieces. Throughout this book, we will use the terms according to our preferences.

Figure 2.11

A two-section, three-variation multivariate test

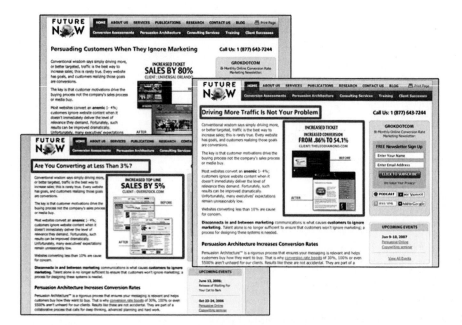

Website Optimizer lets you test up to 8 sections per page and 127 variations per section. However, it limits the total number of combinations to 1,000, which means you can't actually use all your section and variation allotments together. Nor should you need to if you are testing intelligently!

The number of combinations—the factor over which you have the most control—will affect how long you need to run the test to collect meaningful results. Website Optimizer has a calculator (https://www.google.com/analytics/siteopt/siteopt/help/calculator.html; **note the *s* in https://**) to help you gauge how long your test should run; it evaluates these five factors:

- Number of combinations (more combinations to test = more traffic required = longer duration)
- Conversion rate (higher conversion = less traffic required = shorter duration)
- Website traffic (higher traffic = shorter duration)
- Estimated conversion rate lift (greater improvement = the faster statistically significant improvement is confirmed = shorter duration)
- Percentage of your traffic's participation (lower participation = less-effective traffic exposed to the test = longer duration)

Was That So Scary?

When most of our clients bite the bullet and overcome their hesitation, we usually hear, "We missed out on *how* much?" The truth is, *not* testing is what's really scary!

And now you have a free tool—Website Optimizer. You have a substantial list of elements you can race right out and test now (we'll elaborate on these in Part II, "What You Should Test"), and you can figure out how long you should run your test.

So, how crazy should you get? Should you be testing thousands of variables and variations? These questions illustrate the market's misunderstanding of testing. For the vast majority of businesses, testing this way is like throwing lots of things at the wall hoping to find a few that stick.

You can test thousands of combinations in a multivariate test, but being able to doesn't mean you should. Let's compare two example tests and see how long they take to run to get conclusive results using Website Optimizer's calculator.

> **EXAMPLE 1 (NOT RECOMMENDED)**
>
> *1,000* = Test combinations (the number of page sections times their variations in the test)
>
> *10,000* = Page views per day
>
> *100%* = Visitors in experiment (We'll run the experiment with all our traffic.)
>
> *2.4%* = Current conversion rate (average conversion rate)
>
> *20%* = Expected improvement (that is, we expect to go from 2.4 percent to 2.9 percent)
>
> The duration for this test: **3,515.9 days** (about 10 years)

EXAMPLE 2 (RECOMMENDED)

20 = Test combinations (Focus on key drivers.)

10,000 = Page views per day

100% = Visitors in experiment

2.4% = Current conversion rate

20% = Expected improvement (Focus on key drivers in the hierarchy of optimization instead of random elements, and your expectations should rise.)

The duration for this test: **37.8 days** (just more than a month)

Google recommends you run your test for a minimum of two weeks. It runs its own tests for no less than a month. Don't forget that two weeks still includes 28 percent weekend time, which may represent significantly more or less traffic to your site compared to weekday time.

Example 1 selects variables and variations randomly and piles on as many as possible. The second example winnows the kernel from the chaff and is testing only 20 combinations that focus on key drivers of conversion rates. You can see why carefully choosing your variables and variations decreases the outer limit of the time you should invest.

It isn't less scientific to test fewer variables if you know which variables are worth testing and have a framework for understanding what would make a significant impact. Not everything is going to make a difference in your conversion rate, so learn how to invest your time and resources wisely. Testing only what matters is how to recover opportunity costs.

Figure 2.12

Multivariate diagram

More Website Optimizer Tests

The multivariate test (Figure 2.12), in which you test multiple elements on one page, is extremely well suited to finding positive interactions you might not have anticipated between elements that substantially improve the conversion rate. It's also the way to go if you want to evaluate combinations of variables without creating a page for each combination.

In addition to the multivariate test we've discussed here (which you can use to set up a classic A/B test of elements [not pages] or true multivariate test), Website Optimizer provides even more testing options:

- A/B test
- Split-path test
- Multipath multivariate test
- Do anything test
- Linger test
- Click test

Google's A/B Test

If you can call Website Optimizer's multivariate test, in which you run a classic A/B experiment, a "split traffic to multiple variations test" (which is exactly the classic A/B variable and variations test we've just set up together), then the test Google calls the A/B test is more correctly a "split traffic to multiple pages test" (Figure 2.13).

In Website Optimizer's A/B test (which is indeed set up in A/B fashion), you treat the entire page as a section; you are testing *pages*, not *variables* (see Figure 2.14).

Figure 2.13

A/B diagram

Figure 2.14

Website Optimizer's A/B checklist

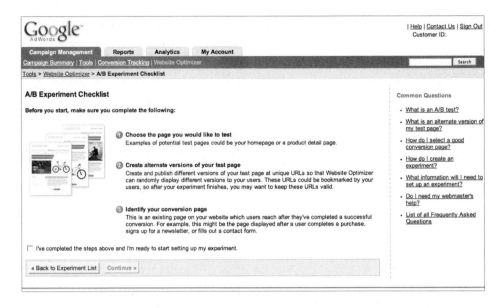

Figure 2.14

Website Optimizer's A/B checklist

To run this test, specify the versions of the page you want to test, each with its own URL. Then you specify the URL of *one* conversion goal page (see Figure 2.15).

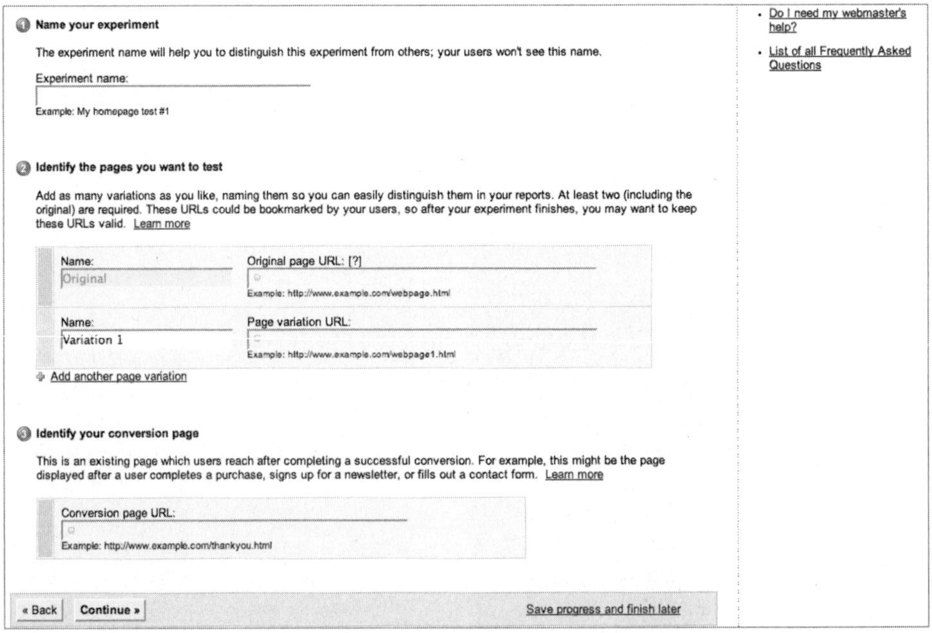

Figure 2.15

Website Optimizer's A/B Experiment setup page

As in the headline test we've just walked you through, Website Optimizer's A/B test uses JavaScript tags to identify your pages and then produces a report telling you which page was more successful in converting your traffic.

This "split traffic to multiple pages" version of an A/B test is handy when you want to test at a larger scale—things such as page designs, page layouts, or different organizations of conversion funnels. It's a good way to identify what works better overall for your visitors. Just keep in mind that testing at the page level means you are not testing at the granular level of individual variables. But you can use this test as a page-level starting point and then turn to the multivariate test to run your classic A/B variable and multivariate tests.

Website Optimizer's A/B test is an easy test to run, so it's good for beginning testers. It works well for testing layouts. Because there are only two combinations, it is particularly suited for pages with little traffic; you don't need a ton of traffic to be able to identify a difference. This A/B test also integrates well with Google Analytics page reports.

Split-Path Test

This test will split your traffic among different linear paths, where each path contains multiple pages (see Figure 2.16). This is different in that you're testing the performance of *grouped* pages against other grouped pages. For example, you could test a checkout process by splitting it into two variations, one with four steps (or pages) and another with only three steps.

Figure 2.16

Split-path diagram

Split-path testing is basically the same as Website Optimizer's A/B test: Each group of pages is treated as a section, and within that section, you have one variation. Each variation of grouped pages has the same conversion goal page—in our example, the order confirmation page. Once you have collected the data, you choose the winner based on which variation converted the highest percentage of visitors.

In essence, Website Optimizer doesn't care how many pages exist between the testing script and the conversion script. Although this can be an easy way to test strongly linear scenarios, you should keep in mind that few visitors navigate your site in a truly linear fashion (even though you might wish they did for analytics-tracking purposes!). Persuasion instead tends to occur along nonlinear paths, although that is a subject far beyond the scope of this book. Further, the longer the "click distance" between testing page and conversion page, the greater the likelihood that some visitors will wander off to other portions of your site, which Website Optimizer may record as a failed conversion for testing purposes, even though such a result doesn't reveal visitor intent.

Multipath Multivariate Test

The multipath multivariate test will compare different sections on multiple pages at the same time, all within one experiment (see Figure 2.17).

Figure 2.17

**Multipath multivari-
ate diagram**

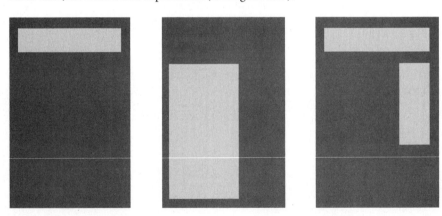

A good strategy is to run this test *after* you have identified a winning combination from a split-path test. For example, you could test images, testimonials, and contact information on the pages throughout your checkout process to find out which combination of elements across the group of pages works best.

Do Anything Test

This useful testing functionality allows you to specify more than one conversion goal page (see Figure 2.18).

You might have a page that has multiple goals: Subscribe to a newsletter, fill out a lead-generation form, download a white paper, and/or buy a product. If a visitor takes any of those actions from your test page, you have a conversion. In the do anything test, you do not have to limit yourself to optimizing one conversion goal page; if the visitor hits any or all of the pages your test page links to, it counts as a conversion.

Linger

Some pages on some websites—particularly content sites—don't have an obvious conversion goal. In these cases, it can be valuable to test the success of the page in terms of how much time a visitor spends on it (see Figure 2.19).

For example, let's say you publish an e-zine and want to test which combination of variables or styles encourages visitors to linger longer. Determine the length of time a visitor needs to stay on that page for you to consider the page successful and then run a linger test to see which version comes closest to or exceeds your definition of success. That is your conversion.

Click

Sometimes you don't want to, or can't, identify a conversion goal page as the end of your experiment, or you just want to measure an action taken on the test page. In this case, you may prefer to target a specific event or click. Suppose you want to test the ability of your copy to motivate a purchase, but the checkout itself is external to your site. (Google Checkout and PayPal are examples of external checkout systems.) To run a click test, you create variations of the link (or perhaps the copy surrounding the link) that will take your customers to the checkout site. You can't specify the off-site page as the conversion goal page in your experiment, but on your site, you can specify the click-through as your conversion goal. The copy that persuades more visitors to click is your best variation.

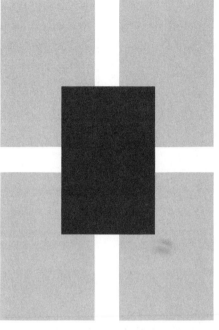

Figure 2.18

Do anything diagram

Figure 2.19

Linger diagram

Also, because you can have the testing script for more than one test on the testing page and because such external off-site pages often include a return page on your site, you could set up two different but related tests to see how many visitors get to the click-through and how many get to the return page. Some interesting opportunities exist here for companies with aggressive testing cultures.

The click test is also a good choice for evaluating forms (clicking the Submit button satisfies the conversion goal) or the optimal way to persuade a visitor to download a white paper (clicking the Download button satisfies the conversion goal).

"Don't think of the click test as the poor cousin; conversion takes place one click at a time, step by step. Without the click, there is no conversion:

"The essence of the Internet experience is how visitors click from one hyperlink to the next. How they feel about that experience is determined by whether each click fulfills the visitors' expectations and needs. Satisfaction with each click (a micro-action) increases their confidence—they'll get what they came for (the goal or macro-action).

"The click, then, is the essence of your persuasive process. Every click represents a question your visitor is asking. It represents your visitor's willingness to try to stay engaged with you (for now). It represents a unique point of conversion. It represents continued persuasive momentum. If your visitors don't click, communication ceases and persuasive momentum evaporates.

"No matter how complex the sale, every persuasive process unfolds click-by-click, one micro-action conversion at a time."

—Jeffrey Eisenberg, *Call to Action*, Wizard Academy Press, 2005.

Avoid Swimming in Data

You have neither the time nor the resources to take endless stabs in the dark. Given the double-edged sword of today's technology, plenty of people strive for miniscule results with brute-force techniques—leave that to your competition. You want to be fast and agile when it comes to testing. Let your competitors be the slow commercial plane carrying lots of luggage, while you concentrate on being as maneuverable as a fighter jet.

The truth is, technology alone won't give you optimal results. Only the professional marketer can intuitively and strategically help you test your way to success. In other words, knowing what to test is still more important than having the ability to do so as cheaply, quickly, and easily as you can today.

The number of contributing factors that affect conversion becomes astronomical when you multiply the 1,100 or so conversion factors we've identified by other elements, including different campaigns, offers, products, keywords, and the biggest variable of all, your visitors' motivations and personality types. When you consider that most of these factors are *potentially* worth testing, you begin to see why having the right talent—a distinctly human trait—is key to figuring out what actually means something. We will discuss how to develop this sort of knowledge-based framework for testing in Chapters 8 and 9.

We believe *any* testing is better than no testing. But informed testing gives you the biggest bang for your buck. The data-collecting possibilities of the Internet can leave you swimming in data; to avoid treading water, understand what to test, how to test it, and how to interpret the results so you can optimize your website's performance more efficiently and effectively.

CHAPTER 3

Understanding Website Optimizer's Report

We've carefully explained exactly how to set up a classic A/B test using the multivariate platform in the Google Website Optimizer, and we've suggested how you can use this test as a full-factorial multivariate test (if these terms have your eyes glazing over right now, don't worry; we'll be explaining them more clearly in Chapter 7). To summarize, the steps you've performed so far are as follows:

1. You've planned which sections (variables) you want to test.

2. You've planned and created variations for each section.

3. You've gone through the mechanics of setting up your test. (Depending on how comfortable you are with inserting code, you may want to have your technical staff do this for you.)

4. Google has calculated how long you need to run the test to feel confident that a reliable winner has been identified.

Obviously, the more effort you put into planning your experiment, the more valuable your results. The same can be said for how long you run your tests. Website Optimizer can help you determine the length of time you might need to run your test to get statistically viable results, based on the number of variables and variations you choose (which determine the possible number of combinations), as well as your traffic volume to each combination and your conversion goal.

While your test is running, Website Optimizer maintains two reports—the combination report and the page section report. These reports can suggest which course of action you might want to take to optimize your site. Each of the columns in these two reports provides a different insight into the performance of your sections, variations, and combinations. In this chapter, we'll cover these two reports and explain what each column means.

Combination Report

When you specify your sections, create your variations for each section, and start the test, Website Optimizer shows one randomly generated combination to a visitor. You'd think you could actually sit there refreshing your page and see how these combinations are displayed, but in reality the first time you visit the test page, Website Optimizer assigns you a combination. Website Optimizer's scripts will write a cookie to your browser for this test that tells your browser which combination you were assigned. From this point on, you will always be shown this combination from the test. If you return to the site in the future, you'll see exactly the same combination as you did the first time you visited the site. As of 2008, the cookie life has been set by Google to two years, so you can be fairly sure your visitors will see the same combination whenever they return in the future, even if it takes multiple visits before they convert.

If you have created sections and variations like the ones in Table 3.1, you will have a total of 24 combinations ($2 \times 3 \times 4$). Thus, the chance that any particular combination will be assigned to a given visitor is a bit more than 4 percent (100 percent ÷ 24 combinations).

Table 3.1

Sections and Variations

	SECTION 1	SECTION 2	SECTION 3
Original (a)	1a	2a	3a
Variation 1 (b)	1b	2b	3b
Variation 2 (c)		2c	3c
Variation 3 (d)			3d

The combination report (see Figure 3.1) shows the performance results for every page combination made from the page section variations you created for your experiment (the first column). By seeing how well a particular combination performs in comparison with the original and the other combinations, you can choose the most successful one to increase your conversion rate. The combination is assigned a number, in no particular order, although, of course, if you follow the combination link, you can retrieve this information, which you'll want to do once the test completes and you have a "winner."

Figure 3.1

Sample combination report

Combination	Estimated Conversion Rate Range [?]	Chance to Beat Orig. [?]	Chance to Beat All [?]	Observed Improvement [?]	Conversions / Impressions [?]
Original	31.2% ± 3.0%	—	0.41%	—	125 / 401
Combination 11	38.9% ± 3.1%	99.0%	85.4%	24.9%	160 / 411
Combination 4	33.6% ± 3.0%	76.8%	4.12%	7.74%	133 / 396
Combination 23	33.4% ± 2.8%	75.9%	2.82%	7.17%	153 / 458
Combination 16	32.7% ± 2.9%	67.8%	1.56%	4.75%	144 / 441
Combination 10	32.6% ± 2.9%	67.5%	1.69%	4.67%	139 / 426
Combination 8	32.4% ± 2.8%	64.6%	1.30%	3.90%	137 / 423
Combination 22	32.0% ± 3.0%	60.0%	1.03%	2.68%	129 / 403
Combination 7	31.6% ± 2.8%	55.1%	0.45%	1.27%	143 / 453
Combination 14	31.4% ± 2.8%	52.2%	0.41%	0.67%	137 / 437
Combination 21	31.1% ± 2.9%	49.1%	0.40%	-0.20%	126 / 405
Combination 18	30.3% ± 2.8%	39.1%	0.11%	-2.79%	130 / 429

Estimated Conversion Rate Range

The second column, which looks like a graph, displays the most immediate insight into overall performance. Ranking your combinations from most successful to least successful, the Estimated Conversion Rate Range graph visually shows you how well each combination is performing relative to your original content. If you're interested in the numerical statistics, you can view the numerical range to the left of the visual performance bars. Bars that veer toward the left of your original (the difference appears in red) mean the combination is not performing as well as your original content. Bars that veer toward the right of your original (the difference appears in green) mean the combination is performing better than your original content.

The estimated conversion rate is simply the number of actual conversions divided by the number of actual impressions, plus a spread. You can read more about such a confidence interval in any good statistics book, but in essence, this means that the true conversion rate is within the estimated range plus or minus the confidence interval. Looking at Combination 57 in Figure 3.2, the true conversion rate lies somewhere between [52.8%, 57.0%] (that's 54.9% + 2.1% = 57.0% and 54.9% − 2.1% = 52.8%).

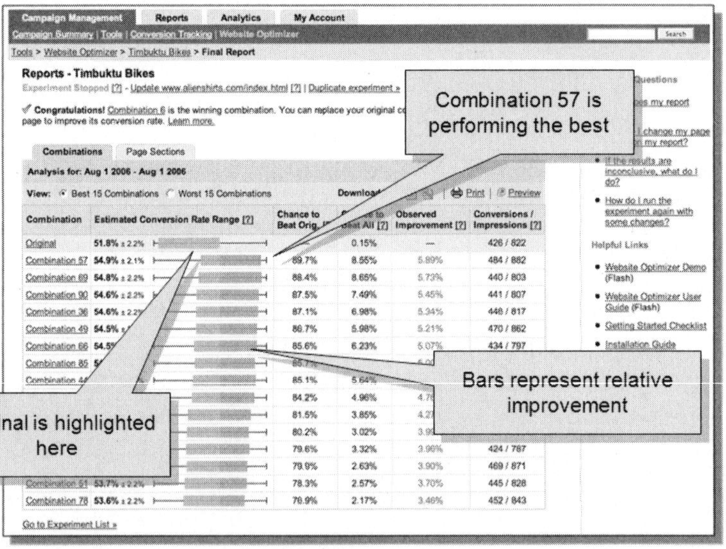

Figure 3.2

Estimated Conversion Rate Range on the combination report (figure courtesy of Google)

Of course, this is the field of statistics, so it's not quite so simple—a confidence interval is based on a confidence level. For our purposes, as of 2008, Website Optimizer uses an 80 percent confidence level to perform this calculation: All else being equal, you can be 80 percent confident that the true conversion rate for this combination lies within that range. You should know, however, that 80 percent confidence is the minimum a hard-core numbers guy would consider acceptable. Think about it: If there's 80 percent confidence that the actual conversion rate for the combination lies within this range, this also means there's 20 percent confidence that the actual conversion lies outside the range. It's a good place to start and gets you directionally correct.

Chance to Beat Original

The third column, Chance to Beat Orig., shows the likelihood, expressed as a percentage (probability), that a particular combination will be more successful than your original content. Although the equation can get complicated, you might like to think of this as the probability that this combination's results are not due to random chance. Again, it's a bit more complex than that, so you should be aware that this is calculated at a 95 percent confidence level: You can be 95 percent confident that this combination is beating the original because of something more than just random chance. In other words, you can be pretty darn sure you didn't just get lucky. You will want to know that the 95 percent confidence level is an extremely common level used by those same hard-core numbers guys, and you can feel, well, "confident" when reporting test results at this level.

As you can see in Figure 3.2, a number of combinations have a very good chance of beating the original page. According to Website Optimizer's documentation, if the Chance to Beat Orig. number is greater than 95 percent, the bar will be all green; if it's less than 5 percent, the bar will be all red.

Chance to Beat All

The fourth column, Chance to Beat All, scores the probability that a combination will be more successful than all the other combinations running in the experiment. This number is usually less (sometimes hugely so) than the related number in the Chance to Beat Orig. column. This makes sense, because the given combination is competing with all the other combinations, not just the original combination.

When numbers in this column are high—perhaps around 90–95 percent or greater— that means a given combination is probably a good candidate to replace your original content. Low numbers in this column mean that the corresponding combination is a poor candidate for replacement.

You might ask, "How can Combination 57 have such a high chance (more than 89 percent) to beat the original yet such a low chance (less than 9 percent) of beating all?" This isn't hard to understand; in fact, all of the combinations shown in Figure 3.2 have a higher than 75 percent chance to beat the original. With so many fine candidates to beat the original, for one to emerge as overall winner is a hard task indeed!

Think about it this way: You're an average reader of this book, and your buddy, a pro golf player, challenges you to 18 holes. Now, couch potato that you are, you might accept anyway. You know you're going to lose, but what's the shame in losing to a pro? It's an understatement to say she has an excellent chance to beat you. But then several of her pro friends hear about the challenge and want part of this action. What are the chances they are all going to beat you? Incredibly good (be prepared to buy lots of drinks at the clubhouse bar afterward). What are the chances your buddy is also going to beat all the other pros? That's a lot less certain.

Observed Improvement

The fifth column, Observed Improvement, gives you the percent improvement over the original combination. This number represents the ratio between the conversion rate of a particular combination and the conversion rate of the original column. It will often vary widely, until the solid group of improvement-combination candidates emerges. Concentrate on the observed improvement when a large amount of data has been collected; it's then that the results are more reliable.

Conversions/Impressions

The rightmost column, Conversions/Impressions, gives you the raw data for how many conversions and page views a particular combination generated. This is the column used to generate the Estimated Conversion Rate Range mentioned earlier in this chapter.

Page Section Report

In contrast to the combination report, which evaluates the combinations, the page section report focuses on which variations to each page section performed best (Figure 3.3). Keep in mind that simply picking the best-performing variations for each page section may not be as effective as picking a winning combination. There may be interactions among variations that the page section report does not capture.

Figure 3.3

Sample page section report

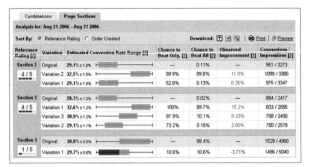

Relevance Rating

All columns except Relevance Rating can be interpreted in the same manner as they appear in the combination report, with the caveat that they're meaningful only among the variations of a single page section and provide insight only into how a variation performs relative to the original variation in that section.

The relevance rating is one of your most important statistics. It tells you how much impact a particular page section has on your experiment. For example, if your headline page section showed a relevance rating of 0, you'd know the headlines you used were not significantly different. If your image section scored a relevance rating of 5, you'd know one or more images were significantly different from the others. This means the images page section has a high impact on conversions. See Figure 3.4.

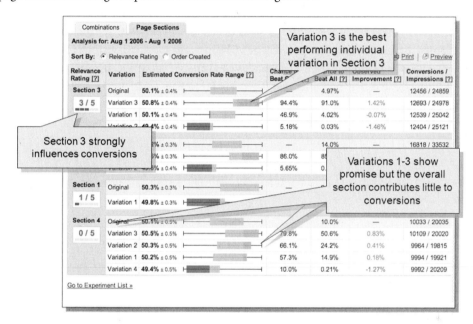

Figure 3.4

Relevancy and Estimated Conversion Rate Range on the page section report (figure courtesy of Google)

Be aware that the implications of relevancy aren't always straightforward. Lower relevancy scores do not necessarily signify a failure, because the test overall may be dominated by another section.

A visitor comes to your page and sees a random combination of your sections and variations. So, the only direct user data you gather comes from combinations. The information provided for combinations (the combination report) reflects what the users actually did when they landed on a page featuring that combination.

To figure out a section's relevance, Website Optimizer looks at the data for all the combinations and then calculates the probable influence of that section based on the differing levels of performance among the variations. In other words, relevance should tell you to what extent a page section appears to be driving results amongst the combinations. If you are testing several sections, wouldn't it be useful to understand which of those sections contributed more to the overall improvement? Wouldn't it be helpful to know that, for example, button color had a large impact on increasing conversion compared to, say, three-dimensional beveling? That would be a powerful piece of insight you could use for future testing, especially when you factor in the opportunity cost of improvement.

Given this, a combination that has a decent chance to beat the original would represent a valid and positive test no matter what relevance score it got for the individual elements. We would like to see a 95 percent or better chance to beat the original on the combination report to consider the score conclusive.

Understanding how Website Optimizer calculates the relevancy rating can often give you more useful information than accepting the statistic at face value.

The combination and page section reports offer you a variety of perspectives on the relationships among combinations, page sections, and variations that let you make informed decisions about how to refine your subsequent tests and optimize your site. In Part III, "Diving Deeper for the Technically-Challenged," we will take a more in-depth look at the basic mathematics behind these reports to help you make better sense of the numbers you generate through your testing.

CHAPTER 4

Optimization Works: Examples for Lead Generation and Retail

Nobody out there knows your business better than you do, and yet sometimes this knowledge leads you to assume wrongly when it comes to predicting what your site visitors will do. We are all at risk for Inside the Bottle syndrome, which leads us to believe the people who come to our sites are just like us—they understand what we mean and know what we know. Of course, they don't. Now that we've stated this so bluntly, you probably find the thought laughable. But it's true. *Everyone* suffers this syndrome. Even those of us at FutureNow.

The most wonderful discussion of this that we've read involves "tappers" and "listeners." Tappers beat out a tune—say, "The Star-Spangled Banner"—on a table, and listeners try to identify the tune. The listeners get it right about one time in forty. The tappers, however, *think* the listeners are getting it right about one time in two! When they realize the listeners can't name that tune, they're flummoxed. How could the listener *not* know "The Star-Spangled Banner"?

Chip and Dan Heath call this phenomenon the Curse of Knowledge.

"It's hard to be a tapper. The problem is that tappers have been given knowledge (the song title) that makes it impossible for them to imagine what it's like to lack *that knowledge. When they're tapping, they can't imagine what it's like for the listeners to hear isolated taps rather than the song. This is the Curse of Knowledge. Once we know something, we find it hard to imagine what it was like not to know it. Our knowledge has 'cursed' us. And it becomes difficult for us to share our knowledge with others, because we can't readily re-create our listeners' state of mind."*

—Chip Heath and Dan Heath, *Made to Stick* (Random House, 2007)

The brothers Heath conclude there are only two ways around the Curse of Knowledge problem: "The first is not to learn anything. The second is to take your ideas and transform them" (Ibid., p. 20).

In our little world of conversion rate marketing, testing is the vehicle for transforming your ideas.

On the other hand, few of us are good at knowing *exactly* what is going to happen when we make a dramatic change in a system. Our intuition gets flimsier the further we get from concrete knowledge. Are more sunglasses sold in Los Angeles or in Seattle? Most people say Los Angeles, for the obvious sunny reasons. The sales data says Seattle. So much for intuition. As John Quarto-vonTivadar usually likes to remind us at FutureNow, "The fascinating thing about intuition is that a fair percentage of the time it's fabulously, gloriously, achingly wrong" (John Quarto-vonTivadar, "Testing add-to-cart buttons: stuck in the middle with you." GrokDotCom; January 25, 2008).

Take, for example, Borders' recent decision to present more books facing out on its shelves. Faced with gloomy future prospects in the three-dimensional book market, Borders is bucking the accepted wisdom, post-Amazon.com, that to compete successfully, brick-and-mortar bookstores need to expand space and stock deep. The new model takes its precedence from grocery and clothing stores, both of which have long known that outward-facing merchandise sells better.

The change has meant Borders will need to reduce its stock by 5 to 10 percent. But in a test case, it found sales increased by 9 percent, encouraging enough for the CEO, George Jones, to require all Borders stores to adopt the face-out strategy.

"Barnes and Noble plans to stay the course; they do not plan on making any changes. They will continue to shelve the majority of their books spine-out and maintain a large stock of 125,000 to 150,000 volumes."

—Jeffrey Trachtenberg, "Borders Tries About-Face on Shelves," *Wall Street Journal*, March 12, 2008.

It's much too early to know whether intuition will beat out experimentation, but clearly, for the tangible-book business, testing new solutions to increasingly desperate problems may be the only thing that ensures survival.

Testing ultimately removes the need to guess or intuit or assume. When you're sitting around the table trying to devise the offer that is going to win you more customers, take the time to set up a little experiment. Test-drive your options. Not many people argue with demonstrated success.

How *has* testing made a difference? How *could* testing make a difference? Let's look at a collection of stories that highlight the benefits of optimization for lead generation and retail sites.

Finding Your Groove

Ethan worked for one of the world's largest staffing companies. He was a dedicated reader of GrokDotCom (back when it was just a newsletter) and believed strongly that he could increase conversions in his online area by implementing and testing our ideas. However, he faced the classic HiPPO problem we discussed in Chapter 1: Management didn't believe testing had value, so they didn't want to invest resources. Ethan had to prove to them that testing and optimization were going to make a big difference in their bottom line, so he decided to pursue a test case, under the radar, to secure funding for further optimization.

When Ethan contacted us, we first did what we do for all our clients; we gave his site the once-over. Informed by our own testing framework (see Chapters 8 and 9), we immediately identified a glaring priority problem: It was virtually impossible for visitors landing on the home page to figure out what this business did. It looked for all the world like a job board. Even we couldn't figure out this business's angle, and it took a little uncovering to discover that Ethan's crew actually had jobs and were trying to fill them.

We suggested a simple change to the site that would immediately communicate the company's unique value proposition: "We're hiring." Two simple words. Ethan removed a header image and replaced it with a banner-like element that linked visitors to a page explaining exactly what the business did and how it went about doing it. The page was unobtrusively outside the structure of the conversion process—a little sidestep.

Ethan saw leads increase by 81 percent. When he was able to demonstrate the financial impact of this small, solitary change, he was able to secure the funding to continue his optimization efforts. Over the course of a year, we worked closely with Ethan. In that time, he increased the site's conversion rate by 875 percent, an improvement that translated into several million dollars for the company.

Ethan took a risk, and it paid off spectacularly. His under-the-radar activity eventually earned him a better salary and a spiffy new job title. Ethan would be the first to encourage you to work the corners and the HiPPOs to get the results that will demonstrate to all the value of testing.

Geico's Disconnect

We often evaluate what businesses are doing and publish our observations in our GrokDotCom blog. The problems are fairly obvious, and when an obvious problem presents itself, you have a golden opportunity for testing solutions.

Here's a simple banner ad that Geico (the insurance company with the branded gecko) ran online:

"GEICO makes it easy. Just click here, mate!" A soft green background features spare copy and the Geico gecko chilling with something in his hand. This banner assumes the viewer is familiar with the branding—"Easy" (implicit: car insurance) is the "scent" Geico creates for the viewer. (We'll talk more about scent in Chapter 9.)

Clicking through the banner ad takes you to the landing page shown in Figure 4.1. Same soft green background. More of the same gecko image. Geico has fulfilled the promise of the click and provides more scent ("save hundreds") and suggests the experience will be customer-centric (or perhaps that the process is so easy, you'll feel downright relaxed, as you would if you were drinking a cup of tea). Fill in your ZIP code and start your quote. Very easy, indeed. We'd guess the conversion rates up until now are fairly good.

Figure 4.1

Geico landing page

All of a sudden, after clicking Start Quote, the prospect of getting a quote doesn't look easy at all (Figure 4.2). All scent falls by the wayside (although the form is prepopulated with the ZIP code information). This is a serious disconnect for the viewer, and we'd bet the rejection rate is astronomical. Where's the soft green? Where's the chillin' gecko? What would a viewer do with search if the goal is to get a quote? What are those questions on the right (as in, isn't the viewer already getting an Internet quote?)? And, get real, what's easy about a six-step process?

Let's take a minute and look at this Geico campaign in a little more detail, from the perspective of *personas*—archetypes that allow you to design your online entities sensitive to the needs of different customers in your audience. We identify four dominant persona types in our book *Waiting for Your Cat to Bark?* (Thomas Nelson, 2006): Spontaneous, Competitive, Humanistic, and Methodical. Understanding personas and what works for them is necessary to framing your solutions.

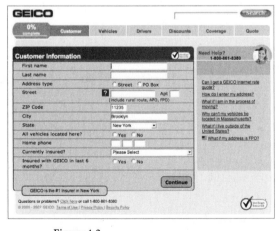

Figure 4.2

Geico's start quote page

The Geico campaign primarily targets the Spontaneous persona. Most Spontaneous visitors likely would never spend the time filling out such a long, multistep form. They just don't have the time. They lose interest the second they see "0% complete." Some may call, but like everyone else in the world, they would never admit they "need help" (especially when *easy* is the operative word). So, what would happen if Geico spoke to their Spontaneous target customers by having the gecko say something like, "If filling it out ain't easy, call me. 800-861-8380."

Bryan Eisenberg quotes FutureNow's senior persuasion architect Holly Buchanan, in an article he wrote. Holly explains how the other three dominant persona types would react to this campaign:

"The Competitive is going to think 'OK, you said you can save me money, but now you're asking for information, and there's nothing to tell me how much more you'll need or how filling out this form is going to accomplish that goal. All I see is 'continue' (really weak Call to Action). What's the benefit in continuing?'

"The Humanistic…is going to feel like 'I want to talk to the lizard, not that white chick. What happened to my milk and sugar? You went from warm and fuzzy to cold and impersonal. You just lost that wonderful rapport you worked so hard to establish.'

"The Methodical is going to think (since they don't feel), 'How many steps are involved? You don't indicate the exact number of steps involved in this process. What is this process? Exactly what information do you require? How long will this take? How will you use this information to save me money? Will I be here for a minute, or two hours? I can't plan ahead because you give me no way to understand the process, how long it takes, or what the process even is. And what's with that annoying icon with a foreign accent about, anyway? My 3-year-old daughter thinks it's cute. Want to sell car insurance to 3-year-olds, do you? Great. Want to sell car insurance to me? Get a life.'"

—Bryan Eisenberg, "Brands and Landing Pages: A Neanderthal Challenge," GrokDot-Com, September 21, 2007

So, what sorts of things would we want to start testing to optimize this lead-generation campaign?

- What would happen if we gave the viewer a quick-answer number contingent on more information?
- What would happen if we echoed the look and feel of the banner ad and landing page?
- What would happen if we got rid of that daunting "0% complete" indicator?
- What would happen if we made the six-step process shorter?
- What would happen if we put the gecko's image up instead of the human operator's?
- What would happen if we removed the search functionality?
- What would happen if we removed the linked questions?
- What would happen if we moved the buried contact phone number to the top and made it bigger?

Our experience working with personas and clients similar to Geico tells us our intuition about the things Geico should be testing is correct, but only testing would give us a solid foundation for solutions.

Doctor FootCare Rewind

A business owner with a conversion rate that averaged 4.6 percent made a number of changes to his shopping cart page—nine changes, to be exact—and watched his conversion rate plummet by 90 percent. He asked us to help him identify the source of his problem so he could get his 4.6 percent conversion rate back. See Figure 4.3 and Figure 4.4.

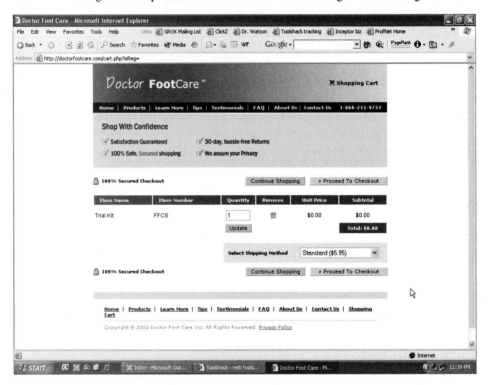

Our business owner had made these nine changes:

- He closed the space between top Proceed to Checkout button line and next line.
- He removed the top Continue Shopping button.
- He removed the Update button underneath the Quantity box.
- He moved the Total box down a line. The text and amount appear in different boxes.
- He added a Discount box above the Total box, with amount in a box next to it.
- He added an Enter Coupon Code box above the Select Shipping Method line.
- He added a Recalculate button to the left of Continue Shopping.
- He put the bottom toolbar on one line.
- He moved the shopping cart icon one space farther from the words Shopping Cart.

Figure 4.4

Doctor FootCare shopping cart page—conversions down 90 percent

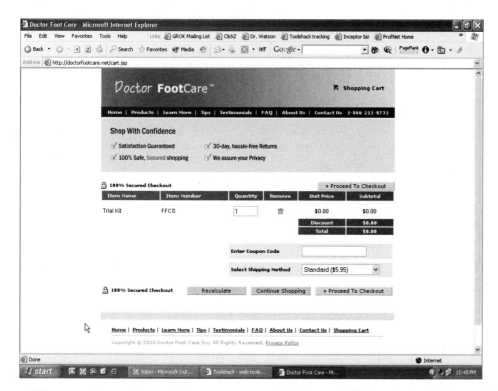

When you change nine variables at once, you are facing a needle-in-a-haystack situation. How many culprits do you have? (This is an excellent argument for controlled testing!) We examined the evidence, came up with several possibilities, and proceeded to test. One variable was fully accountable.

Bryan Eisenberg asked his ClickZ readership which variable they thought caused the decline. Not many correctly guessed the answer (another endorsement for the limited value of intuition). The offending variable for Doctor FootCare's shopping cart page was the Enter Coupon Code field. The feature suggests you can get your items for less if you have a coupon, which is great. But if you don't have a coupon and have no idea how to get one, why would you agree to pay more?

But don't order yet! What's sauce for the goose is not always sauce for the gander. We ran this example past Sam Decker, then senior manager of Dell's consumer e-business, and he said his tests indicated that the same coupon strategy that hurt Doctor FootCare actually increased conversion on the Dell site!

First we say you probably can't trust your own intuition. Then we say you probably can't trust anyone else's solutions. Yes, the entire concept of "best practice" is one of those not-so-sacred cows. The only way you will know what works best for your business and your customers is to make a commitment to your own testing.

Volvo Excavates Leads

Volvo Construction Equipment (CE) is part of the huge international Volvo Group. The Volvo CE site originally launched in 2001 and continued growing as management added applications for prospects, including a build-and-price configurator, request for quote (RFQ) functionality, a dealer locator, and interactive equipment tours. These seemed like features customers would value, but customers weren't signing on as leads.

We provided step-by-step analysis so Volvo could see exactly where it was losing visitors in its lead-generation processes. To submit an RFQ form to Volvo's dealers and become a lead, visitors had to register with the site.

We strongly suggested Volvo CE eliminate this registration requirement and then condense the RFQ form from two pages to one, testing variations to identify the optimal presentation. After testing these changes, Volvo CE increased the number of web leads generated each month by more than 700 percent.

Danica Meets Go Daddy's Home Page

Shortly after the 2006 Super Bowl, FutureNow senior persuasion architect Anthony Garcia created an audiovisual evaluation of the multichannel marketing effectiveness of the Go Daddy ad campaign. He noted one glaring deficiency: When people who viewed the Go Daddy Super Bowl ad went to the website, they found nothing reminiscent of the ad they'd just seen. Not even a picture of the lovely Danica (see Figure 4.5).

Figure 4.5

Go Daddy home page 2006

This is a scent-undermining bad move. Anthony kindly suggested Go Daddy might want to strengthen scent to improve conversion by showcasing both Danica and the TV spots on the Go Daddy site.

Anthony never received a thank you that we know of, but by the next Super Bowl season, the Go Daddy site showcased Danica (Figure 4.6). Go Daddy also played good defense by purchasing relevant keywords and providing a special landing page that featured videos of the ads, including the censored versions (Figure 4.7).

Figure 4.6

Go Daddy 2007 Super Bowl season home page

Figure 4.7

Go Daddy Super Bowl Central 2007

Amazingly, the ad Go Daddy ran during the 2007 Super Bowl season was so stupid, so utterly cheesy, so dot-bomb-era vapid that it was only *half as effective* as the previous year's spot. It generated 48 percent *less* site traffic! That's not even a field goal; it's a punt.

Still, Go Daddy managed to increase its conversion rate and double its revenue! Now, the real question is, "How much revenue did Go Daddy leave on the table last year?" It's a safe bet to say it's staggering, since, aside from these few changes, the site looks exactly the same as it did in 2006. If Go Daddy had an optimization philosophy in place and was routinely testing site performance, it long ago would have identified and remedied these very basic problems.

One of the critical pieces of knowledge to take away from this story is the importance of maintaining scent. Your visitors follow your conversion process as if it were a sort of treasure hunt. They are looking for reinforcement that you will fulfill the promise that originally grabbed their attention. When you abandon your scent trail, at any point, you strand your visitors and destroy the persuasive momentum of your site or campaign. We'll talk more about scent and give you an excellent example in Chapter 8.

Dell's Choices

When we worked with Dell several years ago, the company was trying to improve its online customer experience. Dell had positioned itself as the company that let you build your computer from the ground up to your specifications. It offered excellent online content that helped people understand the differences in the choices they could make, but site visitors didn't seem to be accessing that content. Consequently, conversions were significantly less than we thought they should be.

At each step of the building process, Dell gave visitors a link to "Learn more" (see Figure 4.8). We thought visitors really wanted help understanding what the choices would mean to them, so we tested various alternatives to "Learn more." The Help Me Choose link won (see Figure 4.9).

Figure 4.8

Dell options page before

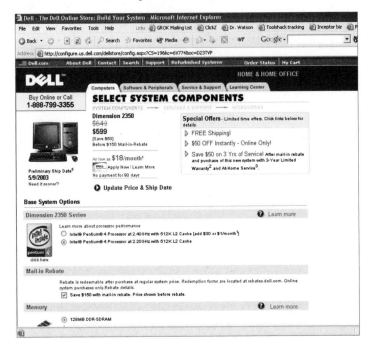

Figure 4.9

Dell options page after

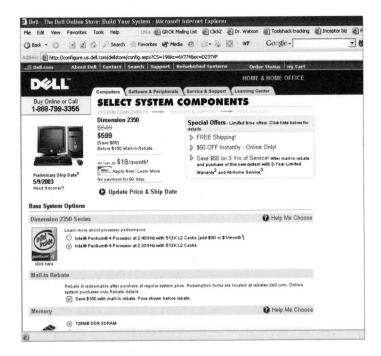

Implementing that small change, Dell saw a dramatic increase in click-throughs to its content and a corresponding lift in completed computers.

Since we worked with Dell, the site has undergone so much change we barely recognize it (this is good). One thing hasn't changed, though (see Figure 4.10).

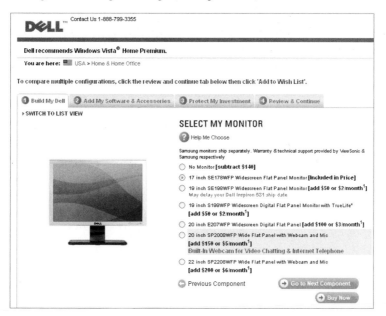

Figure 4.10

Dell's Help Me Choose link

Max Effect's Show-and-Tell

Going through a phone book's yellow pages is rarely a visually exciting experience. Every ad looks the same, as if there were one Yellow Page Ad Designing Agency out there. When Max Effect hired us, we realized yellow page ads didn't need to be dreary. They could be eye-catching, which is, after all, their purpose.

At the time, Max Effect was a one-man operation. That man was Joe; he maintained the site, fielded the leads, and produced all the work. We helped Joe with a simple rede-sign and polished up some of his copy, and then set out to find the most persuasive format for presenting samples of his product. We knew once Joe's site visitors saw what he produced, they'd waste no time contacting him.

We tried a conventional presentation of Joe's work, but the results weren't what we'd hoped to see. It didn't showcase the real difference between Joe's ads and those of the competition. Then we tried a before and after format (Figure 4.11).

Figure 4.11

Max Effect's product presentation format

The results were amazing. Max Effect *immediately* went from generating five to seven leads a month to generating five to seven leads a week. Joe finally had to consider hiring help, and business is still booming.

Testing Is for Everyone

We've looked at a number of retail and lead-generation examples in this chapter, from forms to copy to shopping carts to banner ads and landing pages to product presentations and home page images. It really doesn't matter what business you're in; your ongoing task is optimizing your online experience so you can continuously improve your business.

In between the lines of these stories are certain perspectives central to a successful testing philosophy:

- It's OK not to know.
- It's not OK to assume.
- What works for them won't necessarily work for you.
- There is always room for improvement.
- There are no sacred cows.

Every page has a number of decisions built into it, and many of those decisions get made based on the assumptions and habits businesses have adopted over time. This is inevitable. And it's OK, provided you consider them starting points in your quest to meet the needs of your visitors.

However, the goal is to move beyond the Curse of Knowledge and transform your ideas. You need to develop a degree of empathy for those who use your system but do not have your knowledge. As Tom Leung, product manager for Google Website Optimizer, cleverly asks:

"How would you create your page if your assumptions were wrong?"

—Tom Leung and Bryan Eisenberg, "What to Test," Google Website Optimizer Webinar, March 11, 2008

Now that is a Curse of Knowledge breaker!

CHAPTER 5

The Optimization Life Cycle

Customer control. Those of us who stay on top of our industry can't avoid reading these words. Nor should we. Nor should any business that wants to be successful in the multichannel world that embraces the advantages of the Internet as a hub for marketing efforts, because, increasingly, customers control their own buying experiences, whether this be through blogs, opinion sites, customer reviews and testimonials, banner ads, online searches, and even the persuasive structures of websites.

Despite the lip service marketers have given to the necessity for customer-centricity, the actual practice is still lacking. To succeed, you can't ignore this customer-centricity, because the customer life cycle is also your optimization life cycle.

One of the leading reasons customers find that their online experiences fall short of delightful is the unwillingness of businesses to adopt the level of transparency the market now requires. Transparency depends on how much of your business you reveal to your audience. Today's "experience economy" demands that you commit to a fairly high level of transparency. It's critical. To feel confident, customers need and want information; if they cannot get it from you, they'll get it from someone else. And if you do not provide this transparency for them, they tend to communicate their displeasure, often in ways that, once said, are difficult for you to counter.

You need to acknowledge the essence and substance of your business, even the negatives, so you can communicate and position them in the proper light. This means you need to come to terms with a pair of potentially uncomfortable truths:

- How you view yourself (as a company) is not necessarily how others view you.
- The information you currently provide is not necessarily the information your customers need to develop the confidence to buy.

The remarkable transparency that is available to businesses through the Web allows you to create a level of intimacy with your customers that is unprecedented. It also allows you to use analytics to track and measure the dimensions of the interactive relationship you are trying to create, and then test and optimize them to improve that relationship.

Businesses tend to rely on the traditional cycle of acquisition, conversion, and retention. To support these functions, businesses rely on a variety of tactics and verticals—strategies such as search engine optimization, pay-per-click advertising, and offline marketing initiatives. But these focus on only one (or more, but not all) point in the customer life cycle. Even taken together, they do not account for the big picture.

Suffice to say, this is not part of the customers' experience. Ultimately, it is the experience you want to plan, measure, test, and optimize to achieve true customer-centricity that generates customer delight, word of mouth, and revenue.

Miguel and Denise Need a New Cable Service

Let's take a look at how the customer life cycle interacts with your business cycle. This requires you to think about how the buying decision process takes place.

Miguel and Denise live in Florida. They're dissatisfied with their cable provider and decide to change to a service that supports their new high-definition (HD) LCD television. One day while driving, they hear a radio ad for a satellite service that might meet their needs. Miguel likes the ad; the voices inspire confidence. Denise likes the ad; the presentation seems reasonable and well thought out. That night the topic surfaces over dinner, and both agree to investigate their options.

Miguel, a physical therapist, tends to make decisions slowly; he weighs the emotional benefits of his choices and prefers to think in terms of how each person will be affected by the result. Miguel is the sort of person to whom people reveal their problems; to him, the connections between people define life.

As he begins his investigation, he searches for online feedback from other HD customers. He locates a message board he thinks offers balanced reviews from customers in his area; a lengthy review catches his attention and builds confidence in the business that had created the radio spot he'd heard in the car. So, he goes to that website to find materials that support his impressions so he can share them with his wife.

Denise, a research analyst, makes her buying decisions slowly, but unlike Miguel, she is far more influenced by facts, comparisons, and logic-driven presentations. Denise is the sort of person to whom the Internal Revenue Service sends love letters…if they sent love letters. She isn't interested in other people's opinions; she fundamentally doesn't trust them. Denise would rather find her own answers based on comprehensive knowledge.

She begins her search identifying and evaluating all the HD packages available in their area. She looks for direct comparisons between bundled services, as well as promotions for both cable and satellite. She tries to find materials that address pricing plans, installation fees, and the number of channels offered through each provider. Where possible, she prints out the information she believes is necessary to her family's decision.

As you might suppose, although Miguel and Denise may be trying to accomplish the same goal, they ask very different questions of the providers.

Miguel wants to know the following:

- How will your product or service make me feel?

- Who uses your products/services?

- Who are you? Tell me who is on your staff, and let me see bios.

- What will it feel like to work with you?

- What experience have others had with you?

- Can I trust you?

- What are your values?

- How will this help me strengthen relationships?

On the other hand, Denise is asking the following:

- What are the details?

- What's the fine print?

- How does this work?

- What's the process you use?

- Can you take me through this step-by-step?

- How can I plan ahead?

- What are the product specs?

- What proof do you have?

- Can you guarantee that?

For both, a service provider's ability to maintain scent throughout the early phases of the buying decision process and to answer each buyer's questions creates the persuasive momentum that supports the buyer's deeper personal motivations.

It's important to note that when we visualize our customers, we are not thinking of them in terms of specific demographic qualities. Miguel is not representative of all Spanish-speaking, Floridian physical therapists. He only represents those individuals who share his decision-making style. We will discuss this more in Chapter 8.

The problem with Miguel and Denise's story is that most of the sites they visit will have tested (if they have tested at all) the linear path they expect Miguel and Denise to take through the site's conversion process. And they will have imagined Miguel and Denise (plus all their relatives, friends, and professional colleagues) are subsumed in the Average Person Myth—the prevailing industry belief that all site visitors are average and make their buying decisions the exact same way.

Hitting the Optimization Wall?

Perhaps you've found yourself in this situation: You've done tons of testing and optimization, and you've tweaked your website and your landing pages to the point there's almost nothing else you can do. You've made progress, then SPLAT! You hit the optimization wall. What do you do when you reach a plateau in the optimization life cycle? The problem is, you've tested everything that's there, but what you *don't know* is what's missing.

Holly Buchanan, FutureNow's senior persuasion architect, was trying to explain to a client why traditional optimization can take you only so far. Here's a perfect metaphor—grab a spoon and go with us on this one:

> *"What happens if, [as] an avid ice cream lover (read: qualified visitor), I walk into your ice cream store (read: website), and you offer me vanilla ice cream? Take it or leave it. I might take it if I like vanilla. If I don't, I leave. You notice a lot of people are leaving your store without buying the vanilla ice cream (read: you have a high abandonment rate). You do market research and realize chocolate is a favorite flavor for many people. So, you decide to see which your customers like better, vanilla or chocolate (you A/B test). Turns out, chocolate is more popular (your "B" version of the test resulted in a higher conversion rate). But there are still lots of people who aren't buying from you. I'm certainly not. I like strawberry.*
>
> *"The problem with many optimization projects is that you're testing* what's there *but you don't know* what's missing...*Testing can help you optimize* what is *(i.e., taking action on existing analytics data). But how do you take into account* what could be *(i.e., planning for success in advance)? How do you decide what to test (where do you get your true customer insights)? You're testing vanilla and chocolate, and you see chocolate performs better. Now you can test pricing, different cones, extra toppings, and other variables that can increase conversion incrementally (i.e., measuring local maximums). But what if a lot of people just want strawberry?*
>
> *"And while we're at it, why are people who like vanilla, chocolate, and strawberry all forced down the same pathway? Why can't they each choose the flavor they want and take a different pathway based on that preference (i.e., thoughtfully designed variations)?"*

—Holly Buchanan, "Hitting the Landing Page Optimization Wall," GrokDotCom, March 9, 2007

This illuminates the fundamental difference between conversion and persuasion.

Conversion vs. Persuasion

Persuasion and conversion are two sides of the same coin. Both offer marketers substantial opportunities for growth by providing tools to leverage assets and understand human behavior. Conversion funnels are only one tool in a marketer's toolbox.

Persuasion scenarios, on the other hand, allow customers to feel a seamless, relevant, nonlinear path through your touch points—online and offline.

Conversion: Optimizing the Sales Process

When we first began studying conversion years ago, we observed conversion is about the sales process. By definition, it's always linear. The sales process is about moving consumers along a path that goes from prospecting to close to retention.

In the sales process, you appear to have much more control of the customer's environment. You can optimize clearly defined steps that move prospects forward to a close. But this is an oversimplification of what's happening, taken from the seller's perspective.

In the linear sales interaction, you can easily measure whether you moved people through the sales process. Either the customers took the next step or they didn't. You can see the drop-off between the funnel's steps in Figure 5.1.

Conversion rate optimization assumes people want to participate in your sales process by taking an end-stage conversion action now. If they want to transact now, your job is to help them do so easily. If this is still an issue for your company, priority one is to harvest the low-hanging fruit. Optimizing your sales process is important, but it remains limited in its ability to drive maximum return on your marketing investment.

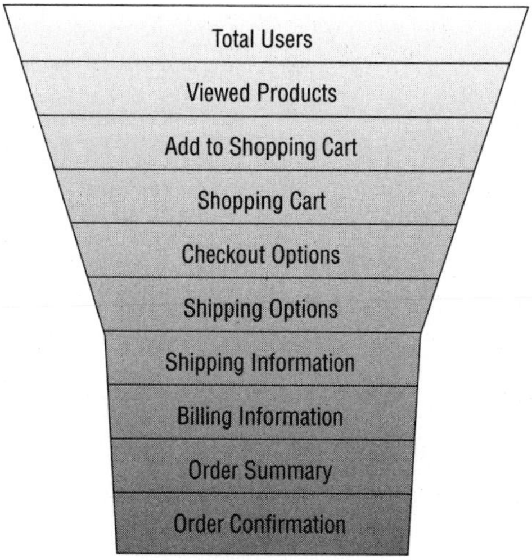

Figure 5.1

Classic conversion funnel

Total Users
Viewed Products
Add to Shopping Cart
Shopping Cart
Checkout Options
Shipping Options
Shipping Information
Billing Information
Order Summary
Order Confirmation

Persuasion: Optimizing the Buying Process

While you're busy optimizing your sales process, customers like Miguel and Denise are engaged in a distinctly different process: their own idiosyncratic buying process. They're in complete control of it. They interact with myriad factors that exist outside of your selling process and outside of your company. These factors are completely out of your control. How can you possibly control your customers' interactions with competitors, word-of-mouth issues, blogs, and product reviews on other sites?

You have the customer's permission to sell inside the conversion funnel. Outside the conversion funnel, even on your own site, the matter is more delicate. Understanding your customers' questions and needs helps you build a predictive model of customer interactions with your site (and any other business entities or touch points). The resulting scenarios are plans to influence their buying decision based on what's relevant to them.

Personas—archetypes of your customers—give you the customer insight you need in order to know what to plan and test. They give you insight into your visitors' motivations and angles of approach. For example, you can test different headlines, but how do you know what verbiage to use in those headlines? Personas will give you that insight.

Planning scenarios allows you to plan for success in advance. You are mapping out the *customer experience* based on how your customers want to buy. And you are creating different pathways to accommodate different preferences or buying modalities. You're thus creating intelligent and thoughtfully designed variations.

While most testing optimizes *what is*, persuasion planning takes into account and optimizes *what could be* by creating hypotheses about who your customers are, what they need, and—ultimately—how you'll address those needs. Holly explains:

"Some customers want to start by picking out their ice cream flavors; some customers want to start with toppings, like asking for a hot-fudge sundae first, then picking ice cream flavors. Other customers want soft-serve. Some want low-cal options. Is it more work to plan for all these different buying preferences? Sure it is. But if you've hit the optimization wall, this is the next logical step if you want to continue to see improvements.

"Sure, it's great that you've optimized for chocolate; you may be selling chocolate better than all your competitors. But imagine the results if you planned persuasive scenarios for all the different ways people want to buy their ice cream."

—Holly Buchanan, "Hitting the Landing Page Optimization Wall," GrokDotCom, March 9, 2007

The persuasion funnel incorporates the nonlinear and multichannel nature of a customer's actual experience, beginning with all the business touch points customers may have to navigate (Figure 5.2). No matter how long it takes, the buying process always begins with customers becoming aware of a problem, need, or want. They then conduct a search (whether in their heads, by being confronted by an offer, by asking others, or with a search engine) to identify a possible solution. These are the driving points where people enter a persuasion scenario.

The experience of buyers evaluating their alternatives can't be linear, although once the consumer makes the decision to purchase, the process becomes somewhat more linear. Persuasion scenarios account for the nonlinear decision-making process based on the motivations and questions real customers have.

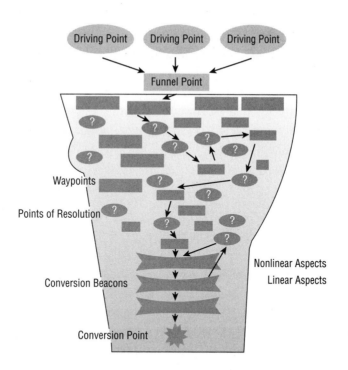

Figure 5.2

Persuasion funnel

Navigating the Phases of the Optimization Life Cycle

Optimization isn't without risk. Many online practitioners dive directly into optimization tactics without any thought to overarching strategy, especially in terms of how they frame their testing goals. They bypass the "intelligent" part of their testing mission.

When effort begins to outsize expected results, many marketers begin to think of site redesign as the only solution. Yet many redesigns throw the baby out with the bathwater. A site redesign may be the riskiest of all tactics, especially if you break what's currently working on your site in the name of having something newer, flashier, and prettier.

A far better strategy is to optimize your optimization. This usually begins with optimizing your linear processes (especially your sales and checkout). Picking at this low-hanging fruit alone can help you achieve dramatic results. But to settle for the results you can achieve here means you will miss out on the even greater benefits to be had from creating a truly persuasive structure that supports the different needs of your buying audience. Persuasion takes you to a higher level in the optimization process; it is the ultimate goal of your optimization life cycle.

As you go about planning your approach to optimization, it is essential that you think outside the box when it comes to your marketing challenges. We will address these challenges later in this chapter.

Optimizing Your Linear Processes

Online marketers need a robust, efficient process to manage their site variables. They need a predictive model of customer behavior—a model that can help prioritize and measure optimization efforts and steer them away from fruitless work. Developing this predictive model often begins with optimizing for conversion, the sales-process clicks, and linear funnels on your site.

This optimization, however, will take you only so far. But it can take you further than you think if you keep these potential problems in mind:

Improper testing methods When testing page elements, you must adhere to proper scientific methods to ensure your data is sound. Many experiments are set up simply as random, uninformed speculation. Many A/B tests compare apples to oranges, when the only valid test would compare apples to apples.

Belief in best practices Someone else's best practice can be your disaster. We had a client who argued about the number of steps we suggested the checkout process should have, citing numerous best practices. But we recognized that the client's goals were different. When he eventually took our advice, he saw checkout abandonment decrease by more than 90 percent. Your business isn't a clone; you have different business goals and customers with different needs. Don't get stuck believing best practices are rules.

Optimization of the unbroken When optimizing for conversion, we often find clients trying to improve engine torque while ignoring a flat tire. What good is optimizing a call-to-action assurance (like a refund policy) on your form page when you have an obnoxious drop-down menu higher on the form that's causing prospects to bail?

The effects of time Things change. People's perceptions, expectations, and needs change. Brand perceptions change. Business goals change. What worked yesterday may not work today. Just because you tested a banner ad six months ago to mediocre fanfare doesn't mean it won't work today. And just because a banner worked brilliantly six months ago doesn't mean it will work as well today.

Knowing the what, not the why We've seen folks replace a problematic page element, like a weak call-to-action button, with an even weaker version that converts horribly. They then label the test a failure, replace the old call to action, and move on to test another page element. They give up too easily. This mistake frequently occurs because they identified what's wrong, but not why it's wrong. Unless you can explain exactly why it didn't work, you weren't practicing the most effective form of conversion rate optimization.

Knowing When You're Ready to Tackle Persuasion Problems

You're ready to undertake optimizing for persuasion if you experience one or more of the following:

- Despite drastic changes to marketing, messaging, and landing pages, you can't move your conversion rate needle more than a point, positive or negative.

- You have one or two marketing channels with a consistent, decent conversion rate. Every other channel or effort you try has abysmal results.

- Perception research, online and offline, shows severe disparity between customer perception and your reality.

- You sometimes get huge spikes after a successful campaign, but you can't duplicate that success.

If you have genuinely done all you can optimizing your conversion process—taking into account the issues we've just discussed—then it's time to start thinking of Miguel and Denise as fully dimensional individuals with different motivations, different questions, and different problem-solving styles. As we well know, it's easy to *say* this. But it is necessary. The challenges that marketers face today require a change in perspective.

Marketing Challenges

We hear the questions businesses ask: How do I increase my sales or leads? How do I get more traffic to my site? How do I get better search engine rankings? How do I get fewer customers to abandon their shopping carts? What do I do with all this data I'm getting from my analytics software? These are important questions.

But there's an even more important question: What makes people buy? When you focus on this question, all the subsequent details fall much more easily into place. We've read publications throughout the industry and listened to our clients. We know the things marketers believe they need. Very often, to help them understand the bigger picture, we ask bigger questions. These are the questions that can help you structure persuasion so your optimization efforts yield truly optimal results.

We Need Better Testing and Usability

Sometimes you simply need better testing and usability. You need to make it easy to buy from you, you need to make it easy for visitors to find what they are looking for, you need to make it easy to checkout, you need to get feedback from visitors, you need to set up tests and watch how visitors vote with their mice, you need to test to isolate which variables are most important to your visitors, you need to test to see which offers work best. . .and variations on this theme.

Here are the bigger questions to explore and ask yourself:

- What motivates people to buy even when sites aren't usability-friendly?
- If usability is the only critical factor, why haven't conversion rates improved in any meaningful way over the past five years, when attention to usability has increased dramatically?
- What if what we're testing is only what we can think of, but the problem lies in what we haven't thought of yet; which variables are truly significant and which are not?
- How do we know that pages further up or down the click-stream don't affect the test we are conducting on one page?
- Do our scientific tests include a hypothesis of the outcome, a theory for why we expect the outcome, and a statistically meaningful sample size so we can validate or refute our hypothesis and learn from the results? Can we apply that learning more broadly to other situations?
- Would different click-through paths for different audience segments give us a cumulatively higher conversion than the best average conversion?

We Need to Redesign

Sometimes you simply need to redesign. You need to scrap what isn't working for you, you need more persuasive copy, you need more persuasive or illustrative images, you need to refresh your company image, you need to update your technology, you need to reconceive the original design because you've added so many pieces to it. . .and variations on this theme.

Here are the bigger questions to explore and ask yourself:

- Do we need a redesign, or do we need to make what we have work?
- Why will the redesigned site better serve visitors?
- How, exactly, will the redesigned site better serve visitors?
- Why are the best-converting sites so often boring in their designs?
- Will our redesign incorporate a scientific testing methodology that will allow us to optimize click-streams based on a prediction of how different audience segments will engage with the site?

We Need Better Metrics

Sometimes you simply need better metrics. You need to measure the impact on conversion of the elements on your website; you need a good web analytics program; you need to turn your data into wisdom so you can act upon it; you need to measure whether your predictions were correct; you need to identify what campaigns, keywords, elements, and audience segments give you the best return on your investment. . .and variations on this theme.

Here are the bigger questions to explore and ask yourself:

- How can we better implement the web analytics program we currently use?
- Do we understand how the data we collect impacts our financial statements?
- Are our metrics based on the way we set up our website to sell or on our visitors' buying cycles and buying modalities?
- Do our metrics help us refine our website to meet visitor expectations?
- Have we identified and planned an intentional path so that metrics can help us separate the signal from the noise, or is our analysis an attempt to divine order from randomness?

We Need a Better Conversion Rate

Sometimes you simply need a better conversion rate. You need a better return on investment on your traffic, you need to remove obstacles to conversion, you need to plug the holes in your leaky bucket, you need to reduce shopping-cart abandonment, you need visitors to complete more lead-generation forms, you need more business. . .and variations on this theme.

Here are the bigger questions to explore and ask yourself:

- How does our conversion rate affect our advertising and promotional budget?
- If we could attract a drastically reduced audience that converts better, we would increase our conversion rate. Are we prepared to reduce our conversion rate if we can generate more sales at an acceptable return on investment?
- If what we are offering is good, what are all the potential reasons why someone wouldn't convert today, in 30 days, in 60 days, and so on?
- What is the percentage of visitors we would expect to lose to each of our potential reasons?
- After identifying all the potential reasons why someone wouldn't convert, if we can't justify why our conversion rate is less than 20 percent, why would we set our goals so much lower than that?
- Is it possible that the strategy that helps us increase the average conversion rate isn't the strategy that would produce the most overall sales or best results?
- Would different click-through paths for different audience segments give us a cumulatively higher conversion than the best average conversion?

Whenever businesses tackle optimization, site design, or redesign, they start with a set of assumptions. Often, these assumptions depend on a granular, detail-oriented view of the problem as the business sees it (from the perspective of the business, not the customer). Very often, the problem is couched in the language of "best practices," a series of tactics. However, to paraphrase Sun Tzu, tactics applied without strategy are the noise before defeat.

Asking a "bigger question" broadens your view of your situation beyond the details; bigger questions often lead you to reevaluate your strategies, which in turn allows you to devise more effective tactics. The critical answers to these bigger questions—the answers that meet your specific needs—can come only from you.

CHAPTER 6

Always Be Testing in Action: Acceller Case Study

We've talked about Amazon.com and its ongoing commitment to optimizing its site. This takes place at the macro level of major overhauls and at the micro level of individual variables. More often than not, the changes Amazon.com puts into place are small enough that most people don't even know things have changed. But over the years, Amazon.com has built up an enormous body of knowledge about what works and what doesn't work for its audience. Amazon.com embodies the essence of a corporate culture of testing, and it has paid off magnificently.

The effects of embracing a corporate culture of testing aren't limited to improving an existing site. The wisdom gathered through testing can make a profound difference in launching a new arm of your business. Acceller CEO Steve McKean didn't need to be convinced of this; he'd already reaped the benefits of continual testing.

Buytelco.com, under the umbrella of Acceller, has been a client since 2003; we often cite its phenomenal success when we promote the value of ongoing optimization and creating a testing culture within a business. Buytelco.com has become one of America's top resources for comparing cable, DSL, and high-speed Internet options. It has carefully identified its business focus and target audience: Convert ready-to-buy, Internet-service-only customers. With a 2,250 percent growth by the fall of 2007, Acceller earned the 54th slot on the Inc. 500, a listing that ranks U.S. companies based on growth acceleration over a four-year period.

Rather than settle for that 2,250 percent growth rate, Steve wanted to pursue further innovations to keep up with changes in his industry. Instead of reinventing buytelco.com, Steve created an entirely new experience and brand: Digital Landing.

Testing, measuring, and optimizing allow Steve to capitalize on what he knows about his current business when he faces many unknowns about the new brand's potential customers and its buying process:

> Do not underestimate the challenge of synthesizing quality data and reporting. You must have the courage to mash together primary (internal) and secondary (external) data. It may not give you drilled-down perfection, but it provides enough of a guidepost to understand. Most of this will depend on identifying personas (abstracting them from visitors) and synthesizing this with transaction data.

We worked with Steve to extend the personas, and particularly the optimization dimension, to offline marketing efforts, retouch efforts, and an inbound call center. This was really pushing the envelope of conversion optimization. The point was to get all efforts to tie together, and this was a continuously ongoing effort. A number of strategies Steve has learned along the way have helped him prepare his new enterprise for success. Combined with rigorous testing, these strategies can work equally well for you.

Assemble an investigative task force. Fill it with people who are experienced with past/current products, new research, and conversion issues. Make sure you ask the right questions and incorporate the lessons you have already learned while testing to see how they apply in the new situation.

Develop customer personas. In Digital Landing's case, Steve didn't have a known customer base, so we had to make assumptions about who the customers might be. But whether you are working with the known or the unknown, testing is the only way you can evaluate your assumptions and optimize intelligently.

Develop and refine the buy-flow. This is the customer-focused, conversion-related aspect of your site structure. Digital Landing was incorporating additional services—for example, phone, video, high-definition—and bundles; we knew the customer's buying process would be complicated. We worked closely with Digital Landing to make the customer experience as smooth as possible, paying careful attention to details that included specific wording of calls to action, shopping-cart usability, and color choices. Optimization was central in confirming whether we got the details correct and providing direction for refining those details.

Use personas to plan your content strategies. Planning content through the eyes of your personas allows you to match the tone and types of content to their individual needs. Digital Landing had to speak to the customer looking for a video on how to install a flat-panel TV, as well as the customer who wants to print an article on how to set up a home office.

Develop top-quality content that answers the questions customers ask. Steve knew the critical value of site content and was not willing to skimp on its quality, whether that content addressed the needs of digital newbies or explained the nature of a custom Internet speed test. Digital Landing didn't have to do that—which, of course, is exactly why they did have to do it. Steve's commitment to a testing culture will help him quickly identify which content is working and where he needs to make changes.

Develop a launch plan. Work with everyone on the team—engineers, researchers, the project manager, the analytics team, designers, and copywriters—to coordinate the launch. If something can't make the launch date, testing will help you prioritize what needs to be fixed as soon as possible.

"Soft launch" ahead of time. A soft launch gives search engine spiders a chance to crawl and index your site. More important, it's a confidence-building exercise that allows you to fix what's obviously not working and avoid exposing your customers to mixed first impressions. Digital Landing officially launched knowing its site contained flaws. Why? Steve knew that the first version wouldn't be perfect and that delaying the launch wasn't the way to fill in the blanks. His customers—the first court of appeal—would do that for him.

Allow customers to interact. Employing a strategy we often use for testing landing pages, open the site to a small-yet-vocal audience—GrokDotCom readers, for instance. Set up a little pay-per-click campaign to generate traffic and monitor how it affects the priorities on your optimization list.

Measure, test, and optimize. Test your original assumptions! Through those tests, listen to what your customers are telling you about their experiences. Figure out who you're losing and where you're losing them, and then test your informed fixes to find the best solution.

Stay cool. This isn't childbirth, even if it does feel like it at times. Putting something new into cyberspace—that "birth"—is only the beginning. The real development of your "baby" takes place over time.

Steve started as a client of ours when buytelco.com had five people and made less than $500,000 in revenue. Since those early days, Steve has demonstrated a relentless focus on execution, the customer experience, and commitment to ongoing improvement. Creating and maintaining a "testing culture" has been central to Steve's business goals. Steve says this:

"[The] culture of optimization is rooted in going from good to great. You need the right people, strategy, and execution as a part of the overall company to have this take hold. Optimization cannot exist in a vacuum in a company. I am convinced it is in the fabric of good to great."

—Steve McKean, personal communication, March 17, 2008

The success he achieved along the way—that phenomenal growth rate in four years—has made a believer of him: Never assume you know exactly what is going on, never assume that what worked six months ago will work now, and continually monitor your performance and test your assumptions. Above all, never settle for "good enough." You are never done optimizing.

CHAPTER 7

Simple Testing Concepts

We test things every day; our lives are full of miniature experiments that matter to us (even if they might have little to do with the success or failure of a business). Let's say you are looking for the dishwashing detergent that truly cuts through grease. You try one. It works to your satisfaction, or it doesn't. If it does, you keep using it. If it doesn't, then you use it as the yardstick against which you measure the effectiveness of the next brand you try. You might work your way through several iterations of dish detergent before you discover the one that does the job you want it to do.

You began your dish detergent search with a set of expectations—goals. The stuff must cut food grease. To this, you may have added other qualifications: cost, availability, environmental impact, ease of use. The one you ultimately choose will be the best fit (not necessarily perfect fit) based on your needs.

To this experimental mix, you bring human attributes that guide your forays into everyday testing. You bring your intuition (instinct, imagination), a wonderful quality that makes it possible for you to see giraffes in clouds and jump out of the path of a bus so it doesn't hit you.

The problem with intuition is that it's often wrong.

You bring your opinions, shaped by your experiences. Experience tells you when the sky gets ominously dark and cloudy, you'd best carry an umbrella with you. You cannot experiment without opinion; if you didn't have it, you would be unable to choose the elements you felt worthy of testing, and you wouldn't be able to establish your parameters for success. You would be unable to form the simplest of hypotheses.

The problem with opinion is that it's filtered through individual perception.

To make predictions about how changes to a system will affect those who use the system, you must have knowledge, and for that knowledge to be valuable, it must be based on some level of accuracy. You must have some way to discover what is true, what is not true, and what is indeterminate.

The problem with knowledge is that it is rarely omniscient.

When people begin testing based on what they think they know or what they believe, they then start looking for more evidence. And, oddly enough, when you look for evidence, you tend to see only the evidence that supports your belief. In short, you support your own fantasy.

If you want to evaluate the physical world of online experience so you can build predictive models for shaping decisions that will make your bottom lines happy, you need a systematic method for creating knowledge that provides far more accuracy than opinion and intuition alone.

You most effectively create this sort of knowledge by applying the scientific method. And the scientific method begins by forming a hypothesis about the outcome of your experiment. To shape the design of your test and evaluate its results, you enter the world of statistics: the collection, evaluation, interpretation, and presentation of data.

Of Variables and Variations

Variables and variations are the building blocks of your ongoing testing, measuring, and optimizing program.

Wikipedia says, "In applied statistics, a variable is a measurable factor, characteristic, or attribute of an individual or a system—in other words, something that might be expected to vary over time or between individuals." Variables are elements of a system that either vary on their own or vary because you change them.

There are two qualities to which you need to pay attention in choosing variables to test. First, you need to identify a suitable scale for your variable. Your entire web page is a variable. You can test it against other web pages if you want. There may occasionally be value in doing this (layouts, for example), but it's going to be difficult to identify what individual variables make one page work better than another. At the page level, the testing sieve is usually too coarse. Variables such as headlines, buttons, point-of-action assurances, and so forth give you a better granular picture of what is and is not working.

Second, you need to isolate the variables that are likely to be responsible for the most significant changes. Your intuition (in a valuable application) might tell you the wording of the opening headline on your home page would have greater weight than the wording of a policy link in tiny type buried well below the fold. Your intuition (and this book!) offers you a place to start testing; the results of first tests then guide your subsequent testing.

Variations are different possible structures of a variable. If color is your variable, red is one variation. Blue is another variation. Thus, a red buy-now button and a blue buy-now button are variations of the variable button color.

Of course, you can always test a bunch of random variables and see which configuration works best with your visitors, but that generally takes too long, adds noise to the data, and makes it difficult to gain any real insight.

The better thing to do is to start with a hypothesis.

The Hypothesis

The scientific method allows you to manipulate your variable and variations in a way that gives you concrete, accurate, and replicable knowledge. You propose a hypothesis, and then you design an experiment that allows you to test your hypothesis. Your design includes a control—a point of departure against which you will measure your results. You include in your experiment's design the conditions for the outcome of your test; this is the piece that tells you whether you have proved your hypothesis. Then you perform the test, assigning page views *randomly* to site visitors, and interpret your results.

Before you run your test, you must decide on these factors:

- A control
- A hypothesis
- A time frame
- A method for evaluating your results

While and after you are running your test, you cannot change your method for evaluating your results!

Hypotheses 101

Your venture into testing begins with curiosity. To achieve success online, you must be curious about *why* things happen and *what* influences them.

Question: Why do so few people add an item to their cart from the product page?

Question: Why do my blog posts with short titles seem to get more comments?

Curiosity is the initial spark to start a learning experience, but to satisfy that curiosity, you need to propose ideas and explanations. This is the source of any hypothesis.

A hypothesis is simply an assumption that provides an answer to the question your curiosity inspired. The ideas and explanations you base this assumption on usually come from real-world examples or basic intuition.

Hypothesis: Making the add-to-cart button larger will increase our conversion rate.

Hypothesis: Using blog post titles with six words or fewer will increase the number of comments we get.

You write a hypothesis, in its simplest form, by stating an answer to your question. Your answer includes the result you expect to find, and it should be readily apparent how your hypothesis would be proven *false*. Your hypothesis provides a framework for the variations you create so you can test them against the original version to see which works best.

To test the "Making the add-to-cart button larger will increase our conversion rate" hypothesis, you create a page with a larger add-to-cart button. You'll probably want to test more than one size.

Let's say the test proves your hypothesis to be valid and you decide to make the add-to-cart button larger. Wonderful, but you might want to hold off on the champagne.

Now it's time to create another hypothesis about the best color for the add-to-cart button. For instance, "A green add-to-cart button will result in a higher conversion rate than a similar red or blue button."

The point is to learn something—anything—about what is and isn't working on your site. Approach testing in a systematic way and record what you learn to guide you through future tests. You may also want to revisit certain tests to see whether they still hold true, especially if you've changed other elements on the page.

Hypotheses 201

Suppose you propose this hypothesis: "All doves are white." How will you design an experiment to test this? You can't possibly find every single dove on the face of the planet. You could hypothesize, "All presidents of the United States are men." As of this writing, there have been 43 presidents. It's not hard to find out whether all 43 have been men. It's a manageable population set. "All doves" is not a manageable population; what you need is a sample, a *subset*, to do some testing. What you ideally want to do is create a mechanism in the dove test that will help you disprove the hypothesis: Can you focus on finding just one black dove (or purple or green or any nonwhite dove)?

From this discussion, you can identify two different types of hypothesis.

The Null Hypothesis

If you have insufficient experience, you simply don't know, or you have contradictory evidence about what you are planning to test, you are operating in the realm of the *null hypothesis*. You create a null hypothesis when you have no preconceived opinions on what the outcome will be of your experiment.

Your expected outcome is to disprove the null hypothesis (in favor of an alternative hypothesis; see the next section). The operating assumption is that there is no difference between variations for the variable you are testing. The null hypothesis is presumed true up until the data no longer supports it.

When you frame the answer to your question as a null hypothesis, you are not specifying a predicted outcome. The hypothesis itself specifies nothing conclusive because you do not have sufficient a priori knowledge to make a conclusion.

Null hypothesis: Doves come in a range of colors; there is no predominant color among doves.

Null hypothesis: The color of the add-to-cart button has no particular effect on the conversion rate.

The Alternative Hypothesis

The alternative hypothesis goes by several other names: *maintained hypothesis*, *research hypothesis*, and sometimes just plain *hypothesis*. When you state an alternative hypothesis, you do have an opinion about the outcome, informed by some degree of knowledge. An alternative for the outcome is implicit in this hypothesis. From Wikipedia again: "Usually the alternative hypothesis is the possibility that an observed effect is genuine, and the null hypothesis is the rival possibility that it has resulted from random chance."

You've seen a dove. It was white. You see another. It, too, is white. In fact, every time you ever think of doves, you think, "Ah, white." You have experience that predisposes your assumptions.

Or, you've seen a site on which the conversion rate is high. The site uses red add-to-cart buttons.

Alternative Hypothesis: All doves are white.

Alternative Hypothesis: Red add-to-cart buttons convert better than other add-to-cart button colors.

The purpose of stating the hypothesis is not to intend to disprove it—after all, you don't pick the expected winner intending it not to be so—but to state the hypothesis in such a way that it is clear (before the testing begins) under which conditions you'd be forced to change your mind in light of the new evidence. That's why there's a strong, compelling reason to state the hypothesis so that it is a true/false statement.

Which Hypothesis?

To recap, you use the null hypothesis when you have no a priori knowledge of the outcome. You use the alternative hypothesis when you have some existing knowledge or informed opinion.

If you start with a null hypothesis, you almost expect to do additional, more-refined testing once you're done, because you're presuming you'll gain enough from the first test to suggest a more refined hypothesis that is not null for the second test. Usually, you use null hypotheses at the start of a new campaign where you might have some inspirational intuition to tell you it should be one way, and you're gathering evidence. On the other hand, with an alternative hypothesis, you have some previous knowledge and evidence that makes you lean toward an alternative, so you want to find (more) supporting evidence in that direction.

Designing the Test

The art of designing an experiment lies in having a very clear idea of what you want to accomplish with your test and how you are going to go about doing it. Let's stick with add-to-cart buttons as an example:

SOME VARIABLES

- Shape
- Size
- Color

SOME VARIATIONS

- Variations of shape: round, square
- Variations of size: small, medium, large
- Variations of color: blue, red, yellow

You have a desired outcome for the experiment: You want to *increase conversion*. And you do have some knowledge about these variables: You expect that button shape, size, and color will affect the conversion rate. So, how might you frame this as an alternative hypothesis?

POSSIBLE ALTERNATIVE HYPOTHESES

- Red buttons convert better than blue or yellow buttons.
- Large buttons convert better than small or medium buttons.
- Round buttons convert better than square buttons.

You might even propose an overarching alternative hypothesis that relates the most effective combinations of variations of the variables to each other:

- Round, large, red buttons convert better than other combinations of button shape, size, and color.

Or you might even propose a hypothesis that describes which variables exhibit more of an impact than others on the goal of increasing conversion:

- Button color matters more for increasing conversion than button shape or size.

You may find this precision of language on the stuffy side, but without it, you run the risk of being imprecise in your experiments. The clearer you can make your language, the more reproducible your results will be. This will provide you with a much higher degree of clarity in the knowledge you acquire.

You can't argue about the meaning of precise language. In the previous examples, you stated what you were testing, and you stated an expected outcome. The results you interpret from these tests will be supportable: The language makes it absolutely clear how you can disprove your hypothesis. It may not be the fodder of titillating dinner conversation, but your stated goal of increasing conversion is a mighty serious business.

Types of Tests

Before we go any further, we'll make our terminology clear. A/B testing is *not* multivariate testing. The most straightforward difference lies in how many variables you include in a single test.

You can call A/B testing *univariate*—one variable. You can have any number of variations on that single variable, but you are still testing one variable. You could call a test that compares an original headline with one variation of that headline an A/B test. If you compare that headline with two variations, you can call it an A/B/C test. You can have an A/B/C/D/E/F test. It still falls under the umbrella category A/B, though. One variable: the headline.

If you put a red button on one page and a blue button on another page, you have an A/B test. If you put a red button on one page, a blue button on another page, and a yellow button on a third page, you have an A/B/C test. And that's still an A/B test.

In Website Optimizer, A/B testing takes place on the page level: Which variation of a single variable works best in the context of your web page?

In *multivariate* tests, you are working with more than one variable—multiple variables. You can have any number of variations on each of those variables. In multivariate testing, you are assuming there is some combination of variables that gives you an overall improvement, but the variables themselves are independent of each other. (Mathematicians would call this *orthogonal*—those folks have a word for everything.) When your variables and variations change relative to each other—when they *seem* to be independent of each other—then you have entered the realm of multivariate testing.

Consider this: You want to test the color of headers and footers on a page. You choose to work with red, blue, and yellow. You set your test up this way:

- Red header/red footer
- Blue header/blue footer
- Yellow header/yellow footer

Have you designed an A/B test or a multivariate test? Many will tell you this is a multivariate test. They are wrong.

In Website Optimizer, headers and footers are different sections. This might lead you to believe you are testing two variables. The header is one. The footer is the other. However, if you only ever associate red headers with red footers on the assumption that, of course, red headers would go with red footers (and would look stupid with blue footers), then your header and footer are one variable. The fact that they are visually separated is incidental.

You are assuming that headers and footers are related to each other—they are dependent. Website Optimizer may call these two sections, but in your test design, you have made them one variable. The previous is simply an A/B/C test. In fact, in Website Optimizer, you'd do better to just set your experiment up as an A/B page test if all you wanted to investigate was header-footer impact on conversion.

So, what would a multivariate test look like? We'll use a different, real-life example, because the words *red header* and *red footer* probably imply some linkage that presupposes red should go with red.

You're at dinner at a fancy new bistro in the warehouse district. Let's say you can choose from one of three entrees (variable 1) and one of three side dishes (variable 2). You wind up with combinations that look like this:

	Chicken	Beef	Fish
Green beans	C/GB	B/GB	F/GB
Squash	C/S	B/S	F/S
Applesauce	C/A	B/A	F/A

This is a multivariate test. You are testing two variables nominally independent of each other. You can pick one from each category for your repast.

In an A/B test, you'll recall, you compare some number of variations across a single variable. In multivariate testing, you have many more combinations to test, because you're testing each variation of each variable alongside each variation to each other variable. You can figure out how many combinations by multiplication: The total combinations equals the number of variations of the first variable times the number of variations of the second variable, and so forth, until you have multiplied all the variations for each variable together. In the bistro example, you have two variables, and each had three variations: 3×3. The total number of combinations you are testing is 9.

If you added another entrée, tofu, to the mix, you would have 12 combinations (4 variations of entrees × 3 variations of side dishes). If you added tofu and two more sides (say, pickled herring and spinach) to your test, you would have 20 combinations (4 entrees × 5 side dishes).

As we've mentioned before, Website Optimizer's sections are not always equivalent to variables.

Now that we've clarified the difference, we'll cover your possible testing strategies in more detail.

A/B (Univariate) Testing

In its simplest implementation, A/B testing takes only two letters to spell (in other words, two variations). It's based on a simple principle with which we're all familiar:

- Compare and contrast alternatives.
- Based upon measurement, act accordingly.

Let's say you want to determine whether Nolan Ryan is a better baseball player than Homer Simpson. How should you proceed? First, you might set a metric for what you mean by a "better" baseball player. You can measure evidence in concrete ways, noting the two subjects' different batting averages or RBIs or the like. What you're searching for is the right metric—a formula that will lead you to a correct decision.

You might decide that considering indirect evidence will lead you to a better decision than comparing pure statistics. In that case, your metric may involve such things as the difference in salary paid for services or a comparison of the prices paid for your subjects' autographs on eBay.

In virtually all such measures, Nolan is the better candidate. If you were choosing a player for your team, you'd certainly pick Nolan, especially if you were also the betting type.

But let's think about that a moment: The reason you feel confidence in signing Nolan stems from your familiarity with the metrics that count when we speak of baseball. Your decision might be quite different if the goal instead is to pick an effective donut quality assurance taster. Suddenly, Homer Simpson is back in the running.

Even then, your confidence may be based on your understanding that "tastes better" is the donut metric and that Homer Simpson is an acknowledged expert in donut consumption. But what does it mean to "taste better"? Are you relying solely on Homer's reputation as an expert? If his expertise is based on consumption quantity, perhaps you suspect he enjoys all donuts equally and actually has little "taste" at all. In other words, it's quite possible you don't have any knowledge at all of what we might call "donut tastiness."

Interestingly, marketers and business owners are asked every day to make more important decisions with less information with undetermined metrics. Oh, they "have" metrics—sometimes several expensive analytics packages—but they don't actually know how to derive actionable information from the various metrics or reports. After being asked, "Do you have any benchmark metrics?" one customer actually told us, "Sure, we do. We can measure anything; just tell us what's important." Let us suggest that if you don't know what's important to measure in your business, no analytics package is going to tell you.

To design an A/B test, you must do the following:

- Identify a metric. *What* are you going to compare and contrast?
- Describe and agree upon metrics (usually a key performance indicator [KPI] such as conversion rate or average order size). *How* will you compare and contrast the differences?
- Optimize the system based on comparisons of two or more tested solutions, which differ in only one respect of how they perform in terms of their KPI.

You participated in a specific A/B test of your own the last time you had your eyes examined. It went something like this:

Doctor: "Which is clearer, number 1 or number 2?"

You: "Oh, number 2."

You hear some clicking, a sure sign of adjustments being performed.

Doctor: "Now which is clearer, number 3 or number 4?"

You: "Definitely, number 3."

More clicks.

Doctor: "OK, final time: Which is better, number 2 or number 3?"

You choose, the optometry gnomes get to work, and soon your new glasses are ready.

Do you see how the examiner ruled out the losing candidates and moved you forward to a final choice while not indicating what the metric was? But you aren't quite focused (pardon the pun) on the metric at that point; you just want to see clearly—and "seeing clearly" is the metric in this example. The examiner steers you toward a solution by means of the somewhat qualitative metric of "which is clearer?"

A/B testing for websites follows a similar pattern. Applied to pages, elements of a page, or the state of the browser at the moment you're viewing it, the metric is the success ratio (conversion) of one candidate page (page element), "A," vs. another candidate, "B."

A typical problem for A/B testing might be "Do more people buy when I use a *red* buy-it-now button or when I use a *blue* buy-it-now button?" The data for this test will come from your Website Optimizer tests. Once you know which candidate converts better, you use the winner and discard the other. You might then test again, comparing the winner to some other variant you have in mind.

The good news about using A/B testing is that you're probably better off using it than if you did no testing at all. You'll almost assuredly do no harm by doing some baseline A/B testing. Even in its simplest application, your business is still likely to see improvement in conversion on a page-centric basis, especially if you've done no previous optimization.

By examining incremental improvements to conversion at the page level, you should be able to move measurably higher on your site's conversion rate vs. what you could expect by random chance—at least compared to your preexisting analytics and your nonoptimized competitors. That's just another way of saying you can use A/B testing to pick the low-hanging conversion fruit.

Imagine you were going to test font size on a call-to-action button. You run tests, gradually increasing the size, until you have reached a font size that gives you a "maximum" conversion rate, past which, increasing the font size further decreases conversion.

Figure 7.1 represents this scenario. You have no idea what your "maximum" might be in real life, although if you look at this curve, you could make a good guess. By comparing the conversion of several page variants via A/B testing, you're able to inch your way further up the conversion curve, closer and closer to your theoretical maximum.

Figure 7.1

**Hypothetical con-
version rate curve**

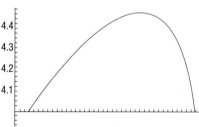

We've heard a number of marketers at analytics conferences remark, "Oh, well, anything more than A/B testing is too hard" or "We're using state-of-the-art A/B testing." We suspect this is a euphemism for "We're doing the same thing as everyone else." The real question is, "What sort of other solutions are available to us?"

You need to understand that A/B testing will get you only so far. If you can take a larger view, outside of page-centric testing, you'll have a much better sense of what sort of A/B testing you should be doing.

You also need to consider some long-term approaches that deal with the issue of multivariate testing and the pitfalls of examining extremely large search spaces. Many large companies already do this when they deal with issues such as "relevance" and "other customers who bought what you did also enjoyed…." Typically, they get wild results because vast search spaces like that are prone to overoptimized solution sets and "backfitting" of data. Such multivariate testing over an extremely large search space is the real problem you need to confront, and the solutions for this problem are not trivial.

Multivariate Testing

Can you test every combination of variable and variation in an experiment? Of course. As long as it's within the abilities of your testing software. This is the idea behind Website Optimizer. It allows you to run what is called a *full factorial* test. It tests all variables against all variations of those variables.

Let's say your content pages have four different headlines—one near the top of the copy, two in the middle, one nearer the end. Each headline is a separate variable. You decide you want to test five different variations for each of those headlines, and you want to know the best combination among the four headlines and each of their five variations. In this example, you have 625 different combinations ($5 \times 5 \times 5 \times 5 = 625$). (Remember, Website Optimizer limits you to a total of 1,000 combinations.)

You set up your experiment. You enter the average number of page views this page gets in a given day (say, 1,000). You decide how much of your traffic you want to expose to this test (say, all of it). You specify the current conversion rate for that page (say your current conversion rate is 2.46 percent), and then you decide how much of a lift you'd like to see in that conversion rate (let's shoot for 20 percent).

According to Google's test duration calculator (Figure 7.2), it might take you 20,518 days to identify a clear winner. That's more than five decades. If we live that long, we plan to be sitting on a beach with a nubile beauty on each arm telling us what hot old geezers we are; we're not going to be thinking about the headline variable test Joe in marketing is still running.

Have you got that kind of time? We don't. It may cost you very little to design your test, and your testing software may be free, but there are always lost opportunity costs even when you do test (as opposed to the even greater lost opportunity costs that come with not testing at all). Any variable or variation you create that doesn't test well represents a lost opportunity cost. The time you invest in testing (especially when you test randomly) represents a lost opportunity cost.

Figure 7.2

Website Optimizer's test duration calculator

Estimate Test Duration	
625	# Test combinations
1,000	# Page views per day
100	% Visitors in experiment
2.46	% Current conversion rate
20	% Expected improvement
Duration: 20,518.75 days	

Back to our example. A 20 percent lift in your conversion rate doesn't seem like much. You might imagine it would be even harder to identify a combination that could give you a really spectacular conversion lift of, say, 500 percent. So, you enter that sublime lift percentage in the calculator—all other numbers remaining the same—and discover it's going to take you only 81.25 days to identify a clear winner. How come?

The answer is fairly simple: If you have a stellar combination capable of giving you that much of a conversion lift, it isn't going to take long for the test to discover it. Either you've got it or you don't. Determining a clear winner for a conversion lift of 20 percent is going to take much longer. Much!

There's nothing wrong with testing everything, and Google's position is if you *can* test everything, you might as well. But if you have lots of variables and variations, you have a monster to deal with. Look how quickly, in our example calculations so far, the number of combinations rockets into big numbers. And if you're going to send a little bit of traffic to each of those combinations, you're going to need a ton of traffic (time and money costs here, too) to achieve useful data.

So, instead of using all the variables and variations, you use a fraction of them. Fewer to test. The duration of your test is shorter. Plus, if your variables are truly independent (varying one will not affect the other), you simply don't need to test every combination. You need select only a representative sample.

Fractional vs. Full Factorial

If you hang around analytics types, you may have heard *fractional* thrown into conversations about multivariate testing. Fractional tests are subsets of multivariate tests:

Multivariate Multivariate tests, also called *multifactorial*, test more than one variable.

Full factorial Full factorial tests are also called *full fractional factorial*, a form of multivariate test that tests every combination of variable variation with every other combination of variable variation.

Fractional factorial When you identify the minimum number of combinations you need to test from all possible combinations and still achieve confidence in your results, you are creating a fractional factorial test. In fractional factorial design, you have to make sure you match each variable with the other variables at least once. When you've run the test—assuming all your variables are truly independent— then you can use statistical computation to infer the values of the combinations you didn't test.

People debate the pros and cons of full and fractional testing (and even different methodologies within fractional testing). As we've said, full fractional testing compares all variables and variations. In terms of thoroughness, this approach is the most thorough. It's what Website Optimizer is set up to handle; there is no functionality in this program to help you identify what subset of combinations would be the best to test, but then the target audience for this software is those who do not routinely test and want to get started. Few marketers and IT people understand the parameters and nuances of the design of experiments and simply do not know how to figure out the best testing strategies for their applications. It's easier to help them test all combinations.

Google writes this:

"It is extremely important to consider how data from a multi-factorial experiment is analyzed. The data that is collected needs to be consistent with the proposed analysis. If, for example, you collect only fractional-factorial data, then only a fractional-factorial analysis can be completed. On the other hand, if you collect full factorial data, then you can still analyze the data using the same assumptions as with a fractional factorial design.

"We believe that the best option for web experiments with no (or low) setup cost is a full factorial allocation of page views to combinations. When traffic is light, you can fall back to a fractional factorial analysis. When traffic is heavy, then full factorial analysis can be contemplated."

—"Fractional vs. Full Factorial Analysis," Google Website Optimizer Testing Guides and Strategies (http://www.google.com/support/websiteoptimizer/bin/answer.py?answer=74818&topic=14314), 2008

Associated values with light and heavy traffic aside, Google fundamentally believes full factorial testing is superior:

"A similar type of experimentation is the 'fractional factorial' model. Taguchi, orthogonal arrays, and other similar types of experiments are special cases of fractional factorial experiments. Fractional experiments are designed to limit (often severely) the number of combinations tested. In real world industries, such as industrial or agricultural, each combination tested carries a significant resource cost. However, the benefit of reducing combinations comes at the cost of limiting the conclusions that can be drawn from the experiment.

"In web site experiments, however, there is no cost to adding additional combinations, which means there's no downside to using a full factorial design. With the same number of impressions, a full factorial design will reach the same conclusions as a fractional design, and—as the number of impressions increases—can yield deeper conclusions. In particular, with full factorial design, you can learn about interactions among factors, such as whether a specific text block influences the performance of a specific image."

—"Website Optimizer Technical Overview," Google Website Optimizer Help Center (`http://www.google.com/support/websiteoptimizer/bin/answer.py?hl=en&answer=61146`), 2008

How do you choose the fraction you are going to test? There are a number of statistical methodologies for selecting your subset. As of this writing, Taguchi, originally designed as a method for improving manufacturing quality, is among the more popular. The pros and cons of the Taguchi method are beyond the scope of this book, although we suggest you begin with Wikipedia's article on Genichi Taguchi and his method (`http://en.wikipedia.org/wiki/Genichi_Taguchi`), and then expand your research to online applications.

It is true that full factorial will yield the most information. However, it is not always true that a full factorial test will yield you significantly better results. The big issue here is time. Full factorial tests with many variables and variations take a very long time to run. The example we ran for 625 combinations in Figure 7.2? It would take you 56 years to perform that test! That's an awfully long time for your conversion rate to remain on hold.

In the end, any amount of time you lose that you don't have to lose to testing is a lost opportunity cost.

The fundamental question to ask in the full- vs. fractional-factorial debate is, if full factorial is significantly better, why isn't everyone doing it? If you knew that button color and shape were important to conversion but not which one of those variables was *more* important, fractional testing would probably help you answer this question more quickly. Doing tests to find highly influential factors gets you stronger results than testing every potential combination.

There's just as much debate surrounding the nuances of fractional testing. A number of analytics and testing firms specialize in fractional factorial testing. They provide insight into what to test and why—often the functionality for selecting your fractional sample is built into the software. They use a particular statistical method—one among many—for determining your subset. The problem? We're back to the "Why isn't everyone doing it?" question. Quite simply, they're not.

Proponents of fractional testing believe this:

"Doing successive tests to find high-influence items with fractional factorial testing will get much higher gains than getting every ounce of information out of one extremely long full factorial test. In addition, with a carefully designed fractional factorial test, you can learn all the major influences and the interactions between elements on the page."

—"Google Optimizer Is Slow," Billy's Blog: Learning about Optimization at Widemile

It is true that carefully designed fractional tests can help you winnow down the most important elements affecting your conversion rate. But we also have a problem getting behind the statement that "much higher gains" are a given in fractional testing. You can *potentially* get gains faster if it turns out that some of the testable variants are much better converting than others. But the point of doing the test is to determine that very fact, not to start with the conclusion. By this logic, fractional testing is *always* better, and that isn't so.

It's not always clear what is important to test. Lots of people say red buttons convert better than any other color. But it's not the redness, the wavelength of the button's color as emitted by your monitor, that aids the conversion, is it? It's really that the Internet is dominated by sites that use cool-color themes (blues or greens), and red is therefore a very contrasty color against blue or green. Clearly, you don't expect red buttons to convert better on a site that is predominantly red. Would crimson or orange or rose buttons (closely related to red) convert better than red on a blue-green site? Should you be testing for color or for contrast?

Fractional testing helps you identify obvious candidates; it can be valuable to identify appropriate factors through fractional testing and then turn to full factorial to refine your results.

Ultimately, the debate between full and fractional testing comes down to whether you are using the right tool for the job.

Once you have an understanding of these testing concepts—the possibilities and the limitations—you are in a position to evaluate what you need to test and how to frame your tests in the context of what most interests your customers: "What's in it for me?" We examine these frameworks in the next chapter.

CHAPTER 8

Developing a Testing Framework

We've mentioned things like scent and personas. We've discussed testing as an essential process for every online business. We've suggested in cases like Overstock. com's movie search feature and Geico's banner ad campaign that even a little bit of the "right" knowledge can help guide your testing strategies.

We opened this book by describing a system for closing, the end phase of which is testing, measuring, and optimizing. Testing can assist in your efforts to get your customers to take the action you've decided is in your best interest. But the other phases of that system for closing help you direct the focus of your testing. So, let's take a step back and look at the bigger picture of marketing and even the science behind successful campaigns.

An online marketing campaign is part of a chaotic system that contains elements both within and outside of the marketer's control. But don't mistake the term *chaotic* for meaningless and random; a chaotic system does have rhyme, reason, and, very often, a purpose.

Those familiar with chaos theory understand that chaotic systems can be extremely sensitive to seemingly insignificant changes. In the movie *Chocolat*, a candy maker stirs up an entire village by adding a secret ingredient—a dash of chili powder—to her chocolate recipe. Successful marketing campaigns, either by accident, by good fortune, or by planned design, simply influence a chaotic system for the benefit of their business goals. Maybe you are one of the lucky ones with a secret ingredient, but you don't need to have one to realize success. Most marketers don't.

We're quite sure no amount of testing can *create* a breakthrough campaign, a successful company, or a worldwide brand. However, informed testing can guide the prudent marketer while navigating the chaotic system of campaigns. Other principles and techniques also can be deployed to successfully improve and sometimes identify profitable campaigns and business opportunities.

So, as you try to whittle down your testing parameters, it's important to understand that the single common denominator in all successful marketing campaigns is this: *Every profitable marketing campaign succeeds at helping the customer reach her goals first.* In other words, your campaign must be relevant to your customers.

Factors That Determine Online Success: The Web Performance Equation

Factors that determine your online success fall into three primary categories: confidence and intent, the personal experience factor (PEF), and environmental and conditional factors.

Confidence and Intent

These factors occur *before* a visitor lands on your site and measure the confidence buildup that occurs prior to that event:

Unqualified How much traffic on your site belongs there? A certain percentage of traffic doesn't belong on your site, simply because the visitor arrived by mistake. Another set of visitors needs a product or service you don't offer.

Customer intent What are your customers' intentions toward your site and products? Will they buy today? Or do they intend to research a product online and then purchase it offline? Keyword research can help determine intent.

Brand confidence How much confidence do visitors have in your products or brand before they arrive at your site? This, in a nutshell, is customers' prior knowledge of your brand. Customers learn this through word of mouth and the impact quotient of your marketing efforts, both offline and online.

Personal Experience Factor

The personal experience factor is the actual experience a visitor has during and after a visit to your site. The following factors contribute to a site's PEF:

Planning Is there a comprehensive, focused understanding of target-visitor buying models? How well do you communicate your unique value proposition in regard to what's in the visitor's heart?

Structure Do the design, information architecture, and technology aspects of the site support the requirements of the buying and selling process? Does the visitor become disoriented or lose interest because of site flaws?

Momentum Does the site's conversion process channel visitor activity and motivate action? Does each page engage the buyer and persuade him to take action? Can you capitalize on up- and cross-sell opportunities?

Communications Does your site content convey your message effectively, and is the copy persuasive? Is it unequivocally clear where visitors are, and why, based on their goals?

Value Does the website communicate the value not only of your products and services, but also of doing business with you? Are the benefits clear?

Service after the sale How do you support customers after the transaction? Do you find ways to exceed their expectations? Can customers find their shipping and product questions on the site easily? At all?

Environmental and Conditional Factors

These factors exist largely outside your immediate control:

Product relevance Do your products deliver on the promise you've made to the customer? How relevant is your offering?

Conversion type Is your site's objective to sell products or services, sell content, or generate leads? We know a significant percentage of all traffic on an e-commerce site won't convert.

Product buy-in and buying cycle How complex is the sales process? Does your product require endorsement from another person, in addition to the visitor? (This is common to many business-to-business sites.) How much time and effort is a visitor willing to devote to the conversion process?

Market potential This is the total dollars available in a product or service category. Keyword research can help determine this.

Competitive environment What are your competitors doing, and how does it affect your sales?

Each of these factors can be taken into account, and each factor can also affect another. For example, all factors being equal, a website with strong brand confidence might expect the same online performance as a lesser-known site with a stronger PEF score.

Online Marketing 101

Whether you are an experienced marketer or just starting out, it's essential you have a firm grasp on a few of the basic principles of online marketing, specifically, how people behave online.

As early as 2001, a Xerox Palo Alto Research Center study indicated humans track information in a similar fashion to the way animals follow a scent. This is according to an article on the study:

"People...engage in what [Dr. Ed Chi] calls 'hub-and-spoke' surfing:

"They begin at the center, and they follow a trail based on its information scent.... If the scent is sufficiently strong, the surfer will continue to go on that trail. But if the trail is weak, they go back to the hub. 'People repeat this process until they're satisfied,' Chi said."

—Angel Gonzalez, "Hot on the Scent of Information," Wired.com, June 8, 2001

People hunting for online data behave remarkably like animals sniffing out prey. It's the most effective means of finding a teensy-weensy squirrel in an awfully big forest. Krishna Bharat, senior research scientist at Google, states it this way:

> *"'We provide strong scent so users don't lose time,' he said. 'We take the text from the page that is relevant to the query, and include it in the summary. . . Advertisers are coming to the realization that ads must have a scent that the user will likely find useful.'"*

—Ibid.

Let's look at a quick example of the presence and absence of scent. Say you want to buy a digital camcorder, so you type your query into Google (Figure 8.1). You see two paid placements in the results, one for Dell and one for Best Buy. Both include linked copy that reinforces your search query—scent. So, you click through.

Figure 8.1

Digital camcorder query on Google

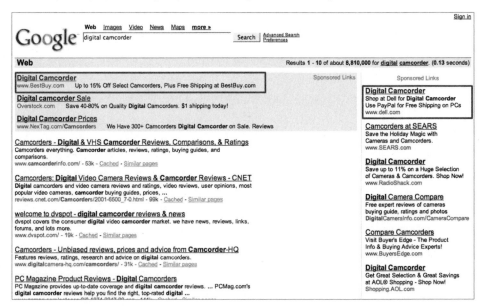

See anything on the Dell page that offers a visual or verbal connection to the keywords you typed in? Compare that to the Best Buy page, which not only includes appropriate words and pictures, but also provides information appropriate to the general (rather than product- or model-specific) nature of your search (Figure 8.2). Best Buy delivers scent.

Eighty percent of visitors leave a site after three pages. One of the biggest reasons for this abandonment problem is the absence of a scent trail.

Figure 8.2

**Dell and Best
Buy landing pages
for digital cam-
corder ads**

A OneStat study of typical metrics for a large sample of sites (from OneStat.com on March 8, 2004) illustrates the number of pages a visitor sees:

1 page view: 9.52 percent

1–2 page views: 54.60 percent

2–3 page views: 16.56 percent

3–4 page views: 8.75 percent

4–5 page views: 4.43 percent

6–7 page views: 1.41 percent

7–8 page views: 0.85 percent

8–9 page views: 0.68 percent

9–10 page views: 0.51 percent

More than 10 page views: 2.69 percent

These results aren't unique to the users in OneStat's study. We consistently observe this same behavior across hundreds of sites. Graphically, these numbers echo Shop.org's study results, shown in Figure 8.3, for customer site abandonment through the conversion process.

Figure 8.3

Typical website traffic drop-off

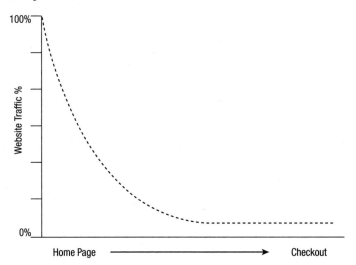

It might take visitors two pages to figure out they are in the wrong place, but we doubt it. More than half of all visitors are interested enough to click one or two steps deeper before they decide to leave. That's a pretty clear indication sites fail to provide enough scent.

A scent trail starts whenever a potential customer encounters one of your messages and decides to act upon it. The beginning point could be a brochure, a television ad, a banner ad, or a radio spot.

The majority of online scent trails start with a search. A prospect types into the search engine the term she believes will give her the result she desires. She intentionally follows the scent trail of that specific term from the starting point, usually the search results page, looking for a specific, relevant answer. She may return frequently to the starting point for orientation. If she doesn't find the answer after several clicks, she starts a new scent trail. She repeats this process until she finds her answer or gives up.

Knowing how people hunt and sniff around for information is certainly useful, but that usefulness is limited until you determine more about what a person is sniffing for.

Most search engine marketing is about getting found. The problem is, most search engine marketing does little more than put signs on every tree that read, "Squirrels in the forest." This is probably true, but the signs don't help the hunter actually *find* the squirrels in the forest.

It's much worse when the marketer doesn't have squirrels but nevertheless lures squirrel hunters. This marketer merely serves a plate of nuts on the landing page.

The search terms a user keys in and follows reveal her intent. The more specific the term, the more transparent the intent. If you want to convert, then your AdWords, banners, landing pages, and site must serve the content and path that match the intent of the search term.

At User Interface Engineering, Jared Spool conducted a study with his team. They asked participants to find a specific item that interested them on a website. Spool's team provided detailed descriptions of what the participants were looking for before they began their search. Each site that participants were asked to search did contain that information. Spool cites the results:

"It turned out that users were far more successful at finding their targets when the description words, which they told us before *they saw the site, appeared on the home page. In the tasks where users successfully found their target content, the description words appeared on the home page 72% of the time. When users were unsuccessful, their words only appeared an average of 6% of the time on the home page."*

—Jared Spool, "The Right Trigger Words," User Interface Engineering, November 15, 2004

Understanding this result allows you to test and optimize the scent trails people follow, both on your site and in your marketing campaigns.

Know Thy Customer

As a marketing vehicle, the Internet is multitalented. Computer technology excels at collecting and collating considerable amounts of visitor data. Compared to other ad media, the Internet delivers more data about who our customers are and what they actually do, and it does so more specifically and quickly than most marketers ever dreamed possible.

Combine such data within the context of site content or a specific ad campaign, and you see accurate snapshots of customer behavior patterns that you can observe, track, and measure. This goes way beyond the typical "target demographic" techniques of yesteryear.

However, although testing and technology give you an impressive advantage, it's the relevant ad *messages* and offers that make the difference in long-term return-on-investment (ROI) marketing efforts. And, in order to create consistently relevant messaging and relevant scent trails, you must first know your customers.

They are a) voluntary participants b) at some stage in the buying decision process who c) embrace one of a handful of identifiable buying modalities.

Voluntary Participants

It may seem obvious, but it is all too often ignored: Every individual actively makes a choice to come to your website. They arrive, task in mind, prepared to participate. While they remain on your site, they agree to continue participating in a persuasive dialogue with you. This is critical knowledge: Behavior on e-business sites (fundamentally a self-service environment) is voluntary, participatory, and goal-directed. Save for those who land on your site by mistake, your visitors are already interested in you and are there for a reason. And they are completely in control of what they will or will not agree to experience. If your visitor refuses to take the next click on your site, your dialogue is over. It is essential to remember you are always one click away from goodbye.

Your visitors:

- Control their experience
- Are goal-oriented
- Are highly fragmented
- Are volunteers
- Are involved in a self-service environment
- Must participate to accomplish their tasks

Propensity to Buy

We can identify four categories of visitors based on their level of motivation and their readiness to make a decision:

- First are the perfect prospects who know exactly what they want. Think of a self-actualizing buyer seeking features, brands, and model numbers.
- Second are prospects who sort of know what they want. Think of shoppers with a strongly felt need who have not yet narrowed down their search criteria.
- Third are prospects who aren't sure they want anything but might buy if what they want were to appear. These are window-shoppers. They have no strongly felt need in mind, but you might be able to suggest one to them.
- The fourth group of visitors aren't prospects, and they aren't qualified to take advantage of the product or service. They're there by mistake. Be happy when they exit gracefully.

You don't know where your visitors are in the process when they land on your site, so your site must be prepared to deal with all possibilities. It also helps to consider that not all your visitors will make a decision when they first visit your site—sometimes a successful conversion is the result of multiple visits.

Buying Modalities

Ever since the great Greek thinkers, people have observed that human personalities, while as unique as a thumbprint, also share much in common. However, our interest in psychographics does not encompass the universe of possibility—it would be a monumental task to sell to every single individual variation. Instead, we examine this issue from the perspective of four dominant temperaments (mentioned in Chapter 4), with a focus on factors that influence how a temperament would approach the buying decision process, such as the following:

- How quickly does the temperament make a decision?
- What level of detail does the temperament prefer?
- Is the temperament disciplined, open-ended, or spontaneous in managing time?
- Does the temperament prefer a business-like or personal approach?
- What sorts of information and documentation appeal to the temperament?
- What is the temperament's primary motivating question?

These four temperaments (see Figure 8.4) represent different buying modalities—natural preferences that influence each of us when we go through the steps of deciding to buy. When you address the needs of each temperament, you are better able to persuade your customers by meeting their wants and needs. The following are the four temperaments as we have labeled them for marketing purposes:

The Competitive wants accomplishment. These individuals have a deep appreciation for challenges. They enjoy being in control, are goal-oriented, and are looking for methods for completing tasks. They are usually quick to reach a decision. They want to know what your product or service can do for them to solve their problem.

The Spontaneous wants action. These individuals want movement, simplicity, and stimulation. They like things that are nonthreatening and friendly. They hate dealing with impersonal details and cold, hard facts. They are usually quick to reach a decision. They want to know why your product or service is best to solve their problem.

The Humanistic wants a relationship. These individuals are people-centered and empathetic. They enjoy helping others and are particularly fond of socializing. They are usually slow to reach a decision. They want to know who has used your product or service to solve problems and, more important, who will be affected by their decision.

The Methodical wants accuracy. These individuals appreciate facts and information presented in a logical manner as documentation of truth. They enjoy organization and completion of detailed tasks. They do not appreciate disorganization. They want to know exactly how your product or service can solve the problem.

Figure 8.4

Decision-making qualities of the buying modalities

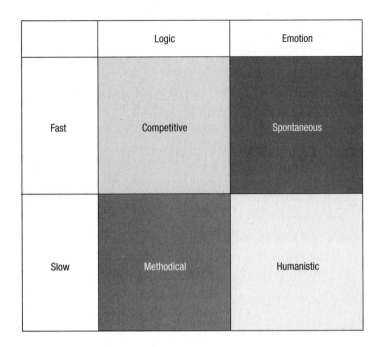

Thinking about your customers in terms of their buying modalities is the easiest way to begin speaking to the psychographic dimensions of your audience segments. It's also the necessary first step on the path to creating profiles.

Profiles

A proven technique to achieve consistent relevance in any marketing effort is *persona creation*.

A persona is a fictional customer who represents one of a company's audience segments. A set of personas, when properly designed, will represent the entirety of a company's potential buyers. These personas provide entire organizations with a framework for engaging customers as the customer prefers to be engaged, leaving no segment unengaged. In addition, personas help businesses realize better marketing opportunities.

Over the past 10 years, our firm has developed and established an extremely robust methodology called Persuasion Architecture. Creating and using personas in developing messages and testing-site scenarios is at the core of this methodology.

The beginning tester, however, does not necessarily have the time or resources to create full persona sets. That doesn't mean you can't benefit from some persona-based principles and techniques.

We recommend creating visitor profiles—entry-level personas who represent each of your customer segments. You can use these profiles to create a predictive model of customer behavior. With this model in place, you can test your campaigns more efficiently.

Creating Profiles That Are More Than Demographic Snapshots

Demographics don't tell the whole story. Underneath all those numbers is a wide array of needs and motivations. They may have little to do with a customer's age, gender, or income level.

Keywords, internal search queries, click-streams, average time spent on individual pages, and other information you can derive from web analytics gives you a clearer picture of those motivations and needs.

Visitors should be segmented by demographics *and* behavior and then targeted accordingly. This effectively answers the questions about where and how to advertise.

But to be more effective in persuading and predicting, your profiles go deeper by attempting to answer the question, why do customers behave this way? Once you understand behavior, you can begin to address the message to which each segment (or profile) is most likely to respond.

The Universe of Buyers

When you combine the stages of the buying decision process with the four dominant buying modalities, you effectively describe your potential universe of buyers (Figure 8.5). It's rare that a site requires more than five to seven personas, but awareness of the buying stages and modalities makes it possible for you to fine-tune your testing in ways that prevent you from spinning your wheels. The path away from randomness starts here.

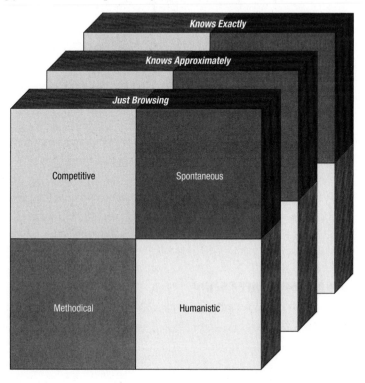

Figure 8.5

The universe of buyers

The Essential Questions

The following three questions ultimately should frame every other question you ask about what to do on your site and underlie every decision you make when you test your persuasive system for optimal performance:

- Who needs to be persuaded?
- What actions does this person need to take?
- How will you most effectively persuade that person?

Let's return to the Overstock.com example we discussed in Chapter 1 to see how the answers to these questions can help guide the elements you test and the variations you create.

Overstock.com Revisited

Recall the Overstock.com case study in which changing one image accounted for a 5 percent lift in top-line sales? (See Figures 1.2 and 1.3 in Chapter 1.) We said when we saw the page, we immediately identified a major problem.

We knew this was a problem because we knew how the four different buying modalities (Competitive, Spontaneous, Humanistic, and Methodical) would respond:

- The Competitive visitors would search movies by actor, title, or director.
- The Spontaneous visitors would be looking for the top sellers and new releases.
- The Humanistic visitors would focus on reviews by others.
- The Methodical visitors would look for films by genre.

Most visitors to a site prefer to navigate by linked categories rather than use a search feature. The categorization of titles on Overstock.com's movie landing page appealed to the Spontaneous visitor—this qualification structure worked reasonably well for them. But the structure did not address the needs of the other three buying modalities at all. When they turned to the search feature as a fallback option, they naturally assumed the search was related to kids' titles, not Overstock.com's entire movie list. And this was the leak in Overstock.com's conversion process.

By changing the image to suggest the search covered all Overstock.com titles, the site managed to convert more of the other three buying modalities. It wasn't as many as it could have if the categorization schemes reflected different priorities, but it was certainly enough to make a significant difference!

The Importance of Scent

In addition to profiles/personas, the other piece of your testing framework needs to focus on creating scent trails for the four buying modalities. Scent is essentially about relevance and continuity in the process, although that relevance may not be the same for all visitors.

You've seen those cartoons where Mickey Mouse catches a whiff of something that smells great. Minnie has set a pie to cool on an open windowsill. The pie sends out tendrils of aroma that target Mickey's nose and pull him inexorably to the source. That's a scent trail.

When the scent trail meets Mickey's nose, it captures his interest. If his interest is strong enough, he'll decide to follow the trail. And if the aroma tendrils remain unbroken, Mickey will follow them until they lead him to the pie. But if Minnie closes the window, the scent trail evaporates. Mickey won't be led anywhere.

It works pretty much the same online. The right scent, carefully chosen, captures the interest of a customer. Instead of using cartoon tendrils, you maintain an online scent trail with words and pictures that reinforce the scent and clicks that take the customer closer to the goal. If you don't interrupt the scent trail, it will lead the customer where she wants to go (which also happens to be where you want her to go).

If you interrupt your scent trail, you leave your customer stranded. The path she was following becomes a dead end. Where's she supposed to go? Do you really want to trust that she's motivated enough to continue on her own? When it comes to scent trails, dropping the ball is one of the leading causes of abandonment!

Establishing and maintaining your scent trail is essential to keeping your persuasive momentum, establishing your credibility, and building your customers' confidence. You simply can't motivate folks to move from click to click without it.

Laying a decent scent trail really isn't that hard. Ask yourself, at every point in your process, what would my customer expect to see next? What promise have I made that I need to keep in the next click? If you're not sure what you've promised, ask others what they think you've promised. Then execute the answers.

Ideally, you want to create unique landing pages targeted to the message that delivers folks, whether that message comes from a banner ad, an email, a pay-per-click, a television ad, a radio spot, a billboard, or a brochure. This is the strongest scent trail you can provide. If you have to use your home page to catch the folks clicking through from your promotional entities, then create a special area that reinforces the promotional messaging so folks can identify the continuity. This was the primary idea behind Go Daddy's second Super Bowl advertising campaign.

Make your scent trail incredibly easy and obvious to follow. Never assume your visitors will take the time to figure out where they need to go next. Remember this caveat: Don't make me think. When you do the work for your visitors, more of them convert.

Lastly, always keep in mind the contract you establish through your scent trail. Avoid hype. It has a habit of creating expectations you might not actually be prepared to meet.

Figure 8.6

Victoria's Secret banner ad

Vicky Creates Scent

Victoria's Secret created a strong scent trail in one of its banner ad campaigns. Let's watch and learn from what Vicky does. She provocatively captures us with the banner ad shown in Figure 8.6. We click. Vicky gently lands us in Figure 8.7.

Notice a few things. The offer, clearly stated on the banner ad, is just as clearly repeated on the landing page. Instructions are easy and concise, and the navigation lends itself to product selection. If the offer is the tipping point in persuading the visitor to click, the landing page has satisfied by emphasizing that offer.

Figure 8.7

Victoria's Secret landing page

If the brand is the tipping point for the visitor, this landing page is as successful as the home page would have been. The top global navigation is clearly evident (breaking more than a few "expert" landing page rules). It provides intuitive entry points into the other products offered and to the home page as well. The landing page has satisfied from a branding perspective because it sustains the corporate spirit expressed in the ad.

If it's not the offer or the brand—and most times, it isn't—you look to the ad itself. In this case, it refers to a specific product, *bras*, and a specific qualifier, *very sexy*. The landing page is within the category of the advertised product and provides the contextual left navigation (chock-full of trigger words, you'll notice) appropriate to provide the visitor with the biggest leap they're comfortable making.

If customers can describe their needs more specifically—by designer or product line perhaps—Vicky can whisk them off to their chosen destination. If not, the graphical clues build on the imagery of the ad. Scrolling down the landing page shows various lines of *very sexy bras*.

Calls to action within these images of *very sexy bras* could (and should) be stronger, more intuitive. Vicky could do a better job motivating the click. However, clicking through cements our perception of Vicky as one hip chick when it comes to getting the customer to the specific goods. Observe the pure satisfaction upon click-through (Figure 8.8).

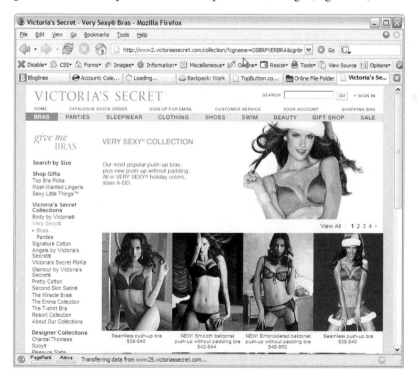

Figure 8.8

Victoria's Secret click-through page

The left contextual navigation is still present, yet the collection we've clicked through to (albeit unknowingly by clicking through the image we found attractive) has been highlighted. We are actually learning to use Vicky's own navigation scheme. Product pictures are cleanly displayed, as the products would be used (or as closely as they can be without a parental warning). Prices are clearly marked, as are product labels, and there are options to view similar products.

This page provides the visitor with a high degree of relevance. Customers have now entered the conversion funnel, and this campaign is much more likely to convert.

Using Scent and Personas as Testing Yardsticks

With the concepts of scent and the differing needs of your customers' buying modalities, you are in a much better position to shape the variations you will test. Understanding these important dimensions of your persuasive system will help avoid testing randomly.

In lieu of an analytics program that helps you identify the biggest drop-off points in your site (though with Google Analytics, there's no reason to be in the dark when it comes to measuring your site), you can focus on certain pages that tend to lose more customers (Figure 8.9). These include landing pages and your home page—entry points to your conversion funnels. Examine the search terms that direct visitors to these pages, and consider the needs of your personas to determine why visitors might leave these pages, focusing especially on your copy.

Figure 8.9

The Google Website Optimizer's page priority graph

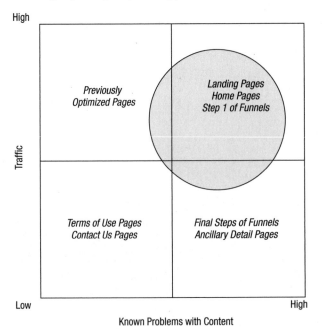

Using analytics software, identify the pages with high bounce rates, high exit rates, and low time spent on page. These measurements will direct you to the problem areas on your site and in your landing pages. An excellent book to help you understand and use analytics to your advantage is Avinash Kaushik's *Web Analytics: An Hour a Day* (Sybex, 2007).

Once you've considered what to test, you are ready to do the following:

1. Define your conversion goals.

2. Identify your customers.

3. Do the creative.

We'll discuss these more fully in the next chapter.

CHAPTER 9

Establishing Testing Goals and Parameters

Only now will we begin to concern ourselves with your company and your goals. This is by design. We understand that your company and its goals are extremely important to you. However, the typical problem with company goals is that most companies put them first, at the expense of the basic tenet of marketing success:

For you to achieve your goals, your customers must achieve their goal first.

Three Steps to Goals and Parameters

In Chapter 8, we concluded with three steps that should guide the prioritization of your testing strategies:

1. Define your conversion goals.

2. Identify your customers.

3. Do the creative.

Define Your Conversion Goals

It is always best to set your goals in the context of what your potential customers need. Willful or unintentional ignorance of this is the number-one reason for marketing and business failure. Simply stating goals will not make them a reality. Of course, not stating goals at all is worse.

With your goals in mind, the next step is to ask yourself what you are trying to accomplish with A/B or multivariate testing. Are you after more subscribers, a higher conversion rate, or a greater return on investment on your pay-per-click (PPC) campaigns? Your goals will determine your testing parameters, which will affect the success of your testing efforts.

You would state your goal as follows:

"I want to increase the sitewide conversion rate by 20 percent from 2 percent to 2.4 percent in the next month."

or as follows:

"I want to decrease the shopping cart abandonment rate by 10 percent from 70 percent to 63 percent by the next quarter."

Key Performance Indicators

Retailers must first establish key performance indicators (KPIs). These are the backbone of ongoing optimization efforts. KPI reporting is really the only meaningful link between the numbers you generate and your business goals.

Eric Peterson, author of Web Analytics Demystified (Celilo Group Media, 2004), elaborates on the qualities that make for a useful key performance indicator in "The Nitty-Gritty Behind the Glamour," http://www.conversionchronicles.com/The_Nitty_Gritty_Behind_the_Glamour.html:

- It offers a succinct definition that summarizes the nature of the relationship between the data that is compared (meaningfully compared, naturally!).
- It establishes an expectation for performance by using business-relevant comparisons over time.
- It is capable of revealing a meaningful change in activity for a selected period.
- It is capable of influencing remedial action.

Here are a few examples of KPIs you may already be measuring:

- Sitewide conversion rate
- Percentage of new and returning visitors
- Look-to-book ratios
- Sales per visitor
- Average order value
- Average number of items purchased
- Shopping cart abandonment rate
- Revenue and profit per product
- Repeat order rate to help calculate lifetime value

Most of these metrics have some correlation to your profit-and-loss statements. Most also provide an incomplete picture of customer behavior. Allen Crane, Dell Computer's senior manager of business process improvement, says this:

"The Holy Grail is a suite of quantifiable, actionable e-metrics that capture behavior patterns and accurately relate them to the key transactional business levers of units, revenue, and margin."

—Allen Crane, "Actionable Metrics," Intelligent Enterprise, February 1, 2003

If you have already been executing campaigns online, it is wise to look at the following for commonalities:

- Your 10 highest-converting/most-successful campaigns
- Your 10 lowest-converting/least-successful campaigns

Now you have all the information you need to begin planning the nuts and bolts of your testing. Only now are you ready to begin thinking about the "creative" component of your campaign.

In summary, what are you trying to accomplish with your test?

- Do you want to increase sales?
- Do you want to generate leads?
- Do you want to generate product-specific purchases?
- Do you want to generate qualified traffic for an on-site purchase?
- Do you want to generate traffic for a self-service or subscription service?
- Do you want to generate online service sign-ups or event registrations?
- Does product image X convert better than product image Z?

Identify Your Customers

You can approach the messaging you will create in several ways. At the most basic level, you can identify where your target customers are in the buying process:

- Are they in the early stages where they are examining the nature of possible solutions and gathering information? For example, they know they want a DVD player, but they really don't know much about their options and how they will go about choosing.
- Are they in the middle stages of the buying process? For example, they have identified the criteria that are important to them and are beginning to locate and compare brands and models.
- Are they in the late stages of the buying process? For example, they know they want a specific brand and a specific model, and they are searching for the right business, the right price, and the right form of customer service options.

At a more sophisticated level, you can work with the qualities that comprise the four different buying modalities: Competitive, Humanistic, Spontaneous, and Methodical. You can begin to flesh out these four perspectives by listing the sorts of questions each might have as they go about making their decisions.

The most sophisticated way to approach testing is to create fully developed personas who stand as archetypes for your actual audience. We discussed this level of persona development in *Waiting for Your Cat to Bark?* (Thomas Nelson, 2006).

When you have an idea how your customers go about accomplishing their tasks with you and the questions they'll likely bring to the table, you can begin to refine exactly to whom you are speaking on different pages of your site or in different advertising campaigns. Not all pages need to speak to all profiles or personas; the same can be said for advertising campaigns. In fact, many site pages and advertising campaigns are stronger when they focus on a single profile (or persona) or on a subset.

Do the Creative

Having defined your conversion goals and identified your target customers, you focus on the elements of your pages, pay-per-click ads, emails, or advertisements (online and off) that drive your prospects to your landing pages:

- Do you have the correct messages for each type of profile and their motivation? You will likely need more than one.
- Do you have the correct message for each stage of their buying cycle? Are they early in the buying process or in the middle, or are they ready to buy?

The Three Essential Questions

Remember the Victoria's Secret scent trail from banner ad to final click-through page? In similar fashion, your site or campaign will probably include several touch points, which could include any of the following:

- Web pages
- Landing pages
- Banner ads
- AdWords
- Pay-per-click
- Emails
- Organic search results
- Offline advertisements
- Affiliate sites

At each of these touch points, you need to ask yourself the three essential questions that allow you to persuade your customers to take the next step. We mentioned these in Chapter 8:

- Who needs to be persuaded? Who has landed on this touch point? Which profiles or personas do you want to click through?

- What actions does this person need to take? Do you want this customer to click through to the next step? Select a product to purchase? Learn more? Subscribe? Register?

- How will you most effectively persuade this person? What questions will this customer be asking at this touch point? How can you answer these questions?

When you've thoroughly planned this, you need to set a benchmark and establish control pages.

Your control page will be the page against which you test all subsequent optimization efforts. If you are just getting started with A/B and multivariate testing, your control page will be your current landing page before you start optimizing. When a new page performs better than the original landing page, it becomes your control page in subsequent testing.

Actually Getting Started

After going through these steps, you may have identified numerous feasible tests and feel overwhelmed by the possibilities. You needn't. You don't have to burden yourself with more than you are comfortable tackling. It is not uncommon for planning to take several months. But time spent planning is time well spent. We recommend testing some of your more problematic entities (see Chapter 8). To narrow your task list, you might start testing the following:

- Your top-five highest bounce rate pages
- Your top-five highest exit rate pages
- Your top-five lowest time spent pages
- Your top-five key pages (checkout, cart, registration, top product, about us)

Of course, five is arbitrary; it could be top three, ten, or seventeen.

Determine Your Time/Quantity Test Interval

This time period should allow you enough time to gather sufficient data to gauge real insight about your A/B tests. Identify the number of unique visitors and/or conversions to test so you can establish good data, and then determine how long it will take you to generate this traffic. This number will vary from business to business, but your decisions should yield enough data to confidently declare a "winner." Many A/B testing platforms, including Google Website Optimizer, will calculate this for you.

Decide Which Elements to Test

Now that you have decided which pages to test, you have to decide what elements on those pages you want to test.

To keep this a true scientific A/B test, you can test, or "contrast," only one element at a time. Also, some elements are more complex than others and do not necessarily lend themselves to testing—among those elements are long copy and page placement. Although it is effective to test messages, headers, and other short copy elements, copy elements such as product descriptions often introduce too many variables that prevent you from gathering meaningful data in the A/B testing structure.

The challenge of A/B testing is not only in identifying the variations of a given element to be tested, but also in enumerating how many elements there are to be varied. When only one element changes and there are two variants of it, exactly one A/B test accomplishes the measurement. When one element changes and it has three variants, there are three A/B tests. You might think of it just as a single A/B/C test, demonstrating that all multivariate testing can be expressed as a series of A/B tests.

But when multiple elements change, the number of A/B tests to be performed rises dramatically because each pairing adds a dimension to the testing. Two elements each with two variants means four A/B tests. Three elements each with four variants means 64 tests. Four elements each with five variants means 625 tests. And that's just for one page, one state of optimization. Scenarios made up of multiple states-with-elements-with-variations quickly become untenable, and testing everything becomes organizationally and computationally impossible.

The trick, then, is in planning how the test will occur so as to maximize your ability to sample the topology, the "lay of the land" as it were, so that in successive testing iterations you can focus in more detail on only those areas of the landscape that indicate potential for increased gain. Rather than a brute-force, test-'em-all approach, intelligence must be used to sample the topology and use well-known but complex techniques to determine the direction of ensuing iterations of tests.

It is important when testing to try to think outside the box—the answer you seek is likely something you would not naturally consider to be a problem, or it may be a problem you thought you had already solved, but your execution is flawed. So, approach this with an open mind, and do your best to put yourself in the shoes of the visitor.

Prioritize by Impact and Resources Required

If you're like most companies, you have a laundry list of things you'd like to do with your site. You know instinctively that all the items on the list aren't of equal value; some probably have more impact than others. You also know these items require effort and resources, some more and some less. So, the obvious question is, where do you begin?

Your overriding priority must be the initiatives that help you meet your company's goals: increasing revenue and reducing costs. Many factors—from the cost of traffic to search engine optimization to site drop-off to page convergence to increasing average order size—will influence your ability to achieve your goals.

Often it is in the company's best interests to gather opinion and intelligence from a variety of sources, including CEOs, sales representatives, customer service representatives, and even customers. In addition, it may be valuable to look to competitive and parallel industry research to see how (if) others have addressed the problems.

Bazaarvoice CMO Sam Decker, formerly of Dell Computers, suggests creating a benefit-model that

---

". . .estimates the impact of each proposed Web site project is expected to have on each challenge. . . Only employees who know what your customers want, which projects best meet those needs, and the relative impact of those projects on the challenges at hand— not to mention the bottom line—should participate in the creation of the [benefit-model]."

Sam Decker, "From Here to Priority," *Dell Insight*, November 2003

You can weight the projects on this benefit-model based on expected ROI compared to the resources you will need to implement them. You could also weight based on each project's "strategic fit" with long-term strategic goals that add to the bottom line or enable future benefits. In general, though, those projects that immediately benefit the business should rank high.

A Hierarchy of Optimization

One of the best ways to help you prioritize your projects is to understand how a hierarchy of optimization helps you identify critical problems and affects your decision-making process. You're likely familiar with Maslow's Hierarchy of Needs, which states that human beings must first prioritize basic needs, such as food and shelter, before they're able to seek higher needs such as social interaction and self-actualization. What good is owning a Harley-Davidson or finding the perfect outfit for a trip to a club if you're starving to death?

Figure 9.1

Optimization pyramid

Looking at your site in a similar fashion will help you better assess where to start or will assist you in knowing exactly what you're optimizing now. The hierarchy also gives insight into optimization's potential impact. The higher you go on the pyramid, the bigger the impact you'll make on optimization. However, the pyramid doesn't indicate the level of effort needed to optimize, because this is as different from site to site as we are different from each other (see Figure 9.1).

FUNCTIONAL

Let's start at the bottom. *Functional* is the most basic requirement. Does your site have long periods of downtime? Do you deliver hundreds or thousands of 404s? Does your shopping cart constantly freeze up on visitors? Can users log in? Do images load? Is your site heavy on customer-facing errors? As a first order of business, work to make your site as reliable as the sunrise.

Another aspect of function is making sure that back-end functions are also in place. We've worked with companies that were spending ample amounts on marketing and great site widgets, but the back-end shipping process was broken, causing an embarrassing number of orders to go unfulfilled. This isn't sexy marketing; it's Business 101. Why go through all the hard work to market and sell a $1,000 dress only to have the customer walk up to a dirty checkout lane with a broken cash register circa 1950?

Having solid, clean user data for analytics also falls into the functional level; otherwise, anything higher up on the pyramid can't be optimized with any accuracy or confidence.

ACCESSIBLE

How *accessible* is your site? Target.com suffered a lawsuit because it didn't include alt tags on its images. Font size, language issues, and pages and sections that don't load correctly are other accessibility issues. In our 2007 Customer Experience Study, we discovered that 38 percent of the retailers had difficult-to-read fonts! Browser-specific issues fall in this level as well. Check your analytics access logs to determine whether you're underserving or ignoring a visitor segment. Optimize for people with disabilities, allow font resizing for users who need larger print, and solve browser-specific issues. Optimize for dial-up users (there are still plenty of them out there). You should also consider access for mobile devices.

USABLE

Are your buttons easy to find and see? Is the search dialog box where users expect it? Do you use drop-downs when you could use a radio button? *Usability* is about moving site elements around and using size, color, and contrast to improve the ease of use of your site. Thousands of great articles have been written about usability. We encourage you to check out publications by Jared Spool's User Interface Engineering.

Call-to-action button optimization is a popular optimization item for marketers. For most, the effort is low, and it can have significant impact. Still, it's only one aspect of the usability equation.

INTUITIVE

Although similar to and often confused with usability, the *intuitive* level is about improving the flow of the visitor's site experience and optimizing elements that are preventing visitors from buying. Point-of-action assurances, product detail pop-ups, customer reviews, up-front shipping costs, and current in-stock messaging all reduce friction in the buying process, anticipate customer questions, and offer answers at the point where the customer asks them.

On a lead-generation site, optimize form questions, try to shorten the time needed to fill out the form, and introduce ways for the visitor to take more control of when and how they're contacted.

PERSUASIVE

At the top of the pyramid are site elements that move a customer toward making a decision to buy your specific product. *Persuasion* issues are almost always high impact.

You improve persuasion on your site by improving copy or product images. Product descriptions, feature tours, demos, and product comparisons (even with competitors) are considered persuasive issues. On a lead-generation or business-to-business (B2B) site, it's your service description, case studies, testimonials, and white papers. Make sure your copy addresses each of your modalities, profiles, or personas.

Brand image and a site's overall look and feel are often persuasion issues, especially if there's a disconnect between the brand promise and site design. Never doubt that visitors will forgive a multitude of site problems when they are intent on a strong, familiar branded product—many of us have endured horrible sites and processes to buy the products and services we really wanted.

Start at the pyramid's bottom and list each of the optimization tests or changes you need to consider. For each item, rank the effort it will take your team to make the change or test possible. Start with low-effort items, even if they're low on the pyramid. Then work your way up.

Allocating Optimization Resources

Any optimization hierarchy must reflect visitors' needs as they approach your site, as well as your sales/conversion goals. The top of the funnel shown in Figure 9.2 is market potential; the bottom is where prospects convert. Almost every conversion rate optimization effort focuses too narrowly on the bottom while ignoring opportunities above it. The best optimization efforts achieve usability. Many companies face persuasion issues, not conversion issues.

As you can see, the sales funnel and the needs pyramid are inversely related.

Any company committing resources to optimization should use these diagrams to determine where in the hierarchy its current efforts fall and what other areas might be more lucrative for optimization efforts. When those in charge of business concerns make the crucial strategic decisions, support staff in IT, Design, and UI can apply the appropriate tactics to meet those strategic goals. When the business side abstains from making these decisions, members of the support staff are forced to make them, even if they don't understand the potential impact their decisions will have on the company as a whole. This isn't a recipe for success. These are some important points to consider:

- Is the value of your product/service too complex for most prospects to understand? If so, optimizing the sales funnel at the bottom, when prospects are ready to convert, isn't efficient. Focus on persuasion issues.

Figure 9.2

**Persuasion/
conversion funnel**

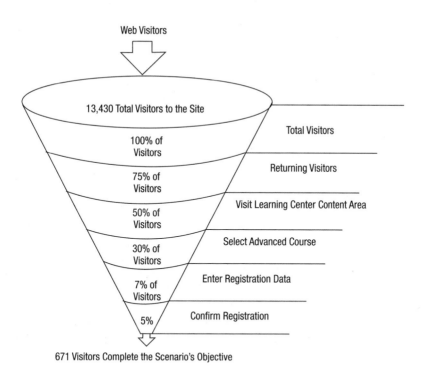

Web Visitors

13,430 Total Visitors to the Site

100% of Visitors	Total Visitors
75% of Visitors	Returning Visitors
50% of Visitors	Visit Learning Center Content Area
30% of Visitors	Select Advanced Course
7% of Visitors	Enter Registration Data
5%	Confirm Registration

671 Visitors Complete the Scenario's Objective

- If you know most of your traffic acquisition focuses on the late stage of the buying process or your product meets a basic, easy-to-understand need, focus on the base of the needs pyramid. This is the place for impulse buys.

- If you have strong brand awareness or are a market leader, optimizing the top of the needs pyramid will bear little fruit. Prospects know what to expect from your company. Instead, focus efforts on the middle to bottom of the needs pyramid. Prospects are already convinced of your brand's value.

- The checkout process and lead forms are where you can see the greatest buyer intent. If your checkout process or lead forms have relatively little dropout, optimize the top tiers of the pyramid to move and persuade more prospects to enter the bottom of your sales funnel.

Before we conclude Part I, "A Marketer's View of Testing: The Power of Optimization," you'll see a real-world example in Chapter 10, in which one company examined various conversion issues (as opposed to higher-level persuasion issues) in the landing page campaign it developed. The example provides insight into a low-hanging-fruit conversion situation, typical to many online businesses, and incorporates a number of the factors we've discussed so far.

Jigsaw Case Study

In September 2007, Inc. magazine ran an article ("Turning Browsers into Buyers") in its prominent *Inc. 500* issue that detailed the importance of conversion and testing's role in improving conversion. (You can access the article at www.inc.com/magazine/20070901/turning-browsers-into-buyers.html.) It was the first time a high-profile publication had acknowledged the value of testing. (So, what are you waiting for?) The article documented two testing success stories, one of which belongs to Jigsaw Health.

Jigsaw Health (www.jigsawhealth.com) provides science-based alternative resources and products for those afflicted with chronic conditions. The company came to us for help improving the conversion rate for its site. We began the process by focusing our attention on a landing page Jigsaw had designed specifically for its magnesium product (see Figure 10.1), examining tactics that could be applied across product pages sitewide.

Figure 10.1

Original Jigsaw landing page

Phase 1: Planning

Before we started actually testing, we planned a set of definitions and tactics that would guide our testing:

- We considered the conversion complete if a site visitor concluded an order and received the order confirmation/thank you page.
- We calculated the conversion rate as the number of visitors who reached order_thanks.aspx divided by the number of unique visitors to the landing page.
- We documented the testing stages and captured screen shots to periodically review our progress.
- We specified a time frame across which we would collect our dataset.

Jigsaw also ran a thorough evaluation of the page's performance. This provided a base point of reference against which we could evaluate subsequent changes.

Analytics revealed the conversion rate for this landing page over the testing period was 2.54 percent—par for industry standards.

Phase 2: Testing

Rather than test randomly, Jigsaw worked with us over the next five months to understand which variables on its landing page were potentially key factors affecting its conversion rate. To identify these elements, we needed to look at things from the customer's point of view, taking into account the questions customers would need answered and where customers were in the buying cycle. Using this information, Jigsaw designed 10 different versions of its landing page to test factors that included its call-to-action buttons, copy, and the wording of key headlines (Figure 10.2).

Phase 3: Putting It All Together

In the final phase of Jigsaw's testing project, it pulled together everything it had learned from its data, evaluated it in terms of the site's selling and buying process, and created an optimized landing page (Figure 10.3).

Important refinements included creating a trimmer header navigation area; regularizing the bigger, yellow call-to-action buttons; removing a "Redeem Promo Code" feature; adding a

Figure 10.2

One version of Jigsaw's landing page in the testing process

list of product benefits (not features) to the copy; and including a "What are others saying?" area at the bottom of the product page.

Figure 10.3

Jigsaw's optimized landing page

Throughout the testing process, the numbers went up and down as Jigsaw tried different combinations of elements, but the trend always improved: The optimized conversion rate was 8.35 percent. This represented a 228.39 percent increase over the original conversion rate (2.54 percent).

Lessons Learned: What Testing Taught Jigsaw About Its Customers

The process of testing this landing page gave Jigsaw critical information about what works best for its site visitors. This is information the company can apply—and test—to improve performance sitewide. What Jigsaw learned includes the following:

- The original top navigation feature was bright orange and offered nine opportunities for visitors to leave the page. Now it's gone. Viewers still have opportunities to move off the landing page, but the design encourages them to engage with the product information.

- Jigsaw discovered this headline:

    2/3 of Americans Are Magnesium Deficient

    was a more powerful headline than this one:

    68% of Americans Are Magnesium Deficient

    A simple change in headline wording (even though 2/3 is actually less than 68 percent) made a significant difference.

- Although Jigsaw still offers the opportunity for site visitors to take a magnesium assessment, the prominence of the option is minimized. Previously, the assessment button was the first big orange button visitors saw and therefore the most prominent call to action. Jigsaw phase 1 analytics revealed that after taking the test, few customers returned to the product page to make a purchase. Now the landing page features three obvious call-to-action buttons, all of which drive the visitor to the Buy_No.aspx page. Jigsaw still allows visitors to take a magnesium test, but the option is much more subdued on the product page: It's a text hyperlink. And the results page of the assessment now links back to the product page.

Not only did conversions increase, but the average time a visitor spent on the site before buying decreased from 25 to 12 seconds.

- If you don't need it, get rid of it! Jigsaw learned anything that doesn't help guide the visitor to a conversion is noise. The company removed promotional code information and a note to retailers from the right column. Less clutter allowed Jigsaw to focus on the product and the calls to action, which, in turn, let site visitors focus on finding a solution to the problem that brought them to Jigsaw.

- Changing copy so that it speaks directly to the emotional needs of visitors is a tactic guaranteed to improve conversion. Jigsaw replaced the following terse, dull introductory copy:

  > Magnesium deficiency is directly linked to heart disease, Type 2 diabetes, hypertension, and many other chronic health conditions.

  with copy that packed an emphatic punch and emphasized urgency (the company put the most important information in bold):

  > Magnesium is **involved in over 325 biochemical reactions**. Some of the early symptoms of magnesium deficiency include body aches, chronic constipation, headaches and migraines, insulin resistance, PMS, leg cramps, muscle twitches, and more. **Left untreated, a magnesium deficiency can lead to more life-threatening conditions** such as heart disease, Type 2 diabetes, osteoporosis, and others. Are you at risk for magnesium deficiency?

The numbers may look small, but the consequence to the bottom line is anything but. During the test range, average monthly revenue for Jigsaw Magnesium was up 63 percent. Meanwhile, yearly revenue companywide was up 150 percent from 2006 to 2007.

Is Jigsaw done? Well, for the next week or so, the employees have every right to gather round the watercooler and congratulate themselves heartily. Then it's back to more testing. Not only are 92.65 percent of visitors to this page failing to convert, but even the tactics that have brought Jigsaw this level of optimization will require further optimizing in the future.

Patrick Sullivan Jr., cofounder and president of Jigsaw Health, said this:

"Having an effective way to test and measure results has saved hours and hours of arguing internally over what might work better. We used to spend two hours a week sorting through web traffic data trying to make sense of it. We literally stopped having that meeting once we began working with FutureNow. Now, we discuss an idea, set up a test, and check back a few days later to see what won."

Keep in mind that Jigsaw's experience was the result of optimizing tactics. The scope of the project did not include developing personas or incorporating persuasion scenarios or even optimizing the click-through experience, which entails everything from what brings visitors to the site through what needs to be in place so they convert. The topics we discussed in Chapter 8 provide an overview on optimizing for persuasion. *Waiting for Your Cat to Bark?* (Thomas Nelson, 2006) provides a more comprehensive explanation.

Fairly straightforward tactical changes brought Jigsaw a 228 percent improvement in its conversion rate. We guarantee this is only the tip of the iceberg. Optimizing for persuasion—planning for the entire customer experience—takes your testing to the next level, where you can realize even more dramatic changes.

PART II

What You Should Test

Now that we've covered the mechanics of using Google Website Optimizer as your testing platform and the frameworks for how to test intelligently, we need to turn to the question of what to test. Over the 10 years we've been helping clients, we've found this question to be the one that routinely stymies most marketers.

In the chapters ahead, we will discuss 30 factors, from big-picture strategies to critical tactical details and from addressing your visitors' buying modalities to decreasing site load time, that affect virtually every business website on the Internet. Some of these factors overlap others, and some often work in conjunction with others so that changes to one factor affect changes to another.

For each factor, we will give you an overview of the key concepts that pertain to it. We'll then help you understand whether the factor applies in your situation and include a series of exercises that explain how the factor works to influence conversion on your site so you can decide whether you need to learn more. In addition to helping you understand the factor, we've created more than 250 testing ideas you can formulate into experiments. Finally, we provide suggestions for how you can apply your results to your website.

CHAPTER 11

Understanding What to Test

We discussed the logical progression of a test from inception to conclusion in Part I, "A Marketer's View of Testing: The Power of Optimization." Let's quickly review them here. You will adopt this ordered procedure with each test you undertake, such that your continued optimization efforts are informed by cycles of tests, each carried out with equal precision.

1. Create a descriptive name.

   - Call-to-action button test: improving product pages.

   - Is this a sitewide or campaign test?

2. Define your goal.

   - I want to increase conversion by [fill in the blank].

   - I will measure this by [fill in the blank], with these key performance indicators (KPIs).

3. Determine how you will achieve your goal.

   - What am I testing?

   - Which test is best suited to evaluating my goal?

   - What are the variables?

   - What are the variations?

4. Define the control variable/variation.

5. State your hypothesis.

   - What is my prediction/hypothesis?

   - What is my reasoning for this prediction/hypothesis?

6. Let the test rip.

7. Measure and analyze your results.

- What did I improve or make worse?

- What did I learn?

- What do I do next?

Create a Descriptive Name

Not only is the descriptive name of your test the one you will probably want to use when you set up your test in Website Optimizer, but it also helps you document the history of your testing efforts. It's not long before the information you gather and the interrelationships of the elements you are testing get complicated. Carefully describing your tests helps you organize your information, allows someone else to find information relevant to their needs within your organization, and, in the event you move on, allows your replacement to become familiar with what you've done (Figure 11.1).

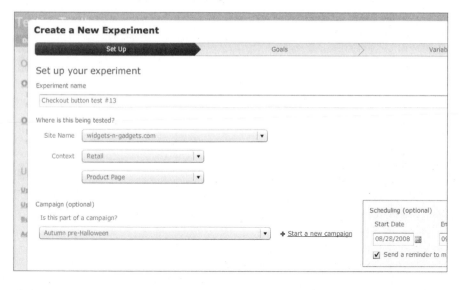

Figure 11.1

Describing your test in Testing Toolbox

It is helpful to note whether your test results pertain to a sitewide or campaign-specific experiment. The elements that work best for a campaign that targets a particular segment of your audience may not apply with equal benefit to your site.

Define Your Goal

You must also clarify your metrics for success. Specify how much of a conversion increase you would like to see for your test. Ideally, you want to identify a realistic goal for how much you want that number to improve. Just remember, even a failure to achieve that goal gives you useful information.

Your goal should also take into account the KPIs by which you will measure success, as in Figure 11.2. These do not have to include conversion per se. They might include increased order value or time spent on page or whether the visitor takes a specific action. As you saw in Part I, Website Optimizer offers more than A/B and multivariate testing options, and as Google continues to develop its testing platform and integrate it further with Google Analytics, you will probably see expanded functionality that will allow you to test more KPIs.

Figure 11.2

Defining your goals and KPIs in Testing Toolbox

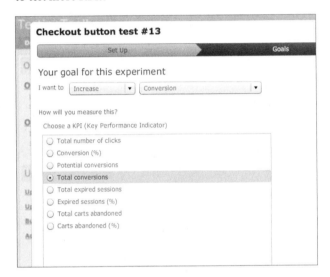

What, within the parameters of your test, would constitute a failure? What would qualify as an indeterminate result? Not every inability to increase conversion signifies a failure. It's perfectly legitimate to run a test to see whether a change simply doesn't make things worse. For example, you might increase the amount of white space on a page between elements and between blocks of text. It may have no effect on conversion, but you know it's going to make interacting with the page easier. Tests aimed at keeping conversion the same or not diminishing it are fair game!

Avoid being vague in defining your KPIs. However you describe your goal, base it on concrete metrics on which everyone agrees up front.

Determine How You Will Achieve Your Goal

In determining how you are going to achieve your goal, you will want to specify your test page and your success page. You will specify your variable(s) and variation(s), and you will select which testing platform is best suited for handling the sort of experiment you want to run.

As you consider the parameters of your experiment, you must make sure you avoid creating variations that confuse your results. This is probably the single biggest mistake people make when they design their tests.

We've seen far too many useless test designs. Here's a fairly typical bad design applied to copy. The perspective of your copy—"we" focused or "you" focused—has a strong impact on your conversion rate. Many people identify a paragraph of copy, say Copy A with its "we" focus, and then create a variation, Copy B, to test a "you" focus. But when they create Copy B, they often change more than the one attribute. Copy B not only has a "you" focus but also has been formatted differently and presented in a different font.

Can you see why comparing these two variations gives you useless results? This test does not isolate the effect of the copy perspective. Formatting and font have become hidden variables you can't tease from the results.

The test itself won't tell you your thinking is cloudy—only you can do that. When you carefully create variations that allow you to identify the effect of *one variable*, you avoid the proverbial "garbage in, garbage out" that so often plagues results.

Define the Control Variable/Variation

Every experiment has a control against which you test other variations. This control is the element that is already in place on your web page; it's the element you are trying to improve upon. If, after you've run a test, you discover a different variation worked better, that becomes your control for the next experiment you run. Figure 11.3 shows a way to document your variations.

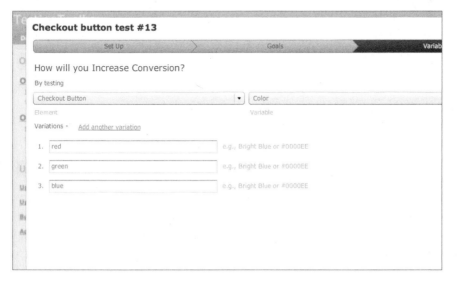

Figure 11.3

Defining your variations in Testing Toolbox

State Your Hypothesis

Every test you create must have a hypothesis. You need to pick a winner. Which variation will it be? Why will that variation win? Defining these up front will help you create subsequent tests and hypotheses to optimize further. Also, in the spirit of thoroughly documenting what you are doing, your hypotheses and reasoning can influence how you structure your tests and interpret your results later.

Let the Test Rip

After you decide how long you plan to run your test, you are ready to launch. Often it is not necessary to run a test for the full length of time the duration calculator specifies. In some cases, several weeks or a month can give you the essential information you need.

Measure and Analyze Your Results

You complete the cycle of testing when you analyze your results and use them to shape your next move, which almost always means another test. Virtually every test will teach you something, including those that do not bring you the results you expected. Spend the time thinking about what happened. Did you achieve your goal? Did you fall just shy or wildly below your goal? What does this information tell you about your hypothesis? (See Figure 11.4 for a sample result.)

Figure 11.4

Testing Toolbox results for evaluating returns on testing and opportunity costs

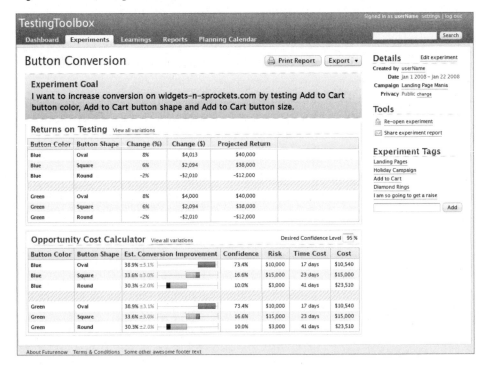

There is an inherent limit to what a testing platform can do for you: It will run; it will give you results. It is what it is—a police officer standing at an intersection directing traffic, a number cruncher. The intelligence you bring to the design of the test determines whether your results have value.

How might you apply this to a simple button test? Figure 11.5 gives you an idea of how you might define an A/B/C button test based on the steps of the testing cycle.

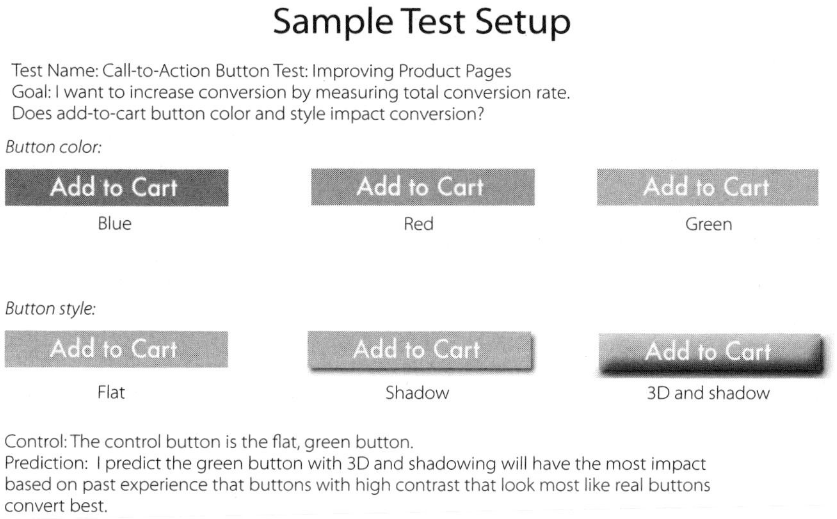

Figure 11.5

Sample call-to-action button setup

Sample Test Setup

Test Name: Call-to-Action Button Test: Improving Product Pages
Goal: I want to increase conversion by measuring total conversion rate.
Does add-to-cart button color and style impact conversion?

Button color:

Add to Cart	Add to Cart	Add to Cart
Blue	Red	Green

Button style:

Add to Cart	Add to Cart	Add to Cart
Flat	Shadow	3D and shadow

Control: The control button is the flat, green button.
Prediction: I predict the green button with 3D and shadowing will have the most impact based on past experience that buttons with high contrast that look most like real buttons convert best.

Keep in mind when you state your hypothesis that a guess is perfectly acceptable; you do *not* have to know. You may have taken the reasoning behind your hypothesis based on something you read or on what another company finds successful. Or you may simply be operating on instinct.

Because we've kept the color and the font the same in the sample test setup in Figure 11.5, we can be sure the results we get will address the performance of our call-to-action button with respect to style variations (shadow and three-dimensional beveling).

To get an idea of just how complicated it can be limiting the variable you actually test for, let's look at the range of options you have to choose from in the realm of button design.

The Lowly Button

Making sure you are testing apples against apples, as opposed to apples against oranges, can be tricky. Let's look at all the variations you could apply to the lowly little add-to-cart button (and what's in the following sections isn't even the sum total of what's possible).

Wording

Just think about all the possible ways you can say "add to cart." Then think about how all those ways reflect what they would do if they were buying from you. Are you a basket business? A bag business? A grocery-store-cart business?

- Add to Cart
- Add to Bag
- Add to Shopping Bag
- Add to Basket
- Add to Shopping Cart
- Buy
- Buy Now
- Add Item(s) to Cart
- Add Item(s) to Bag
- Add to My Bag
- Add to My Shopping Cart
- Order Now

Figure 11.6

Various button shapes

Rectangle

Rectangle with Rounded Corners

Oval

Irregular

Representational

Shape Variations

There are rectangles, squares, ovals, circles, and oddball combinations. Corners can be pointy or rounded (Figure 11.6). Is there a shape that works better for you?

Colors

You have a world of color from which to choose—there's really no "wrong" color. How can you use color to increase the contrast and visibility of your buttons? Could color help you categorize the functionality of different types of buttons on the same page?

Nongraphical Buttons

There are also nongraphical add-to-cart "buttons" created from plain text or simple HTML that have the traditional gray background (Figure 11.7). These can also be styled somewhat using Cascading Style Sheets. Would plain and simple be the best way to go?

Figure 11.7

Nongraphical button samples

Plain Text

[Add to Cart]

Simple HTML Code

Style Variations

Two-dimensional or three-dimensional? With or without shadowing (Figure 11.8)? Does your audience have a preference?

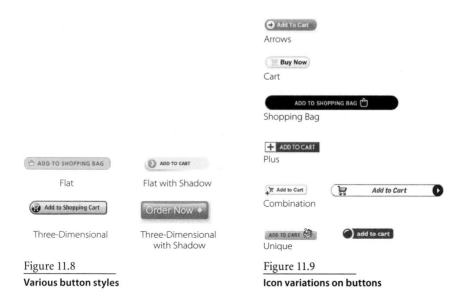

Figure 11.8

Various button styles

Figure 11.9

Icon variations on buttons

Icon Variations

Little images of arrows or carts or baskets or bags may or may not help distinguish your add-to-cart buttons from the other elements around them (Figure 11.9). Is there an icon that makes sense for your business and improves conversion?

Size Variations

Larger is not always better (Figure 11.10). Will size matter?

Legibility

The factors we have discussed work in combination to affect the legibility of an add-to-cart button. Font choice, font size, and text/background contrast will also affect how readily a visitor identifies the call to action and acts upon it. The possibilities are limitless, but Figure 11.11 shows some examples of potential problems.

Location Variations

Where should you put your button? Above the fold? One above and one below? On the right, middle, or left of the page? How far should you place it from neighboring elements?

Look at all the possibilities you can associate with a single website element! Perhaps you can understand why it can be difficult to make absolutely sure you are testing apples against apples. We empathize and in the same breath encourage you to weed out those oranges!

Figure 11.10

Various button sizes

Small

Medium

Large

Figure 11.11

**Legibility problems
in button design**

Small, undistinguished

Low contrast

Serif letters can break up at this small size.

White text on a black background hurts the eyes, and color choice
may not distinguish it well against black text on a white background.

Stacked text is hard to read quickly.

Trendy fonts and presentations often work against visitor
expectations of what an add-to-cart button should look like.

The Bottom Line

Most of us wouldn't bother with testing if we were merely looking for laughs and giggles.
We test because we want to maximize our return on investment. There are costs to testing; there are greater costs to not testing.

Remember two things:

- Setting your sights to test at the optimal level, particularly when your experience
  with testing is still nascent, may lead you into the realm of the Infinite Monkey
  syndrome (the idea that if you gather enough monkeys in a room and give them all
  typewriters and tons of time, they could eventually produce a Shakespearean-quality
  play). Instead of taking on too much, consider that sometimes performing a little
  bit better is better, and that if it's worth doing at all, it's worth doing for lower incre-
  ments of improvement.

- You have no a priori knowledge of your optimal configuration. Only afterward can
  you know what you lost before you started testing. Testing helps confirm that it's
  possible to stop the leaky holes in your conversion bucket or, at the very least, get
  them to leak less.

Website Optimizer works wonderfully. It offers an easy and elegant testing platform
and a phenomenal support base through users and consultants. Who else but Google
would have had the moxie to conceive this tool, make it free, and keep it up-to-date?

The piece you need to bring to the table is the knowledge of what to test, why you need
to test it, and how you can design tests in such a way that you are actually testing what
you think you are testing.

CHAPTER 12

WIIFM: What's in It for Me?

When visitors arrive on your site, they are coming, questions in hand, to solve a problem. Their biggest question is: What's in it for me? WIIFM evaluates the degree to which the site addresses the needs of the four dominant temperament types:

- Competitive
- Spontaneous
- Humanistic
- Methodical

In addition, each of these temperaments can arrive at your site at different stages in the buying decision process. It's important for your site to acknowledge the preparedness of each temperament to buy (see Figure 8.5 in Chapter 8):

- Visitors who know exactly what they want
- Visitors who know approximately what they want
- Visitors who know they have an interest but may not have committed to active buying mode
- Visitors who arrive at your site by accident and don't want anything

When you combine the four temperament types with the different stages of the buying decision process, you essentially have your "universe of buyers."

Studies have shown that different temperaments have different preferences for navigating a website and interacting with the content. Our interest here focuses on how each of these four types represents a particular "buying modality." Individual temperament contributes substantially to how people prefer to buy, but sometimes the nature of the product or service requires a visitor to "operate" in a particular buying modality. The visitor evaluating a company-wide software solution necessarily must be more methodical in her approach than she might be were she considering the purchase of an art print or a good book to take along on holiday.

This chapter will review each of these types and describe them within the context of the buying decision process, helping you understand their attitudes, the questions they ask, how they prefer to use their time, and how you can meet their emotional and logical needs.

Competitive/Assertive

These attributes characterize the Competitive personality type:

Attitude: Businesslike, power-oriented. Logical, quick decision preference.

Time: Disciplined, strategically paced.

Question: What can your solution do for me?

Approach: Provide options, probabilities, and challenges.

Personality: Competitive types seek competence in themselves and others. They want to understand and control life. Driven by curiosity, a Competitive is often pre-occupied with learning and has a deep appreciation for challenges. They enjoy being in control, are goal-oriented, and are looking for methods for completing tasks. Once their vision is clear, they usually reach decisions quickly. They fear loss of control. Those who are Competitive are highly motivated, success- and goal-oriented, hard-working, image conscious, good planners, and good at promoting their ideas. They are able to subordinate their present needs to develop future success. They can be intense, are very persuasive about getting their own way, and are particularly irritated by inefficiency.

These individuals are looking to win at everything they do and are searching for those products/services that will most effectively help them win.

Competitive types are generally the hardest to sell to. The information that captures them is compelling, honest, and blunt.

They can easily sniff out the truth; therefore, you must offer obvious information that demonstrates your credibility and the amazing value you offer through the quality of your products/services.

Place information for the Competitive first on each page. They are direct, they are too impatient to dig for information, and they also ask the most relevant questions that will apply to all of the personality types.

Spontaneous/Amiable

These attributes characterize the Spontaneous personality type:

Attitude: Personal, activity-oriented. Emotional, quick decision preference.

Time: Undisciplined, fast-paced.

Question: Why is your website best for the problem?

Approach: Address values and provide assurances and credible opinions rather than options. Offer immediate gratification where appropriate.

Personality: Spontaneous types must live in the moment. Their sensing preference makes them most grounded in the immediate world of the senses. This, coupled with their perceiving preference, helps them remain poised and present in any situation. They are available, flexible, and engaged in a personal quest for action and impact, which defines who they are. For the Spontaneous, integrity means the unity of impulse with action. These individuals appreciate the personalized touch and are in search of new and exciting experiences. They dislike dealing with traditional details and are usually quick to reach a decision. They fear "missing out" on whatever life has to offer.

Address the needs of the Spontaneous visitor next on the page after you take care of the Competitive.

These people ask the second-most relevant questions, and they will not spend a lot of time reading content; rather, they are skimming for interesting and captivating information within the most obvious sections of each page.

This is where you need to explain your unique value proposition (see Chapter 13).

Humanistic/Expressive

These attributes characterize the Humanistic personality type:

Attitude: Personal, relationship-oriented. Emotional, deliberate decision preference.

Time: Undisciplined, slow-paced.

Question: Who has used your solution to solve my problem? Who will these solutions affect besides me?

Approach: Offer testimonials, and tell the visitor who you are.

Personality: Humanistic types have a tendency to put others' needs before their own and are often uncomfortable accepting gifts or allowing others to do anything for them. They are very creative and entertaining. They enjoy helping others and highly value the quality of relationships. They are usually slow to reach a decision. They fear separation. Those who are Humanistic are good listeners and are generally willing to lend a sympathetic ear. They focus on acceptance, freedom, and helping. They generally prefer the big picture. They greatly value human development, including their own.

After you've answered the Spontaneous visitor's questions, offer information for the Humanistic.

The first two sections will be useful to the Humanistic, and they will take their research one step further and want to learn about previous clients, hear testimonials, and learn about your company.

Adding testimonials will help Humanistic types build confidence and trust. They will tie the possibility of working with or purchasing from your company to the existing pleasant experiences people have had with you. Also, offering a personal tone to some of your content will capture the Humanistic's interest. When adding testimonials or any other reassurances, add them to the right side of the page where the eye is trained to look for them.

Methodical/Analytical

These attributes characterize the Methodical personality type:

Attitude: Businesslike, detail-oriented. Logical, deliberate decision preference.

Time: Disciplined, slow-paced.

Question: How can your solution solve the problem?

Approach: Provide hard evidence and superior service.

Personality: Methodical types need to be prepared and organized to act. For them, task completion is its own reward. These individuals appreciate facts, hard data, and information presented in a logical manner as documentation of truth. They enjoy organization and completion of detailed tasks. They do not appreciate the "personal touch," and they abhor disorganization. They fear negative surprises and irresponsibility above all. Those who are Methodical have a strong internal frame of reference. They prefer to think and speak about details and specifics. They compare everything to a standard ideal and look for mismatches (what's wrong or what's missing).

The last questions you must answer on each page are the Methodical questions.

Methodical types want an abundance of information with evidence and facts. These people want to do all the research they can before they make a decision to purchase.

The other personality types will generally never scroll this far down a page; therefore, make information you place here relevant to the methodical personality type. (You needn't worry about addressing other needs down here!)

Further down on each page, present facts, hard data, and information in a logical manner. Graphs and tables are appropriate formats for presenting this material. You do not need to focus on the personal touch (the personal touch generally does not impress the Methodical); this is to document evidence for those people who want to research further into the details of your offerings before making a decision.

One Page, Multiple Needs

What would it actually look like to address the needs of more than one temperament on the same page? Figure 12.1 shows an example of how copy from the Leo Schachter Diamond site speaks to Competitive and Methodical customers.

Figure 12.1

Leo Schachter addresses Competitive and Methodical needs on the same web page.

This copy speaks to the Competitive. It appears at the top of the page because Competitives want their information quickly.

This graphic appeals to the Methodical and suggests the page will offer something of value.

These calls to action help move the Competitive off the page and return her to the sales process.

The remaining copy on the pages speaks to the Methodical, who will make the effort to keep reading and values the education. This copy would bore the Competitive.

The graphics appeals to the underlying motivation of the Methodical: the desire to fulfill a loving commitment.

Let's look at some sample copy for similar products. Note the trigger words for each of the personality types:

Competitive

Our approach is timed to meet your objectives. The **bottom line** is that your **results** are **guaranteed**. Explore our methodology to discover how thousands of clients just like you have been delighted.

Spontaneous

Our approach is **timed to meet your objectives**. The bottom line is that your results are guaranteed. Explore our methodology to discover how thousands of clients just like you have been delighted.

Humanistic

Our approach is personalized to meet your objectives. The bottom line is that your results are guaranteed. Explore our methodology to discover how **thousands of clients just like you** have been delighted.

Methodical

Our approach is timed to meet your objectives. The bottom line is that your results are **guaranteed. Explore our methodology** to discover how thousands of clients just like you have been delighted.

Here is another example of different messaging for the same product:

Competitive

Our remote PC access software lets you get a competitive edge. Instantly access key data in meetings, impressing your clients. You'll never be caught unprepared.

Spontaneous

Our remote PC access software lets you make the world your office. Work whenever and wherever you like. Break the ball and chain to your office.

Humanistic

Our remote PC access software lets you finish work at home instead of staying late at the office so you can spend more time with your family.

Methodical

Our remote PC access software lets you be more productive, increasing efficiency and saving time.

Questions to Ask

Here are some questions to ask yourself:

- Does the site use language designed to appeal to the different personality types?
- Does the site establish multiple navigation paths based on "personality scenarios"?
- Are these navigation paths interlinking—is it possible to switch from one predominant personality path to another?
- Does the site address the needs of visitors with different perspectives?
- Does the site address the needs of visitors in different stages of the buying process?

Exercise

For each of the four buying personalities (Competitive, Spontaneous, Humanistic, and Methodical), write 20 keyword phrases that would describe your products and services. Remember, these phrases should reflect what will "speak" to these four buying personalities. Some keywords will work with more than one personality preference. For example, the same person who searches for *diamond certification* (Methodical) is not likely to search for *perfect diamond* (Spontaneous).

What to Test

Here are different ideas on what you can test when thinking about WIIFM:

- Test your headlines to see which ones most influence each personality type and on which pages.

- Test the wording on your hyperlinks. Try going from a logical point of view to an emotional one. Remember the Dell example: "Learn more" became "Help Me Choose."

- Test different images to see which one has the most impact for a particular personality type.

- Test different styles of landing pages in an A/B split to match your personality preference for each of your keywords. For example, try more competitive language on your landing page for a keyword term meant for Competitives.

- Test the order of your bullet points in your copy.

- Test the order of the blocks of text in your copy.

- Test putting relevant testimonials on the site with links to read more testimonials. This tends to engage Humanistics.

- Test adding a more detailed section to your page, and fill it up with all the facts. This tends to engage Methodicals.

- Test adding an interactive component to your page, like a quiz, poll, or some sort of fun tool. This tends to engage the Spontaneous.

- Test adding some bottom-line facts and challenges. This tends to engage Competitives.

- Test adding reviews to your site.

- Test different featured products on landing pages (most popular, sale items, new arrivals, seasonal, highest rated, top savings).

NEED TO LEARN MORE?

You can learn more from the following articles:

"You Want Them to Buy? Sell Benefits" by Bryan Eisenberg. ROI Marketing, ClickZ.

http://clickz.com/article/cz.3722.html

"Emotionally Speaking." The Grok. GrokDotCom by FutureNow.

www.grokdotcom.com/writingforemotions.htm

"Personality 101—Who Are They?" The Grok. GrokDotCom by FutureNow. January 1, 2002.

www.grokdotcom.com/personalitytypes.htm

"Fine-Tuning the WIIFM Dial: Personality Revisited." The Grok. September 15, 2002.

www.grokdotcom.com/personalityonline.htm

"Persuasive Online Copywriting for Beginners (and Dummies!)" by Robert Gorell. GrokDotCom by FutureNow. May 1, 2006.

www.grokdotcom.com/topics/copywritingforbeginners.htm

"Are You Designing for Usability or Sales? Part II" by Bryan Eisenberg. ROI Marketing, ClickZ. January 16, 2004.

www.clickz.com/experts/design/traffic/article.php/3299801

"Are You Designing for Usability or Sales? Part III" by Bryan Eisenberg. ROI Marketing, ClickZ. January 23, 2004.

www.clickz.com/experts/design/traffic/article.php/3302291

Apply This to Your Site

Review your site pages, especially your top landing pages, for language that speaks to each of the buying modalities (temperaments). In your copy, how many times are you using the keywords and key phrases your visitors use in their searches? Consider including more keywords and associated trigger words that will catch the visitor's attention, because they are the words the visitor cares about.

Provide multiple navigation paths based on "personality scenarios." Develop navigation throughout the site that uses internal text links, directly within the active window, as well as both global and local navigation.

Plan your site and advertising campaign paths so the scent trails you create fulfill your visitors' buying needs. You may find it's more effective to target a campaign to one temperament so you can develop appropriate scent and content.

CHAPTER 13

Unique Value Proposition/ Campaign Proposition

One of the first things a site must do is reinforce the visitors' feeling that they are in the right place through a unique value proposition (UVP).

A UVP isn't a slogan or phrase designed for advertising, although that's a potential use for it. Rather, it is the concise and memorable statement that powerfully describes the unique value of the business and creates excitement in the visitor. Its purpose is to answer the question always implicit in visitors' minds: "Why should I do business with you and not somebody else?"

Drop-off rates are frequently due to a website's inability to present a credible answer to this question, certainly on the home page but also on critical landing pages. This can also happen when a visitor follows a scent trail you established in an ad but failed to reinforce in the click-through; in essence, you undermined your unique campaign proposition (UCP). (You might recall the Geico insurance example we presented in Chapter 4.)

Here's a positive example of how to reinforce your UVP and maintain the scent you offer in an ad. The UVP of this banner ad is "Learn the Secrets of Self-Running Email Campaigns."

The visitors will expect the landing page to reinforce this UVP. Let's look at the landing page and see how well Responsys maintains the continuity of this scent (Figure 13.1).

The click-through delivers satisfaction. Not only does the headline from the banner repeat on the landing page, but the same report cover image appears again. Even the color palette from the banner to the landing page retains the same look and feel.

To create your UVP or UCP, find a statement that explains the concise and unique value of your business (or your current campaign) and creates an emotional sense of excitement or desire in the visitor. Your UVP (or UCP) should be one of the first things the visitor sees.

Figure 13.1

**Responsys's
landing page**

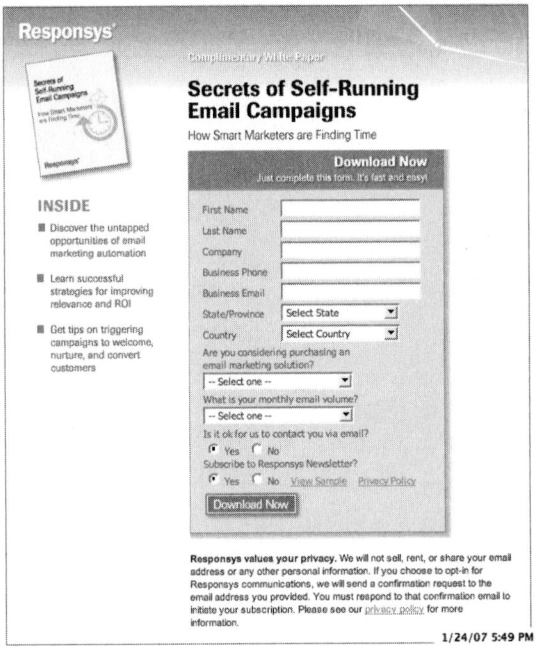

Your visitor must be able to identify who you are and the value you offer before she will engage with your site. Notice the screen shot of site 59 (now Lastminute.com) in Figure 13.2; its UVP is "last-minute weekend getaways—Save up to 70%." In this clear, concise UVP, site 59 suggests it understands our love for spontaneity and helps us achieve it through deep discounts.

Figure 13.2

site 59's UVP

A couple of years ago, Morgan Stanley (quick, off the top of your head, tell us what it does) ran an advertising campaign with the tagline "One Client at a Time." This tagline also appeared on its website (Figure 13.3). Although this makes a good advertising slogan, when a visitor lands on a page trying to figure out what this company does, you don't want them to answer Morgan Stanley "does" one client at a time.

According to Google search results, Morgan Stanley is a global financial-services firm and a market leader in securities, asset management, and credit services. Does that help?

Figure 13.3

Morgan Stanley's UVP

Questions to Ask

Here are some questions to ask yourself:

- What is the initial impression you get of what the business has to offer you when first landing on the home page?

- Does this impression create a feeling of enthusiasm, curiosity, or confidence that encourages the visitor to engage and find out more?

- What offer would it take to make certain customers buy today?

- Is there an asterisk next to the UCP? If so, this could raise doubt in the visitor's mind.

- Is the value proposition reinforced throughout the site, especially on key landing pages?

- Does the site pass the "man-from-Mars" test? That is, would someone who had never even heard of the company understand the site or the offer within 4–8 seconds?

- What is it about your company that makes it special? (This addresses why someone would do business with you—perhaps "all the employees have been here 10 years or more.")

- Does the site clearly answer the question, why should I do business with you and not someone else? (This is the practical, logical reason you're the best choice—for example, "no-questions-asked returns.")

- What is the *hook*, the emotional benefit to the visitor, for engaging with the site? (This is the emotive, relationship reason you're the best choice—perhaps "we walk with you every step of the way.")

NEED TO LEARN MORE?

See the following to learn more:

Persuasive Online Copywriting: How to Take Your Words to the Bank by Bryan Eisenberg, Jeffrey Eisenberg, and Lisa T. Davis (Wizard Academy Press, 2002). (It's out of print, but you can still find it used on sites such as Amazon.com.)

"Landing Pages & the Value of First Impressions" by Melissa Burdon; March 8, 2007.

www.grokdotcom.com/2007/03/08/landing-pages-the-value-of-first-impressions/

Made To Stick: Why Some Ideas Survive and Others Die by Chip Heath and Dan Heath (Random House, 2007).

Exercises

The following are some exercises for you to try on your own:

1. List the UVPs for each of the following sites:

   - Dell.com

   - Kayak.com

   - 1800petmeds.com

   - landsend.com

   - Americanexpress.com

   Which of these sites has the best UVP and why?

2. List the UCPs for three competitive advertisers from each of the following pay-per-click terms:

   - Pink Roses

   - Sony DSC W80

   - VOIP Office

   - Austin DUI

   - Pick one of your website's popular terms

   Which of these sites has the best UCP–scent combination and why?

What to Test

Here are different ideas on what you can test when thinking about UVP/UCP:

- Test different versions of your UVP to see which resonates best with your visitors.

- Test different offers to see which ones convert best. Test features such as free shipping, flat-rate shipping, free gifts, % discount, and so on.

- Test the effect on conversion to show the UCP from the landing page through to the conversion page. Does maintaining it throughout help? Or does most of the "bang" come from repeating it early and phasing it out (thus releasing extra real estate)?

- Test how you display the UCP—is it in a banner or a headline?

- Test using the same image on the landing page as appears in the banner ad vs. an image that is similar to it (like the Victoria's Secret example we showed in Chapter 8).

- Test slightly different versions of your headlines to match your UCP.

- Test using an image next to your UCP to reinforce its message and draw attention to it. Be careful the image itself does not overpower the UCP.

- Test adding your UCP near the call-to-action button.

- Test adding the UCP on your product image.
- Test landing pages for UCP–scent combinations based on click-throughs from emails you send.

Apply This to Your Site

Using what you've just learned, answer these questions:

- Can you find a UVP on your site?
  - If yes, then:
    - Is the UVP concise?
    - Is it memorable?
    - Is there uniqueness to it?
    - Does it create excitement?
    - Does it answer the question, why should you buy from them?
- Can you find a UCP on your site from your key pay-per-click and/or banner campaigns?
  - If yes, then:
    - Is the UCP concise?
    - Is the scent reinforced?
    - Is there uniqueness to it among your competitors?
    - Does it answer the question, what's in it for me?

CHAPTER 14

The Buying Decision

People rationalize buying decisions with facts, but they make the decision to buy based on feelings.

The buying decision is the flip side of the selling process. It is a series of steps visitors go through—consciously or subconsciously—and it operates in tandem with selling. A website's execution must present opportunities for the visitor to satisfy each step.

The steps of the buying decision process are as follows (see Figure 14.1):

1. Identify the problem.

2. Search.

3. Evaluate.

4. Decide.

5. Purchase.

6. Reevaluate.

Many factors affect the buying decision process. Let's look at three of the most important ones.

The Complexity of the Sale

When planning a website, it is important to consider how people buy the products or services offered. How much time generally goes into a decision to make a purchase of this sort? How many people are required to make this decision? Does the product or service offer an improvement over what's generally available?

The complexity of your sale has four dimensions. You need to understand how your visitors perceive their relationship to each of these dimensions so you can provide the messaging that satisfies their needs:

Need We can describe need on a continuum that ranges from critical to necessary to luxury. How urgent is the need for your product or service? How fast are your visitors likely to make their decisions to buy? Will the need be satisfied by a one-time purchase (either impulsive or momentous), or is the need ongoing? People might be willing to compromise their thoroughness for a casual one-time deal. But if that one-time deal is something like a house or if they are choosing a long-term relationship to satisfy an ongoing need, things get significantly more complicated.

Risk Risk can be perceived as pertaining to the physical body, a career, self-esteem, or self-actualization. How risky, especially with respect to issues of finance, is the sale? Although price may not be an ultimate decision factor in a purchase (for many, safety and trust trump price), increasing financial risk necessitates a more intricate persuasive structure. Risk may also be associated with compromises to health, such as when individuals or medical professionals have to make treatment choices, or even, for that matter, when someone simply evaluates the safety of an herbal remedy.

Knowledge Knowledge contains depth and breadth, which can widen and deepen. How difficult is it for visitors to understand the nature of your product or service or the procedures for buying? What do they need to know? Your persuasive process must eliminate the friction generated by confusion or lack of knowledge. Knowledge dimensions for the buying decision can differ based on who is doing the buying: Is the customer buying for herself (she will be the end user), or is she buying on behalf of another (as in the case of a purchasing agent)? The knowledge assumptions and language—especially jargon—that work for one may be totally inappropriate for the other.

Figure 14.1

The buying decision process

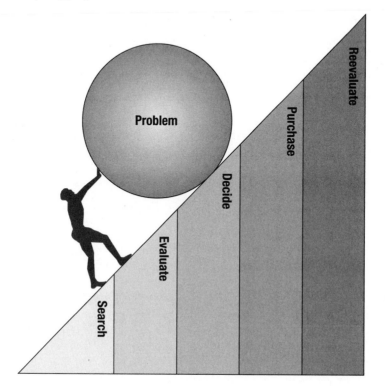

Consensus You can think of consensus issues as decisions that are made anonymously, personally, or by groups. Just how many people do you have to persuade? An individual? An individual and his significant other? Several end users and heads of departments? Your ability to understand who is involved in the decision-making process allows you to provide copy and content that appropriately informs, reassures, and persuades.

These factors apply differently depending on the nature of your sale. For example, home computers aren't a terribly high-risk product anymore, but lots of people find them unfathomable, and they'll take their time acquiring information before deciding to buy one (unless the one and only computer upon which their sole-proprietor business depends just got zapped by lightning and must be replaced by noon tomorrow). By the same token, you might take a while to consider the purchase of a water heater if you are building a new house, but if your existing water heater goes belly up, you need to replace it quickly. Almost no one would say a pencil is a considered purchase—knowledge of pencils isn't much of a problem, and there's generally no risk associated—but if the purchase of a case of pencils or a single pencil from a new vendor requires several departments to sign off, consensus is an issue.

These factors can also be interdependent. Take knowledge, for example. The more you know about something, the more you may perceive the risks involved. Conversely, more knowledge may afford you the perception of less risk. The individual facing heart surgery will consider the relationship between knowledge and risk differently than will the heart surgeon. As will the individual investor staking his life earnings on options, compared to the options trader for whom these transactions are daily occurrences.

When you understand how your visitors perceive the complexity of your sale, you can begin to address their needs in the buying decision process.

Scent Trails

We described scent and discussed its importance in Chapter 8. You must maintain your scent trail from your visitors' initial touch point with your brand to the final conversion. Your visitors need to either see the information they are searching for or find links relevant to the content they are searching for in order to continue moving forward. We call this *persuasive momentum*. The buying process that someone goes through looks roughly like a funnel (see Figure 5.2 in Chapter 5). They will be able to make their way through that funnel more easily and are more likely to purchase from you if you provide an uninterrupted scent trail.

Point-of-Action or Shop-with-Confidence Messaging

When you provide your reassuring policies on privacy, returns, guarantees, shipping, and so forth (and you do offer these, right?), put them at the point of action (POA). See Figure 14.2.

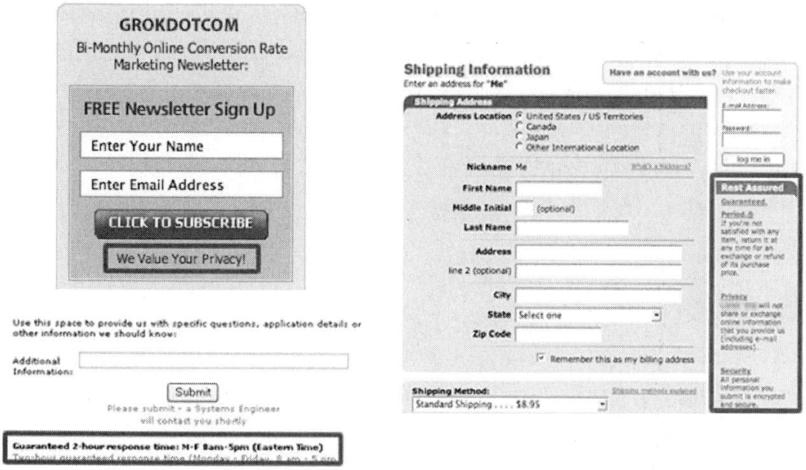

Figure 14.2

Examples of confidence messages placed at the point of action

If you want to subscribe to GrokDotCom, you have to share a little information—not tons of it, just your name and email. But some people are understandably squeamish about doing even that, so the Grok has a privacy policy. You can scroll all the way down to the bottom of the page and read this: "We will never give, lease or sell your personal information. Period! If you have any questions at all about our privacy policy, please email us." That policy is clear, concise, and compelling, but it's at the bottom of the page, while the opt-in subscription box is at the top. You might never get to the bottom to read how sincerely concerned we are about your privacy. So, what did we do for the Grok? We put a concise little statement right under the Subscribe Now button, right at the POA: "We Value Your Privacy!"

As soon as we did that seemingly minor thing, subscriptions went way up! By putting the information at the POA, the impact was immediate and dramatic.

Think about how often information that's critical to your customer gets buried in tiny type at the bottom of the page (or in some other place where it is not immediately visible) at the precise moment when the need to know it is foremost in your customer's mind. If you walk into a store, it's fairly easy to find out product warranty information. You can read the box in your hand or chat with a salesperson. Online, why not give your customer this same option at the point of action, where she'd figuratively be examining that box. Link right there to product warranties, your company's specific policies, and even optional extended service plans.

At the exact point your customer has to start filling in a form with personal information, let her know her privacy is sacred to you. At the point she might be curious about your company's shipping costs, make them concretely available. Just when she's wondering whether she can return the item if it doesn't suit her, make sure she knows you have a no-questions-asked return policy.

And don't limit yourself to policies. Some shoppers value what other people have to say about a product or about doing business with you. Offer testimonials, but also be sure to put them where they need to be seen, when the question is in your prospect's mind. Think about other aspects of your sales process. What else does your customer want to know, and when will it have the most impact on his or her decision? It's not only about making sure it's on your site, it's also about making sure it's located where it will have the greatest impact on your sales.

Questions to Ask

Here are some questions to ask yourself:

- Does the site provide options and information that satisfy each stage of the buying decision process?
  - Identify: Is there a clear starting place? Are there content markers for each of the different buyer perspectives?
  - Search: Do I know where to go next? Is there a clear path I can follow to find information?
  - Evaluate: Is information provided that answers the visitor's questions?
  - Decide: Is that information persuasive? Does it address the product's emotional benefits—not just features—to help the visitor make a decision? Does it help overcome all the buyer's possible objections, fears, and doubts?
  - Purchase: How easy and intuitive is it to make a purchase?
  - Reevaluate: Do you provide assurances? Do you make the visitor feel like they made the right purchase? Is the product nicely packaged and presented?
- Is this material presented in places appropriate to where the visitor is within the process?
- Does the site present information in a way that reflects how visitors approach the buying decision process for the particular products or services offered?

Exercise

Write a specific scenario, in story format, for the following:

An executive asks his (very Methodical) secretary to research and come up with the very best toy to give to his 2-year-old nephew. It must be a toy he'll never let go of, and one he'll remember when he's in his 70s.

This is someone early in the buying process, with little knowledge, who will have to present a case for her recommendation. She will, by nature, present her choice methodically. What questions might she ask?

What to Test

Here are different ideas on what you can test when think-ing about the buying process:

- Test adding additional copy content on the page or linking to additional pages that answer your visitors questions.

- Test adding assurances near the point of action.

- Test the placement of elements in your forms.

- Test your form labels and field size. You may need your designer to use Cascading Style Sheets (CSS) to modify the form font size to accommodate more text in the same space.

NEED TO LEARN MORE?

You can learn more in the following articles:

"How Much of My $1,000 Rock Climbing Budget Do You Want?" by Melissa Burdon. GrokDotCom. August 18, 2006.

`www.grokdotcom.com/2006/08/15/how-much-of-my-1000-rock-climbing-gear-budget-do-you-want/`

"Conversion Funnel Folly, Part 1" by Bryan Eisenberg. ClickZ, ROI Marketing, February 17, 2006.

`www.clickz.com/showPage.html?page=3585516`

"Conversion Funnel Folly, Part 2" by Bryan Eisenberg. ClickZ, ROI Marketing, March 3, 2006.

`www.clickz.com/showPage.html?page=3588626`

"The Equation that Matters." The Grok. GrokDotCom by Future Now. July 1, 2006.

`www.grokdotcom.com/topics/salestopology.htm`

- Test adding more product images/screen shots in order to provide more visual infor-mation about your products.

- Test marking up your images with labels to highlight key features and benefits.

- Test using video to explain your more complex products/solutions. Don't forget that if the video doesn't stream effortlessly, you might've done better with no video at all.

- Test reformatting your content with additional subheadlines, bullet points, and addi-tional supporting images to make it easier for visitors to scan for the information they want.

- Test adding "microconversions" to see whether you can get buyers in the earliest stages to engage with you before buying. These microconversions include download-ing a white paper or viewing a demo, which are evidence of interest if not prepared-ness to purchase.

- Test relabeling products or services so that they are easier to understand.

Apply This to Your Site

When we build a site structure that is sensitive to the way people buy, we often use the Methodical buying modality as our "test" case. Methodicals are the most comprehensive information-gatherers of the four types, so if you can satisfy the Methodical's informa-tion needs, you've probably satisfied everyone else.

Imagine you have a Methodical visitor who is early in the buying process (just research-ing), and one who is late in the buying process (ready to click the Buy Now button). What questions will they want you to answer? Make a list of their questions, then go to your site and see if you have provided answers exactly where they would ask them. If you haven't, begin incorporating ways you can help these people get their answers from you.

CHAPTER 15

Categorization

Visitors arrive with different degrees of certainty about their task. There are those who:

- Know exactly what they want
- Know approximately what they want
- Don't know what they want, but if they found it, they would buy it
- Got there by accident and don't want anything

A website must have categorization schemes that acknowledge and address solutions to each of these approaches.

User-interface engineering studies have shown that visitors prefer to navigate through categories rather than search by keywords. This is largely because an overwhelming number of keyword searches return irrelevant results. Make sure your categories are relevant, easy to understand, and easy to navigate.

Use effective categories within the active window and navigation to quickly orient visitors to the value you offer. The persuasive copy should be "above the fold" (in other words, your visitor should not have to scroll down the page to find it) and should easily guide the visitor to the information they seek.

A good example of a site that is categorized well is www.kineticfountains.com (Figure 15.1). It speaks to different types of visitors in different ways using trigger words that help capture interest. Not all visitors conceive of classification schemes the way you do. Kinetic Fountains' home page helps visitors quickly identify categories based on their preferences: by category, by accessory, and by price. A visitor can choose from a list of "I need a. . ." or "I'm looking for a. . . ." The scheme offers featured products, an in-site search, and even a buyer's guide for those unfamiliar with these products and the features they may or may not want.

Figure 15.1

Categorization scheme for Kinetic Fountains

Questions to Ask

Ask yourself the following questions about your site:

- Are there clear starting points and paths for each type of visitor?
- Does the website make it easy for visitors to satisfy their needs based on their level of certainty about why they are on the website?
- Does the site make it possible for visitors to determine immediately where they want to go (in other words, is the categorization part of the active window of the conversion process)?

NEED TO LEARN MORE?

You can learn more from the following resources:

"Three Steps to Creating Better Category Pages" by Bryan Eisenberg. ROI Marketing, ClickZ. July 21, 2006.

www.clickz.com/showPage.html?page=3622915

"Building Better Category Pages" by Bryan Eisenberg. ROI Marketing, ClickZ. September 14, 2007.

www.clickz.com//3627012

- To what extent does the site leave this function entirely up to supplemental navigation?
- Do the categorization schemes make sense based on how visitors shop for these products or services? Is the categorization scheme comprehensive enough—and cross-referenced—to identify most requests? Is the "men's yellow North Face down ski jacket that's good to –30 degrees" in the "Men's," "Ski Jacket," "North Face," and "–30 Degree" categories?

Exercises

Figure out how many different ways you can come up with to categorize the following products:

- Women's yellow North Face down jacket good for –30 degrees (Hint: There are many more than five.)
- A wireless presentation device
- A beige lap poodle
- A housecleaning service

Figure out how easily you can find the following products if you don't know the exact name of them:

Figure 15.2
A whatchamacallit toy

- The toy in Figure 15.2
- A digital camera that allows you to take pictures rapidly one after the other. You know, one that you don't have to wait until it finishes saving it so you can take that next picture of your kid really quickly and not miss those magic moments.

What to Test

Here are different ideas on what you can test when thinking about categorization that is based on the visitor's buying process rather than your selling process:

- Test adding pages that are designed as buyer guides to help people narrow down their selections.
- Test adding more information points on your category page that could help visitors narrow their choices.
- Test relabeling the terms used in your navigation.
- Test relabeling your category names, using terms your customer is familiar with rather than professional terms your industry favors.

- Test descriptive headlines for products and services.
- Test new ways of categorizing your products (maybe by season, by use, by level of knowledge needed, and so on).
- Test placing products in additional (multiple) categories; however, if you do this, it is vitally essential for search engine optimization (SEO) purposes that the products still have a single product page, no matter how many categories with which it's associated.
- Test the products you list as featured products.
- Test using images of sample products next to your category or subcategories to help distinguish them.
- Test adding bullet points to describe each category/subcategory.
- Test the number of category subcategories you show. For example, show the top five and a link for additional categories. Do you even know what portion of your total sales come from the top-five categories?

Apply This to Your Site

Pick two or three of your products or services, and list all the possible categorizations.

CHAPTER 16

Usability

Usability addresses the ways in which a site effectively implements the body of knowledge concerning a visitor's ability to interact successfully in an online environment. The goal of usability is to remove any obstacles impeding the experience and process of online interactions. Here you want to identify problems with mechanical usability, not persuasive usability.

It is important to understand that usability removes impediments but does not, by itself, provide momentum. It's like removing detours on a road so you can travel more easily, but a detour-free road can't tell you where you should go or how you should go about getting there.

Questions to Ask

Here are some questions to ask yourself as you evaluate your own site for usability issues:

- How does the site function?
- Are font sizes appropriate for reading online?
- Does the site employ drop-down or cascading menus that are difficult to use?
- Do people know where to click? (Visitors decide where they are going to click before they move the cursor, so hover elements do not always support good usability design.)
- Does the site employ any gimmicks that interfere with usability?
- In a general way, what roadblocks (both structural and content) impede the shopping process? What elements require the visitor to think (the imperative being "Don't make me think!")?

NEED TO LEARN MORE?

You can learn more from the following resources:

"Beyond Usability." The Grok. GrokDotCom by Future Now. September 15, 2000.
www.grokdotcom.com/beyondusability.htm

"Beyond Usability 2: Is Your Website a Tool?" The Grok. GrokDotCom by Future Now. March 15, 2003.
www.grokdotcom.com/beyondusability2.htm

"Prioritize Usability Testing and Web Analytics" by Bryan Eisenberg. ROI Marketing, ClickZ. February 18, 2005.
clickz.com/3483671

"Does Usability Actually Sell Anything?" by Bryan Eisenberg. ROI Marketing, ClickZ. December 5, 2003.
www.clickz.com/experts/design/traffic/article.php/3116541

"Color and Usability." The Grok. GrokDotCom by Future Now. June 1, 2003.
www.grokdotcom.com/usability-of-color.htm

Tool: Morae by TechSmith Morae is software for usability testing and user-experience research that helps you identify site and application design problems and share them with stakeholders.
www.techsmith.com/morae.asp

Free and helpful tools: UITest.com. User Interface Engineering offers a huge collection of free tools, from browser emulators to an image compression service to font determiners, that help you evaluate and improve your site's usability.
uitest.com/en/specials/

Designing Web Usability by Jakob Nielsen (Peachpit Press, 1999).

Don't Make Me Think: A Common Sense Approach to Web Usability, Second Edition, by Steve Krug (New Riders Press, 2005).

Web Site Usability: A Designer's Guide by Jared Spool et al. (Morgan Kaufmann Publishers, 1998).

Exercise

Go shopping on three different sites for a computer that would be great for 3D-intensive games. Write down any obstacles impeding your experience.

Which one gave you the best experience? Why? What questions did you still have that would have helped you feel more confident in your decision?

What did you learn by the end of the exercise that you didn't realize was involved in shopping for such a computer at the start of the exercise? And was the last of the three sites you shopped the beneficiary of the knowledge you gained during your research? Did site 1 do the hard work of educating you while site 3 reaped the benefits, or was site 1 so much better that you would actually go back there to buy?

What to Test

Here are different ideas on what you can test when thinking about usability:

- Test increasing the font size of the text and/or headlines on your pages.
- Test using free-form fields instead of drop-down menus.
- Test different ways to attract attention to your landing-page forms. Use features such as colored backgrounds, graphics, and text headers to draw attention to it.
- Test the color and underlining of your hyperlinks.
- Test using a Flash movie vs. a static image with copy in it.
- Test increasing the size of your call-to-action buttons.
- Test making your buttons more three-dimensional and shadowed to make them more obvious.
- Test adding callouts or labels on your forms to provide instructions.
- Test removing or adding navigation through your funnel.
- Test adding or changing your progress indicator on forms.
- Test having breadcrumb navigation vs. not having it.

Apply This to Your Site

To apply this to your site, perform the same exercise from this chapter, but with your site and two of your competitors. Go to your own site first so that you put yourself at the worst disadvantage. This will make it easier for you to honestly appraise how much better or worse your site is compared to your competitors' sites.

CHAPTER 17

Look and Feel

Look and feel is a subjective factor to evaluate. We discuss other layout elements in this book, so for this one, evaluate the congruence between the appearance of your site and the image of your business.

Questions to Ask

Here are some questions to ask yourself about your site:

- Is the appearance attractive, pleasing, and professional?

- Does the appearance support the image the business is trying to convey? Needs to convey?

- Do all the design elements (choice of pictures, colors, type styles, and so on) support the tone of the site?

- Do layout and functional elements support the site's goals?

- Is the same look and feel supported throughout the site?

NEED TO LEARN MORE?

You can learn more about this topic with the following resources:

The Non-Designer's Design Book: Design and Typographic Principles for the Visual Novice, Third Edition, by Robin Williams (Peachpit Press, 1998).

"Help Their Eyes Find It." The Grok. GrokDotCom by Future Now. May 1, 2003.

www.grokdotcom.com/helpeyes.htm

"The Eyes Have It." The Grok. GrokDotCom by Future Now. September 1, 2001.

www.grokdotcom.com/eyetracking.htm

"Set Up Scanning and Skimming So They See." The Grok. GrokDotCom by Future Now. November 1, 2001.

www.grokdotcom.com/scanning-skimming.htm

Exercise

Take a look at these top websites, and find out what look-and-feel elements they have in common. (Hint: There are at least eight things in common.)

Amazon.com	Sun.com
Staples.com	Landsend.com
SAS.com	Accenture.com
Ticketmaster.com	Travelocity.com
ADP.com	eBay.com

What to Test

Here are different ideas on what you can test when thinking about the look and feel of your pages:

- Test simplifying your landing page to increase/decrease the amount of white space.
- Test different-colored page backgrounds to see what impact they have on making your main area's contrast higher.
- Test using more or fewer rounded corners on your images.
- Test your choice of font.
- Test using sharper-quality graphics.
- Test adding elements throughout your checkout, registration, and lead form processes to make them look more uniform to the rest of your website or landing page. This is especially an issue when taking people to a third party to complete your offers.
- Test the color palette used on your landing pages.
- Test a new layout of your page elements on a landing page.
- Test whether you should use a one-column, two-column, or three-column layout. Landing pages offer you the best beginning point for evaluating column layouts.
- Test using stock images if you are currently using any clip art.

Apply This to Your Site

What elements add to the look and feel of your pages that you should incorporate on your site? What are you currently using that you feel may detract from your intended look and feel?

CHAPTER 18

Searchability

How can your visitors find what they are looking for? This is another category that includes information presented in other chapters. A site that is easily "searchable" will include many or all of these factors:

- Effective categorization of products or services

- Effective supporting navigation

- Effective use of white space in layout and design to help the visitor visually identify appropriate information

- Visual differentiation of key copy

- Visual groupings of related content or functions

- Truly functional and useful on-site search. (It is important to understand in-site search is most effective when it works in a support capacity—not every site needs or should have an in-site search option, and even those that do should not depend on it as a replacement for navigation frameworks.) Sorting is also important to keep in mind.

Questions to Ask

Ask yourself the following questions about your site:

- If you have on-site search, what does it accomplish? What would a visitor use it for? How well are you explaining the value of your search tools to visitors?

- Does searching acknowledge different terms for related items (for example, *stationary* for *paper*) and accommodate misspellings?

- What happens when nothing comes up in a search? Do you just leave the visitor there guessing at what else to search? What are the top 50–100 in-site search terms visitors use, and how many of them give no result? Can you come up with a way to record searches that yield no results and then figure out how to ensure future such searches result in something a visitor might enjoy, related to that search term?

- Does the search engine display results that are pertinent to the terms? (Some search engines search by the description and end up just showing items that are incorrect because a word is used in the description that isn't actually the correct item.)
- Is the search engine in an easy-to-find location on the page?
- When can the visitor further refine search results? Are the search results displayed in an easy-to-read manner?

Exercise

Pick your top-10 products and come up with as many ways as possible to reasonably misspell them. Search for them on Google and on your website.

What to Test

Here are different ideas on what you can test when thinking about the searchability of your site:

- Test showing your most popular products on your search results page.
- Test showing products on your search results page when you return no "results."
- Test what information you show in your description on your search results page.
- Test search results pages with and without images.
- Test the formatting of your page to make it easier to skim and scan.
- Test what you display when your visitors misspell a term in your in-site search engine.
- Test the placement on your site of your search box/form.
- Test the wording on the Submit button of your search box.
- Test different ways to allow visitors to refine their search results.
- Test making your in-site search more or less visible depending on how often it returns relevant results for visitors.

NEED TO LEARN MORE?

You can learn more from the following resources:

"Make a Good Investment in In-Site Search Engines" by Bryan Eisenberg. ROI Marketing. ClickZ, April 9, 2004.

www.clickz.com/showPage.html?page=3337221

"How Will They Buy It if They Can't Find It?" by Bryan Eisenberg. ROI Marketing. ClickZ, November 12, 2001.

www.clickz.com/showPage.html?page=920611

Search tools from in-site search engine expert Avi Rappaport.

www.searchtools.com

Apply This to Your Site

Search your site (or Google) for the terms your visitors type in your in-site search function. Evaluate the results, and question whether the search has provided satisfying and relevant results from the visitor's point of view. Make all necessary changes to increase relevance.

CHAPTER 19

Layout, Visual Clarity, and Eye Tracking

Compare the information in this chapter with what we discuss in the look-and-feel chapter (Chapter 21). Here you want to focus on the effective layout of information in each of the general areas of the computer screen. This should include factors such as scanability, skimability, the amount of helpful white space, whether information is grouped together in ways that make sense, and the degree to which information is placed where the visitor is most likely to look for it.

Designing web pages is challenging. Unlike almost any other medium, a web design's integrity is compromised by the nature of a fluid medium. In other words, just because you want something to look a certain way doesn't guarantee it will—differing browsers, resolutions, screen sizes, monitor calibrations, and operating systems all distort the experience.

The one good habit we've picked up over the years is learning to compromise. Compromise, however, should be done intelligently and accountably.

One of the more contentious issues in web design presents itself when deciding where specific elements should go and how much space they should occupy. This is especially true in cases where politics (read: Who's the most important person in the room?) rules. In print, such as in catalogs, you can evaluate the accountability of your screen real estate by determining cost and revenue per square inch. We'll do something similar.

A popular technique we've developed over the years for removing politics from these important decisions is the Battleship grid. For this technique, you divide a page into a grid of horizontal and vertical lines of approximately equal size. (We'll explain why it's approximate shortly.) The main purpose for using this tool is to spark conversation. Figure 19.1 shows an example for a page from Dell.com.

How does the Battleship grid work?

Figure 19.1

Battleship grid overlaying a Dell.com web page

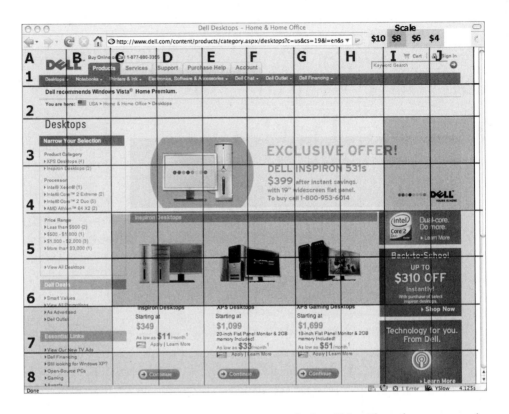

Let's say you're reviewing a page at 1024×768 resolution. Using Photoshop or an equivalent graphics program (or have your designer do this for you), work across the page, drawing vertical lines up and down the screen. Create 10 rows, labeled "A" to "J." Then, start drawing horizontal lines across the page. The first horizontal line is right underneath the top navigation. (Do this because your visitors are already subconsciously focusing on the center area, or *active window*. This is why we said "approximately equal size" earlier.) After creating this line, add lines every 10 pixels, labeling them "1" to "8."

In Photoshop, add a layer where you can overlay the grid with different colors at 30 percent opacity (just enough so they are visible and you can see the elements behind them on the page). Next, begin to assign values to the different areas of the grid. The values you assign to each of the shaded regions aren't absolute; they're relative values, and you should view them as rough guidelines. You can follow what we set out in our example. We came up with these values for the sake of simplicity, based on certain eye-tracking, design composition, and vision physiology guidelines.

The area we assign the highest "value" is the active window (see Figure 19.2). As Jakob Nielsen pointed out as early as January 2000, "My studies have shown the same user behavior: Users look straight at the content and ignore the navigation areas when they scan a new page."

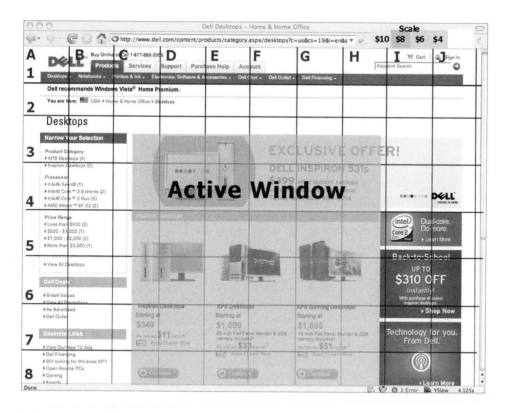

Figure 19.2

Battleship grid indicating the active window

Every eye-tracking study in which we've participated has shown the same visitor behavior. It's also important to understand human physiology and how the eyes view a page. Any artist who has studied composition knows the rule of thirds. It's a good guideline for understanding how people's eyes naturally take in what they see so you know where to place things you want to draw attention to.

> The characteristic behavior of eye tracking, by the way, is why it's so important to test your headlines; they are the things virtually everyone sees on your page. Make them count.

How do you use the Battleship grid?

Take a screen shot of the page in question at a 1024×768 resolution. Overlay this grid on top of it. Then, work with your team to agree to the values assigned to differing zones. Review elements in the high-value real estate zones. This is all about deconstructing the size, design, and placement of elements for maximum impact.

For each design element, ask yourself:

- How much space does it occupy? Should it take more or less?
- What calls to actions are there? Are they obvious?

- Can it hold its own weight? Should some elements be moved to maximize effectiveness?

- Do the visual elements attract the different personality types? (You can also gray out anything customers don't actually care about and ask these questions again.)

Now, take another look at the Dell.com Battleship grid in Figure 19.1. What are your observations of the design? Is Dell underutilizing any areas?

LIMITATIONS

Please be careful with this tool. It's not meant to be scientific; it is, however, meant to help you subjectively judge the relative importance and accountability of your site elements.

Depending on your design, you can skew how visitors engage with the site by doing the following:

- Use strong, contrasting colors. You may place a form you want filled out in the right column with, say, a monochromatic design or one with minimal color compared to the rest of the design. If so, try placing a color-shaded background behind the form to make it stand out.

- Use a powerful image or consider image placement. Most eye-tracking heat maps show that visitors spend virtually no time looking at loosely framed "lifestyle" images (for example, a picture of executives shaking hands over a conference table). On the other hand, having a single close-up image of someone's face can draw a lot of attention—especially when it's "above the fold." Keep in mind that if you use this technique, the person in the image should have their eyes facing the action—or content—on which you want them to focus. Never have the subject looking straight at the visitor. It will distract them.

- Use different column widths. The active window for people who read left-to-right begins just beyond where the left column ends. If there is no left navigation, make sure to have enough empty "buffer" space from the browser for visitors' eyes to settle.

- Use bigger text for headlines and larger-sized versions for key visual elements. Make sure the copy is formatted so people can scan and skim. Make headlines and sub-headers stand out next to the body text.

- Contact information is critical on every page.

- Testimonials are most effective on the right side of the page where the eye is trained to look for this information.

- The center area, the active window, is prime screen real estate and where you will want to present copy that captures interest and motivates visitors through to the next step of their buying process and your selling process.

- The right side of the screen is valuable space to communicate confidence—a good place to showcase "shop with confidence" messages, guarantees, and policies.

- When evaluating shopping cart processes, always check whether the site has progress indicators and clear calls to action that say exactly what each step involves.

- Forms should be nicely designed, should be concise, and should not ask for excessive information.

Visitors demonstrate a consistent eye-tracking pattern (in cultures that read left to right) when they land on a web page: They start first in the top left, checking that they are in the right place (this is typically where they find the address bar of their browsers), scan along the top of the page, drop diagonally to the center of the screen, scan left, then cross center again to scan right, and then return to center.

You can use this information to provide a sort of template for where to place various categories of information. It's not meant to be a rule but a general principle that depends on the nature and specific goals of your business. Not all sites have or even need three-column layouts. So, within the general parameters of eye tracking, see whether your site satisfies basic needs.

In general:

- Global information appears along the top. This is not information the visitor will interact with often; they turn to it as a fallback option.

- The central area of the screen is where the eye naturally wants to land. This is the active window, the area where the site must focus on the buying process, the selling process, and the AIDAS process (the business acronym for the selling process that guides the buyer through Attention, Interest, Desire, Action, and Satisfaction; see Chapter 26), as well as provide multiple navigation paths, calls to action, and so on. When a visitor disengages from this area, you want to get the visitor quickly reengaged.

- On the left is a stabilizing area where visitors generally look for comprehensive (local) navigation when the information in the active window has ceased to engage them. Its goal is to get the visitor quickly back into another active window.

- The eye treats the right as a peripheral area of the screen. (Often, visitors use scroll bars without even looking at them!) The visitor generally does not pay a lot of attention to this area but is always aware of it. This is a good place for assurances, action centers (newsletters, communities, registration options) and overall calls to action on product pages.

- The questions you ask as you go through your own site will depend on how effectively the site takes advantage of eye-tracking tendencies by placing categories of information and handling the conversion process across all its pages.

Questions to Ask

Ask yourself the following questions about your site:

- Is information visually presented well, within columns and other key areas?
- Are there any jarring elements (for example, animations, revolving banners) that appear as visual distractions and pull the visitor away from the conversion process?
- Are there other design elements that undermine visual clarity?
- Does the site employ effective layout in the available space—within the active window, on the left, on the right, along the top, below the fold?
- Are there elements that contribute to an impression of clutter?
- Are there elements that seem inappropriately placed?
- Does your site group elements (navigation, persuasion, confidence, action centers) in a way that reinforces your visitors' native eye-tracking habits?
- Have you checked the "overlay" function in your web analytics tool? (Please note that not all analytics programs have this function.)

Exercise

Try the following exercise:

1. Pick any three pages on your site. Do a Battleship grid on them.
2. List all the potential actions or links someone may take.
3. Next, let's assume you have $100 to split between all the actions/links. How would you divide this up? For example, your privacy policy may be worth 10 cents of your $100.
4. Now, based on these values, which are the most valuable ones? Which are the most visible on your site?

What to Test

Here are different ideas on what you can test when thinking about your layout:

- Test moving important elements that are below the fold to above the fold.
- Test different sizes for your elements. Make some larger and others smaller.
- Test moving key supporting messages or testimonials to the right side of your page.
- Test what elements are in your active window.
- Test how much space in your active window is taken up with images vs. copy.
- Test removing elements to create more white space on your page. In this test, having a zero impact on conversion could still be a good thing. If you can simplify the page without impacting sales, be happy.

- Test the length of your forms.
- Test having form fields next to each other on a line or below each other.
- Test the offers in your active window.
- Test elements to engage the different personality types at different points on the page.

Apply This to Your Site

Are your most valuable calls to action most visible on the page and above the fold? Do you offer any secondary calls to action for people who are not ready to commit now?

NEED TO LEARN MORE?

You can learn more at the following resources:

"Layout and Visual Clarity: Not a Matter of Taste" by Bryan Eisenberg. ROI Marketing, ClickZ. October 17, 2003.

www.clickz.com/showPage.html?page=3092801

"Five Critical (and Overlooked) Design Elements" by Bryan Eisenberg. ROI Marketing, ClickZ. May 27, 2005.

www.clickz.com/showPage.html?page=3507666

"The Eyes Have It" by The Grok. GrokDotCom by FutureNow. September 1, 2001.

www.grokdotcom.com/eyetracking.htm

"Where Oh Where Did My Eyeballs Go?" by Bryan Eisenberg. ROI Marketing, ClickZ. September 3, 2001.

www.clickz.com/showPage.html?page=877131

"Eyetracking, Heatmaps & Gaze Plots!" Oh My..." by Howard Kaplan. GrokDotCom by FutureNow. September 5 2007.

www.grokdotcom.com/2007/09/05/eyetracking-heatmaps-gaze-plots-oh-my/

CHAPTER 20

Purchasing

Visitors on e-commerce sites need to have confidence in their purchasing options. They prefer to have all shipping costs clearly stated and presented early. Sites that convert well make every effort to "get the cash!" and offer as many options as possible for visitors to tender payment. They also offer the gift purchaser as many gift-buying options as possible.

Many B2B visitors are doing their research for multiple decision-makers. They often want to gather all their presentation material before speaking to a salesperson. It is also helpful to let people know when they are submitting a lead form what they should expect in terms of response times and what kind of information they can expect.

Questions to Ask

If the site provides multiple options for payment, does it offer the following?

- A variety of credit cards
- Non–credit card payment methods such as PayPal
- Third-party payment options
- Fax number
- Telephone number (toll-free, if possible)
- Online accounts
- A corporate mailing address
- Online forms that can subsequently be mailed

If the site does not accept credit cards online (and sometimes certain small businesses have reasons for not doing this):

- Does it encourage the visitor to call in an order (and provide the phone number)?
- Is there an order form that can be printed?

- Does it provide an address to which the form can be mailed?

- Does it include specific check-writing information? What about services like PayPal?

- Does it offer the option to submit the form online and make subsequent payment arrangements?

- Does the site require you to establish an account before making a purchase? (If a lot of people are bailing out, this can really hurt your sales.)

- Is the checkout process easy to use without any excessive steps?

- Does the site provide shipping costs early in the process? What about shipping time estimates?

- Does the site provide gift certificates, gift cards, and wrapping options?

- Do lead-generation forms provide additional contact information?

- Do lead-generation forms tell visitors when they can expect a response?

- Does the lead-generation site provide enough details so that people don't have to speak to a salesperson if they are not ready to do so?

Exercise

Try the following exercise:

1. List how many types of payments are available on the Web. (Hint: You should be able to find more than 15.) How many different types do you offer? How many do your competitors offer?

2. Here's a tough one: Learn about some of the more esoteric forms of payment online, and determine which ones would actually hurt your ability to make a sale. Some payment forms, rightly or wrongly, are associated negatively with rip-off schemes. Don't offer more choices just to offer more choices; do so because it meets a customer need.

3. Have someone submit an anonymous lead to you and two of your competitors. Did anyone set an expectation of how long it would take them to respond? How long did it take each to respond? Would you want to receive the email you received as a response?

NEED TO LEARN MORE?

You can learn more from the following resources:

"Why Must I "Register" Before Checkout?" GrokDotCom. October 3, 2007.

www.grokdotcom.com/2007/10/03/yes-or-no-why-must-i-choose/

"How to Increase Shopping Cart Abandonment," GrokDot-Com. April 24, 2008.

www.grokdotcom.com/2008/04/24/shopping-cart-abandonment/

"Yours for Just 3 Easy Payments of…," GrokDotCom. August 2, 2007.

www.grokdotcom.com/2007/08/02/yours-for-just-3-easy-payments-of/

"Screencast: Hunting for Early Bird Persuasion, Part 1," GrokDotCom. September 14, 2007.

www.grokdotcom.com/2007/09/14/screencast-early-bird-thinking-part-1/

"Screencast: Hunting for Early Bird Persuasion, Part 2," GrokDotCom. September 19, 2007.

www.grokdotcom.com/2007/09/19/screencast-hunting-for-persuasion-part-2/

"Screencast: Hunting for Early Bird Persuasion, Part 3," GrokDotCom. September 21, 2007.

www.grokdotcom.com/2007/09/21/screencast-hunting-for-early-bird-persuasion-part-3/

What to Test

Here are different ideas on what you can test when thinking about the purchasing options you offer:

- Test adding stock messaging to your product page.
- Test letting visitors know when products will ship or arrive (you can give a range).
- Test adding free or flat-rate shipping information near your add-to-cart buttons.
- Test adding your gift return policy to your product pages during high gift-giving seasons.
- Test adding an average response time to get back in touch with a lead.
- Test adding some benefit messaging above your lead form. Try taking away all copy.
- Test reducing the number of steps in your checkout process.
- Test reducing the number of form fields.
- Test adding an open-question form field to find out what additional information people are looking for.
- Test adding gift-wrapping and card options. Make it easy for visitors to know you offer them.
- Test offering more or less information before asking for a lead.
- Test offering a white paper or buying guide before they commit to speaking to sales.

Apply This to Your Site

What have you learned that makes buying easier on sites you frequently buy from? What elements can you use from them to make your site easier?

Add different purchasing options to your checkout or lead forms in order to make it easier for visitors to buy or contact you. What can you do to reduce the number of steps and the time it takes to purchase from you?

CHAPTER 21

Tools

Websites use a variety of "tools" to enhance the shopping experience. These can include virtual models, interactive tours, wish lists, forms, and the like. To be beneficial elements in the conversion process, all tools must be efficient, intuitive, and truly helpful.

Apple has a great tool for specifying engraving on the back of an iPod. However, the placement of this tool, in the add-to-cart process, may not be the most advantageous (Figure 21.1). This would be an important element to test.

Figure 21.1

Apple iPod engraving option tool

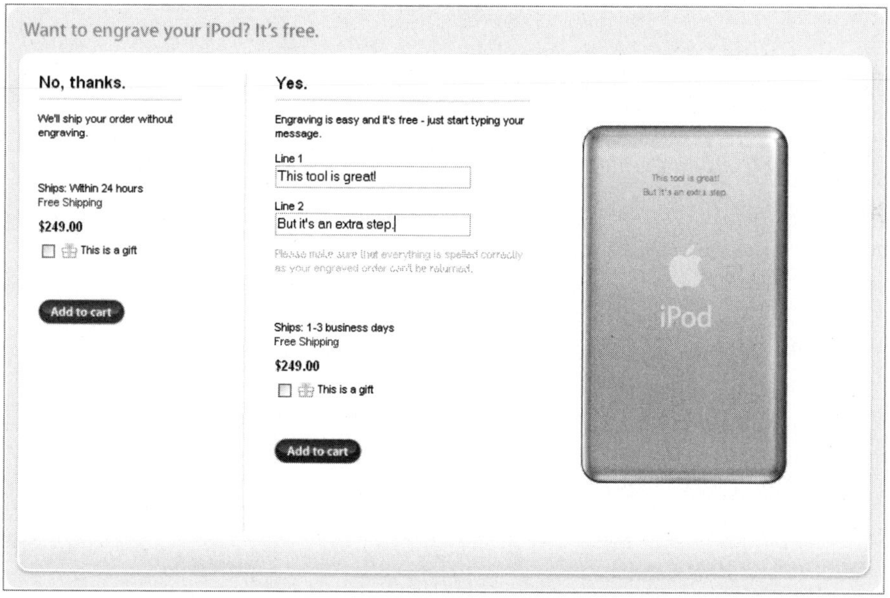

Want to engrave your iPod? It's free.

No, thanks.

We'll ship your order without engraving.

Ships: Within 24 hours
Free Shipping

$249.00

☐ This is a gift

Add to cart

Yes.

Engraving is easy and it's free - just start typing your message.

Line 1
This tool is great!

Line 2
But it's an extra step.

Please make sure that everything is spelled correctly as your engraved order can't be returned.

Ships: 1-3 business days
Free Shipping

$249.00

☐ This is a gift

Add to cart

This tool is great!
But it's an extra step.

iPod

Another useful and simple tool helps visitors visualize the use of your products. Knowing whether the straps of a bra will show under shirts with different necklines is important to women. Check out how HerRoom offers simple image changes based on which "style" of outfit you plan to wear over the bra pictured underneath it (Figure 21.2 and Figure 21.3).

Figure 21.2

**HerRoom
product page
with fitting tool**

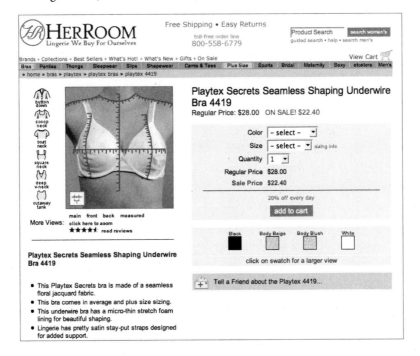

Questions to Ask

Here are some questions to ask yourself about your site:

- What tools/applications does the site employ?
- Are they easy to use?
- Do they provide real value to the visitor?
- Does the tool help the visitor buy?
- Are the tools essential or peripheral to the shopping experience?
- Are the tools error-free?
- Do visitors have to download plug-ins to use the tools?

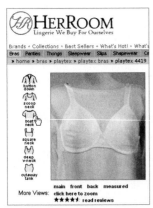

Figure 21.3

**HerRoom detail
of bra-under-shirt-
style tool**

Exercise

Try the following exercise:

1. What types of tools could add to or detract from traffic or sales? How would any of these impact your site positively or negatively?

2. What tools do your competitors use? As we asked in an earlier chapter, does everyone in your industry use the same tools for a specific reason, or do you all just sit around and copy each other?

What to Test

Here are different ideas on what you can test when thinking about tools for your site:

- Test adding instructions next to your tool.

- Test adding calculators to your landing page, if appropriate.

- Test using video vs. an interactive tour. Add a way for
  visitors to "demo" your product or service.

- Test using an interactive tour to explain your service
  or product benefits.

- Test using a male voice vs. a female voice in your
  voice-overs.

- Test adding ways for people to visualize using your products, such as a virtual model.

- Test getting people engaged in your tool before they have to give any personal
  information.

- Test offering pages, or alternate paths through the site, that do not require any tools
  like Flash.

- Test the sequence in the selling process where you present the tool, as in closer to the
  end of the checkout or before the checkout.

- Test tools such as zoom or rotate on your products.

NEED TO LEARN MORE?

You can learn more here:

"Why Free Web Tools Make Customers Want to BUY NOW"
by Melissa Burdon, GrokDotCom. March 27, 2008.

www.grokdotcom.com/2008/03/27/free-online-
marketing-experience/

"Interactivity: For a Call to (More) Action" by Bryan Eisenberg. ClickZ, May 23, 2003.

www.clickz.com/showPage.html?page=2211111

Do It Wrong Quickly: How the Web Changes the Old Marketing Rules
by Mike Moran (IBM Press, 2007).

Apply This to Your Site

Not every website lends itself to using an interactive tool or widget. Just because you can
do something cool doesn't mean you should or that it will necessarily help your visitors
through their purchase process.

It is often better to test a new tool on a landing page or microsite before you roll it out
on your website.

CHAPTER 22

Error Prevention

It isn't always possible to come across an error in a site. But it's incumbent to try. Do what you can to make something not work. (After all, if it can be done, someone will find a way to do it.) In particular, fill in forms incorrectly, submit them, and see what happens.

Mistakes also can happen when updating a website—especially if you regularly update your site. Giving the visitor a personalized error message helps keep them engaged. Figure 22.1 shows a great example of an error report that provides the visitor with options to move forward or backward in the process; it is not a dead end.

Figure 22.1

BMI's 404 error message

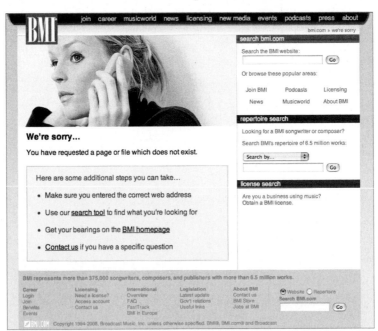

When customers do something that creates an error, never phrase the error message in a way that blames them. Error messages should be genial, not condescending. No one is persuaded when they receive a message implying they are stupid, especially if within several clicks they can shop somewhere else that makes them feel smarter and valued.

Questions to Ask

Here are some questions to ask about your site:

- What did the error message look like?

- What was the cause of any error you found?

- How was the error language phrased?

- If an error occurred, how easy was it to return to the process? Errors are mini–dead ends. Your site must make every effort to get the discouraged visitor immediately back into the process.

Exercise

Go to a variety of popular sites, such as Amazon.com, and type in **/test** or **/crazy404page** after the name. This will show you the site's Page Not Found message.

How are the best ones worded? Which ones lead people to do something valuable on the site next?

> **NEED TO LEARN MORE?**
>
> You can learn more with the following resources:
>
> "Honey vs. Vinegar." The Grok. GrokDotCom by FutureNow. September 1, 2005.
>
> www.grokdotcom.com/topics/errormessages.htm
>
> Tool: Xenu's Link Sleuth: Use this online tool to find broken links on your site.
>
> home.snafu.de/tilman/xenulink.html

What to Test

Here are different ideas on what you can test when thinking about preventing errors:

- Test the error messaging when a mistake is made by trying a more polite approach and suggesting the fault was with the site, not the visitor.

- Test clearer indicators near areas where there was an error, such as highlighting instead of putting an asterisk near incorrect fields.

- Test the text on a 404 error page.

- Test removing all optional fields from a form and state that everything is required. Ask for only the information you actually need.

- Test different ways of illustrating what fields are required.

Apply This to Your Site

See what errors you can create on your site:

- Put bad data into forms.

- Subscribe with a wrong email address (for example, with no .com).

- Try to "break" your system.

What do your error message(s) look like? Can you find a way to phrase them inoffensively?

CHAPTER 23

Browser Compatibility

Not all browsers render or display your website the same way. Test your pages in all the top browsers. Browser popularity can be fleeting and fickle, although Internet Explorer, Firefox, Safari, Opera, and Mozilla (formerly Netscape) continue to rank high. Different browsers array pages in a variety of ways (see Figure 23.1), so make sure—on several test pages—that important information appears appropriately and that links function as expected.

Look for errors in your coding that may contribute to any problems. In addition, test the way your page looks on several mobile browsers such as the ones for the BlackBerry and iPhone phones.

Questions to Ask

Here are some questions to ask yourself about your site:

- Is your site compatible with all major browsers? How about the same browser version but on different platforms (Windows, Mac, and the like)?
- Is your site compatible with previous versions of each browser?
- Does page layout change dramatically from browser to browser, or is it relatively uniform?
- How does your site look with images turned off?

Exercise

Try the following to test your site:

- Look at the site using different font sizes.
- Look at the site through browser compatibility programs such as www.delorie.com/web/lynxview.html and http://browsershots.org/.

- Print your pages to see how they look.
- Check how your emails render in all the top browsers.
- Review how your site looks on a mobile device.

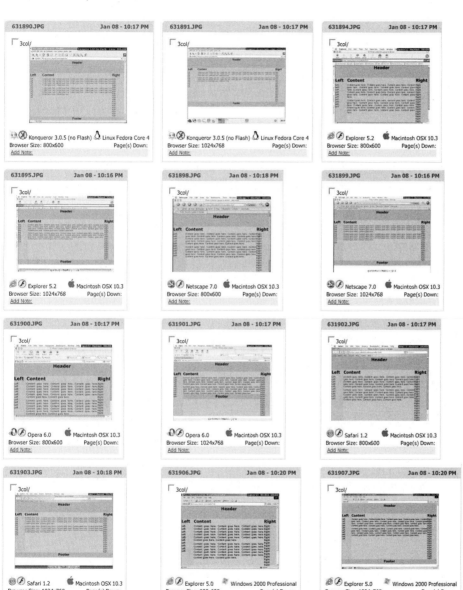

Figure 23.1

Browser compatibility results from BrowserCam

What to Test

Here are different ideas on what you can test when thinking about browser compatibility:

- Test using more descriptive `alt` tags for your images.

- Test using fewer images on your pages.

- Test using different Cascading Style Sheets (CSS) elements for mobile, print, and screen rendering.

- Test what you name text navigation links.

- Test using tables vs. CSS for certain elements to see whether they render better in different browsers and devices.

NEED TO LEARN MORE?

The browser compatibility tools let you see what your website would look like for people using older browsers and different operating systems. BrowserCam is a good tool to get screen shots of multiple browsers—although you will need to register for a paid account. BrowserCam can take screen shots of different browsers in different versions with different resolutions. Each shot is tagged with the browser, version, and resolution on the top.

www.browsercam.com

Free browser tools you can use include UITest.com.

http://uitest.com/en/specials/

Lynx Viewer allows web authors to see what their pages will look like (sort of) when viewed with Lynx, a text-mode web browser.

www.delorie.com/web/lynxview.html

Browsershots makes screen shots of your web design in different browsers. It is a free open-source service created by Johann C. Rocholl. When you submit your web address, distributed computers will open your website in their browser, take screen shots, and upload them to the central server at Browsershots.

http://browsershots.org

Apply This to Your Site

Make sure your site works on multiple platforms, operating systems, and browsing technologies.

Determine who is responsible for doing such testing. Make a one-page checklist and review once each quarter to see how your site renders. Assign it to someone who is not involved in the day-to-day site operations so that there's a fresh face watching for inconsistencies.

CHAPTER 24

Product Presentation

One of the best ways to improve persuasion on your site is by improving copy or product images. Product presentation, feature tours, demos, and product comparisons (even with competitors) are considered persuasive issues. On a lead-generation or business-to-business site, it's your service description, case studies, testimonials, and white papers.

Once your visitor has narrowed down her potential product, it is your responsibility to do your best job presenting it so that she can understand and desire what you offer in a tangible way, even through the intangible medium of the Web. This is a great place to invest your persuasive resources.

Questions to Ask

Ask yourself the following questions about your site:

- Is the presentation undermined by slow download speed?
- Is it simple for the visitor to determine the most appropriate product from the product category page?
- Does the image provide enough context to discern the most important benefits?
- Do the images entice on their own even without copy?
- Is product information presented so visitors don't have to scroll down for the most important product information (that is, does it appear within the active window and above the fold)?
- Does the presentation make the best possible use of the available screen real estate?
- Is the choice of graphic material appropriate to the presentation?
- Does the presentation incorporate benefit-oriented language?
- Is it important to include specifications (feature-oriented facts)? If so, is this information available?
- Does product presentation include calls to action?

- Is pricing clear on the product page?

- Are calls to action above the fold, or are you requiring visitors to scroll before they can act? Do your calls to action stand out?

- Does the product presentation stir desire?

- Does the product image show enough details to make a purchase decision?

- Are there multiple views of a product?

- If the product is complex, is there a download available for continued reference during the purchase decision process?

- Are there reviews? If so, are they high quality, fresh, recent, and specific?

NEED TO LEARN MORE?

You can learn more about product presentation in the following resources:

"Online Product Merchandizing and Persuasive Momentum" by Bryan Eisenberg. ROI Marketing, ClickZ. July 9, 2004.

www.clickz.com/showPage.html?page=3378361

"Online Merchandising Tips from TigerDirect" by Bryan Eisenberg. ROI Marketing, ClickZ. July 16, 2004.

www.clickz.com/showPage.html?page=3381101

"Optimizing B2B Demand Generation" by Bryan Eisenberg. ROI Marketing, ClickZ. March 16, 2007.

www.clickz.com/3625240

"How Changing Your Product Image Can Boost Sales 147%," GrokDotCom by FutureNow. February 7, 2007.

www.grokdotcom.com/2007/02/07/how-changing-your-product-image-can-boost-sales-by-147/

"How a Pretty Face Can Push Visitors Away," GrokDotCom by FutureNow. October 4, 2007.

www.grokdotcom.com/2007/10/04/how-a-pretty-face-can-push-visitors-away/

Exercise

Identify ways you are presenting products on your sites, particularly those that you know for certain your competitors also sell. Pick your top-10 products and take screen shots of them.

Go to two or three of your competitors' sites, and do the same thing for these products.

Which one presents the best? Why?

Which of your competitors present the same way you do? Do you all do it the same way for a reason, or are you a lemming? (It's OK for your competitor to be a lemming, but not for you.) But don't be different solely to be different; can you find a way to be different that helps your customers achieve their goals?

Ask 10 people to compare the pictures:

- Can they tell the difference between yours and your competitors'? You want yours to stand out.

- Do they think the pictures give enough details to buy your product?

What to Test

Here are different ideas on what you can test when thinking about your product/service presentation:

- Test the default size of your product image.

- Test video vs. a static image.

- Test different backgrounds on your images.

- Test using a single image vs. multiple images. How many are ideal?

- Test adding a call to action to your product detail pop-up page.

- Test using callouts to point to key benefits/features of your product.

- Test how you let visitors know they can enlarge or zoom products.

- Test product images with and without people.

- Test adding information, such as reviews or secondary images, on your product detail pop-ups.

- Test different ways to present your different product options on the same page.

Apply This to Your Site

Apply the insights you have gained from your tests more broadly to your product presentation across your site.

If it is appropriate, make distinctions in product presentations between categories, if tests indicate this has value.

Can you think of better, more effective ways to present your products? What are they?

CHAPTER 25

Load Time

You express download speeds in raw numbers based on actual download time. (Be sure to clear your cache before evaluating this—in most browsers you can click Tools → Internet Options and clear your cache to delete all temporary Internet files.) It is important to test these speeds on a variety of connections, including dial-up at 56Kbps. You'd be surprised how many people, even as of this writing, still use dial-up or have slow connections.

Do you still remember being on dial-up? Why did you switch? You wanted sites to load faster. What has the market done as broadband speed has increased? We've added to page weight. Do you feel you are still waiting too long for some pages to load?

Your goal should be for pages to load in less than eight seconds, as measured on a 56Kbps connection, because that equates to roughly less than a second on a T1 connection.

However, speed of download is also a perception the site can influence by getting certain information, particularly headers and other text, to the visitor more quickly.

Questions to Ask

As yourself the following questions about your site:

- If downloads are longer than ideal, does the site employ a strategy for prioritizing the order of the information downloaded? (This might include key copy and navigation elements.)

- Is the site broken into several tables instead of one for layout (knowledge of HTML necessary), or does your site use Cascading Style Sheets (CSS)? If you're not using CSS, you should be.

- If there are images with text in them, could you replace them with text-based headers?

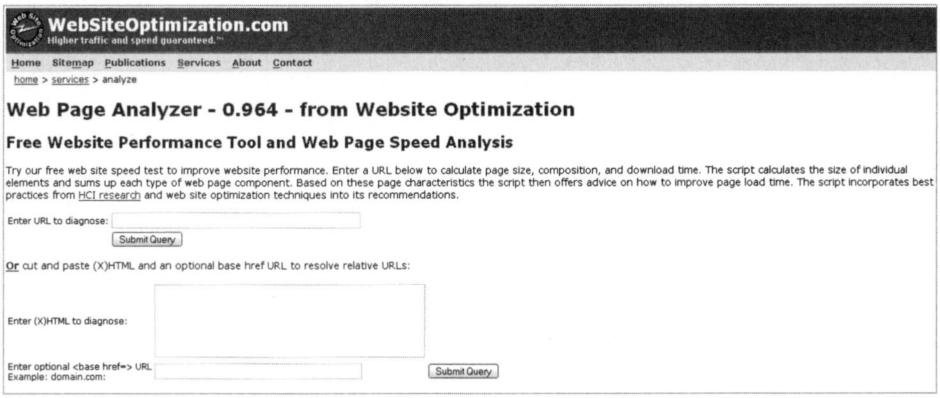

Figure 25.1
**WebsiteOptimiza-
tion.com entry
fields for page/site
analysis**

Exercise

Using WebsiteOptimization.com in the "Need to Learn
More?" section, test your site, as well as your competitors'
sites. Which one's pages load faster? Try to compare like
products.

What can you do to lower your load time?

What to Test

Here are different ideas on what you can test when thinking about load time:

- Test the default size dimensions of your main product
  image.

- Test the default file quality of your images or videos.

- Test a table-based layout of your page vs. a CSS-based
  layout.

- Test reducing the number of elements on your page.

- Test splitting up long pages into multiple shorter ones.

- Test changing your images to GIFs, JPGs, or PNGs to see which one maintains the
  quality while reducing the load time.

- Test placing scripts (such as JavaScript) into external files.

- Test specifying height and width for your tables and images. It's a good idea to also
  have descriptive alt tags.

NEED TO LEARN MORE?

Go to www.websiteoptimization.com/services/analyze/,
and use the free tool to analyze your website. Run your
analysis on your page/site by entering your URL (Figure 25.1);
then copy the download speed report from the site or take
a screen capture (and include the information on page
objects as well as your analysis and recommendation) to
share with your team (Figure 25.2).

Speed Up Your Site: Web Site Optimization by Andrew King
(New Riders Press, 2003).

*High Performance Web Sites: Essential Knowledge for Front-
End Engineers* by Steve Souders (O'Reilly Media, 2007).

DynamicDrive's Image Optimizer optimizes your GIFs, ani-
mated GIFs, JPGs, and PNG images so they load faster. It will
also convert image formats for you.

`tools.dynamicdrive.com/imageoptimizer/`

Figure 25.2

WebsiteOptimiza-
tion.com analysis
report

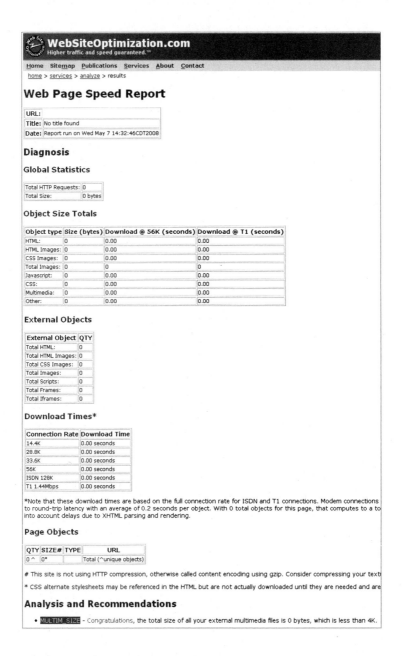

Apply This to Your Site

Take all the images you have optimized using DynamicDrive's Image Optimizer (mentioned earlier) and replace your unoptimized images.

Apply table-based or CSS-based page layout based on your testing results.

There are also many more suggestions to speed up your site in the books we recommended earlier.

CHAPTER 26

AIDAS: Attention, Interest, Desire, Action, and Satisfaction

AIDA is the classic business-school acronym for moving customers successfully through the sales process. The letters stand for Attention, Interest, Desire, and Action. We add an *S* for Satisfaction—you always want to do everything you can to leave your customers delighted and looking forward to returning.

AIDAS always functions at two levels: the individual page experience (the micro level) and the overall site experience (the macro level). Consider this an extension to the concept of scent on your landing pages. Each page has to provide enough information about what someone should click and what they are likely to see on the next page after they click. Content on that page should satisfy the visitor by being relevant to the scent the visitor followed to get there, and each link from this page to another likewise generates a "contract" to deliver relevancy on the ensuing pages.

Questions to Ask

Ask yourself the following questions:

A: Grab their *attention*

- Is material immediately relevant?
- Is it difficult to figure out what your page/site is about?
- Is key text differentiated?
- Does key text speak directly to what matters to the visitor?

I: Strengthen *interest (customer-focused)*

- Is it obvious how your site can meet visitors' needs?
- Is important information presented where it will do the most good?
- Does the copy speak in the visitors' language (customer-centered) or in your language (business-centered, talking more about you than them)?
- Does the site make it easy for visitors to find what they are looking for?

D: Stimulate *desire (benefit-focused)*

- Does the copy appeal to benefits rather than features?
- Where technical specifications are appropriate, are these available (but subordinate to benefits)?
- Does copy use language that helps visitors imagine themselves center stage, enjoying the value of your product or service?

A: Get them to take *action*

- Does the action you are trying to motivate make sense to the visitor based on where the visitor is in the buying decision process?
- Does your site make it easy to take action?
- Is it always clear exactly what the visitor must do to take action?
- Does your site reinforce a sense that taking action is safe?
- Does your site "ask" the visitor to take action?

S: Satisfy *them*

- Does every click satisfy the implicit question the visitor is asking?
- Is it always clear what the visitor should do next?
- Is language always aimed at the visitors' needs, from the visitors' perspective?
- Do some clicks produce error messages? (How easy does your site make it to refuel satisfaction in this case?)
- Do some on-site searches produce null results? (How easy does your site make it to refuel satisfaction in this case?)
- Would visitors find the experience of interacting with your site delightful?
- Can visitors feel good about doing business with your site?

Exercise

Take your top-10 keywords. From those keywords, decide what you want your visitors' final action to be and work backward to identify how you can help visitors get there. There are often multiple ways to get to the same goal.

What to Test

Here are different ideas on what you can test when evaluating AIDAS on your website:

- Test different keywords/trigger words in headers, links, and banner windows.
- Test using bulleted lists of benefits near the top of your page to summarize what will be covered in the rest of the page.
- Test the location of call-to-action buttons.

- Test the size of your calls to action.

- Test adding more white space around your call to action.

- Test the "thank you" page text. This space is often underutilized for offers.

- Test what words you use in your hyperlinks.

- Test what images, headlines, and copy you present when visitors click from page to page to add more scent.

- Test adding more secondary calls to action to offer visitors a choice of paths on your landing page.

- Test the elements and copy you place next to your calls to action.

Apply This to Your Site

Remember that your sales process matters to you, but it doesn't really matter to your visitors, who care far more about their buying process. Identify the critical steps in your sales process and then communicate them to your visitors in ways that meet their needs. Work toward making the steps in your sales process as unobtrusive as possible. Provide your visitors relevant and intuitive paths from your landing pages to your goal/success pages.

NEED TO LEARN MORE?

Learn more about AIDAS with the following resources:

"Hey, It's Music to MY Ears," The Grok. GrokDotCom by FutureNow. June 15, 2000.

www.grokdotcom.com/aidas.htm

"Do the 5 Step … and Dance Your Way to Higher Sales," The Grok. GrokDotCom by FutureNow.

www.grokdotcom.com/stepstosellingonline.htm

"If You're So Good, Sell Me" by Bryan Eisenberg. ROI Marketing, ClickZ. July 16, 2001.

www.clickz.com/experts/design/traffic/article.php/843851

"How to Fill Your Customer's Needs," The Grok. GrokDotCom by FutureNow. September 1, 2003.

www.grokdotcom.com/customerneeds.htm

"Are You Designing for Usability or Sales? Part II" by Bryan Eisenberg. ROI Marketing, ClickZ. January 16, 2004.

www.clickz.com/experts/design/traffic/article.php/3299801

"Are You Designing for Usability or Sales? Part III" by Bryan Eisenberg. ROI Marketing, ClickZ. January 23, 2004.

www.clickz.com/experts/design/traffic/article.php/3302291

"Qualify Your Visitors," The Grok. GrokDotCom by FutureNow. November 1, 2002.

www.grokdotcom.com/qualifying.htm

CHAPTER 27

Security/Privacy

We discuss elsewhere privacy issues associated with the buying decision (Chapter 14) and how to communicate those at the point of action (Chapter 33), so we will keep our discussion of privacy brief in this chapter. But even when customers trust *you* to safeguard their privacy, they may find it difficult to trust the medium as a secure venue for exchanging money and personal information. Your attention to security and privacy reassurances are necessary whenever credit card transactions are involved. Your visitors need to know they can trust your company to process the order, that you won't overbill them, and that their payment information cannot be hacked.

Although the visitor's perception of security and privacy is what's really at stake, you can use technology creatively to reassure customers that they have made a safe, smart transaction.

For instance, notice how the "submit" button in Figure 27.1 turns gray and dims once the visitor clicks it. A simple change like this can help your customers feel safe and will increase the likelihood of future purchases.

Better Business Bureau or VeriSign logos can also help e-commerce newbies have confidence in your site's security, but the look and professionalism of your site will ultimately be what inspires the most confidence.

Questions to Ask

Ask yourself the following questions about your site:

- Is your site secure?
- Is your site encrypted?
- Are there verification services?
- Is the transfer of information secure?
- Does the site look credible?

Figure 27.1

A TypePad strategy for promoting confidence in site security

Exercise

Check your site for the following:

- Ensure lock icons appear in browsers when visitors enter an HTTPS connection.

- Access your site using various security settings to ensure you don't get any security messages.

- Consider including functionality that protects your visitors from double ordering. Some sites offer a reminder not to hit the "submit" button twice, although providing the protection is a more customer-friendly way to handle the situation.

NEED TO LEARN MORE?

Learn more about security/privacy here:

ComPass Security AG offers a secure document exchange solution.

www.csnc.ch/en/

www.sicherheitstest.ch/static/

Scanalert.com, a McAfee product, provides a security solution that offers protection from hacking, credit card fraud, and identity theft.

www.scanalert.com

What to Test

Here are different ideas on what you can test when thinking about security and privacy:

- Test the language on your security and privacy policies.

- Test adding one-line summaries of your policies near the calls to action or forms you want people to act on.

- Test letting visitors know they are progressing to a secure area by adding it to your calls to action.

- Test adding "We value your privacy" next to any form where you are collecting information. Test whether making it an actual link to the privacy policy helps or hinders the conversion rate.

- Test adding icons of a lock to let visitors know they are in a secure area.

Apply This to Your Site

Although visitors are always concerned for their privacy and security, they rarely will read your policies. However, it is helpful to let them know you are aware of their concerns and will address them up front. Very often, all you really need to do is acknowledge their concerns in copy that you place exactly where they will question your commitment to security and privacy—how you apply this will depend on your test results.

CHAPTER 28

Trust and Credibility

Trust and credibility are interwoven, often unintentionally, into many of a site's features and functions. At the most obvious level, your site's association with agencies verifying its integrity (VeriSign, Better Business Bureau, Hacker Safe, and so on) will influence the visitor's perceptions. Even more important are your point-of-action assurances, business policies, and the tone of your copy.

Questions to Ask

Ask yourself these questions about your site:

- Does your site look professional?
- Is your site affiliated with certifying agencies?
- Are your certificates up-to-date? (Nothing kills confidence quite like clicking through on a VeriSign logo and discovering your certificates have expired!)
- Does your site make active use of point-of-action assurances?
- Are these assurances to the right, where the eye is trained to look for them?
- Does your site employ "shop with confidence" messages?
- Does your site offer secure transactions?
- Does your copywriting inspire confidence and make the business appear credible?
- Does your site offer online and/or offline help?
- Does your site display a toll-free telephone number? (Be sensitive to international communication issues if your reach is more global.)

Exercise

Review your site's and your competitors' About Us page. Score the following on a scale from 1 (low) to 5 (high):

SITE	PERFORMANCE	TRUST	COPY	HELP	PHONE #
Your site					
Competitor #1					
Competitor #2					
Competitor #3					

After you've done this, have someone else (for example, a customer or a business associate) do the same thing to see how your scoring compares to theirs.

What to Test

Here are different ideas on what you can test when thinking about building trust and credibility:

- Test using third-party verification logos, such as Hacker Safe and VeriSign.
- Test putting links to your About Us page throughout the site.
- Test adding staff images to your About Us page.
- Test putting your physical address in the footer.
- Test putting more assurances related to security, privacy, returns, and the like throughout the site.
- Test putting your phone number in the header. Test making it larger.
- Test offering different ways to reach customer service such as phone, chat, and email.
- Test letting people know the hours that customer service is available.
- Test changing the voice/tone in your About Us page to a more approachable and friendly tone.
- Test changing the language in any of your policies (such as your privacy policy) to make them more approachable.

NEED TO LEARN MORE?

You can learn more about trust in the following article:

"Would You Trust This Face?" The Grok. GrokDotCom by FutureNow. October 1, 2000.

`www.grokdotcom.com/trustperception.htm`

Apply This to Your Site

In addition to making sure you have the products or services people want, you need to understand that trust and credibility are the make-it-or-break-it of converting visitors.

Be aware that the appearance of your site and the quality of your content reflect your trustworthiness and credibility. Your primary goal is to find a way to present these in a manner that works for your audience (and there is no one correct solution here). Also be aware that your attention to the concerns your visitors bring with them—their questions and needs—will greatly improve your visitors' perceptions of trust and credibility.

Always keep in mind that you cannot "tell" visitors you are reliable; you must "show" them through image and deed.

CHAPTER 29

Product Selection/Categorization/ Search Results

Helping visitors identify where to look and getting them quickly to the products or services they want is critical. The site must skillfully help visitors qualify their needs through scenarios that make sense to the visitor and are sensitive to how visitors tend to buy that product or service. In the brick-and-mortar world, a salesperson would begin a dialogue. Online, a site makes the questions implicit in the linking strategies it offers.

There are four types of visitors:

- Visitors who know exactly what they want.

- Visitors who know approximately what they're looking for.

- Visitors who know they have an interest but may not have committed to active buying mode.

- Visitors who arrive at your site by accident and don't want anything.

We'll use a retail example to illustrate the issue, but lead-generation sites could have the same issues if you are trying to get visitors to choose from different services or products.

Imagine you step into a typical garden-variety department store. Today, you're purchasing a burgundy leather belt. You orient yourself; you scan for visual cues that may steer you in the right direction. Hanging from the ceiling in the far corner of the store is a sign that reads "Footwear." You start in that direction.

Why?

We have a lifetime of experience with shopping and learning the way retailers categorize and lay out their selling space. Belts are considered accessories and are usually surrounded by other accessories, typically near the shoes. In the grocery store, milk is usually near eggs; both are perishable and require frequent replenishment at home. When buying one, you're likely to remember you're out of the other, so they put the items together.

Likewise, with belts, you're usually thinking of them in the context of shoes and having to match a belt to shoes, so they put the belts near the shoes. As a consumer, you're so used to this that you don't even think about it anymore; as a retailer, you think about it all the time.

The offline shopping world is rich with textures, colors, tastes, smells, lights, sounds, and the bustle of people. Buying offline is a richer experience, because the retailer has more control over the shopping environment. On the downside, it's short on space and therefore product choices and information.

The online world is a flat, two-dimensional screen. It's often daunting, overwhelming, and lonely. The upside is product choices are endless, information abounds, and you have 24/7 access. Buying online should be a more convenient experience because the buyer has more control.

By trying to mimic the offline experience, many online retailers only underline how inferior the sensory experience is. Other online retailers present a tangled pile of links and images, leaving prospects confused and frustrated. It's often a surprise that the same retailers who know where to put what offline suddenly seem talentless on their websites. Shoppers don't notice this consciously, of course—well, unless they read GrokDotCom regularly (shameless plug!)—but shoppers do unconsciously feel something is amiss, even if they can't put their finger on it.

It's no surprise more and more people shop online but buy offline. Is this because the offline world is a much better experience? Or is it because most e-tailers have failed to create convenient online shopping experiences?

Online, Expectations Are Different

Not only do we surf the Web with a life history of offline buying experiences and expectations, but we've also developed additional expectations. We demand immediate relevance.

Online, we're a teeny needle in a haystack of bits and bytes, searching through a maze of interconnected digital data. It's not like we feel lost; we know where the Back button is. Heck, we know where the nearest department store is. What all those billions of bytes of surrounding data do is magnify our sense of urgency toward finding relevancy, finding the data we seek, and finding the product we want.

For the online retailer, the center of this struggle is the category page. This is where the experiences of the offline world seem to clash with the realities, advantages, and limitations of online. How does an e-tailer present wares effectively for maximum selling opportunities while meeting the plethora of needs a prospective customer has when she arrives? How do we present her with immediate relevance as she shops? Worse, how do we categorize, present, and introduce potentially thousands of SKUs on a flat, two-dimensional, 800×600 screen?

Answering the following three questions will bring you closer to better category pages.

Who's on This Page?

Start by making a list of who will be visiting this page. If this is a category page, it's likely a long list. Don't consider just demographics; also list specific needs and motivations as they relate to the products you sell. Sort these into different visitor types, or even create personas.

What Do You Want Them to Do?

Now that you've identified several visitor types, you must assign at least one or more actions you want each type to take on this page. Do you want to give them the opportunity to dig deeper, to buy now, to browse, or to do all of these actions? Again, the list of actions could be long. That's OK. Later, you can prioritize these actions on the page. (One good way is to assign a dollar value to each action.)

The ultimate purpose of a category page is to help the visitors evaluate alternatives and choose the product that's right for them based on their needs as they define them. If visitors don't see this on your category page, you'll see *pogo-sticking* in your analytics. If visitors engage in too much pogo-sticking and keep clicking back and forth from category page or search results page to product page, they'll abandon your site. That leads to the third question.

What Must the Visitor See to Take Your Desired Actions?

Take into account where the visitor type is in the buying cycle and her needs and motivations:

> If she knows exactly what she wants, does she perceive how she can quickly get there from your category page? If she wants a Versace Ingenue burgundy leather belt, is there any reason to not immediately present her with one?

> If she knows approximately what she wants, does she have a way to browse products in the context of her specific need or use, or is she forced to browse your self-named categories? If she's looking for a burgundy leather belt, is there any reason not to show her the various burgundy leather belts you have for sale?

> If she's early in the buying process and she's just identified a need, do you provide a way to learn more about the category? Are you doing what you can to narrow her choices? Can you let her know that burgundy leather products are "in" this year?

FutureNow's senior persuasion architect, Anthony Garcia, was shopping for a RAM upgrade for his Apple notebook. Having an account at MacMall, he arrived at the memory category page. The active window presented him with a clear question: "Need Memory?"

Of course, he did. The question Anthony really needed answered, however, was "What type of memory does my notebook need?" A sharp retailer would have followed up "Need Memory?" with "Pick the Right Memory for Your Laptop," but on this site the answer was difficult to find. He bailed.

He ended up spending about 33 percent more on his memory upgrade on Apple.com because it answered his question quickly with a clear and easy-to-understand process.

Plan to Help Visitors Find the Right Product

Any profitable brick-and-mortar retail store meticulously plans its lighting, floor plan, product presentation, and so forth. The idea is to provide shoppers with a path through the store that allows them to find what they're looking for with minimal effort and, along the way, to be presented with additional products. You can do this with your online category pages. Simply plan your category pages by answering and accounting for the answers to the previous three questions.

Questions to Ask

Ask yourself these questions about your site:

- Does the copy on the home page and category pages help the visitor know why they should see particular items?

- Can the visitor do a product ID search? Maybe your visitor got the product ID from another site that frustrated him. Wouldn't you like to be the happy recipient of his money when you quickly and easily show him what he wants?

- Do you include buying guides or educational information on your site?

- Does your site offer "buy/act now" options as well as "learn more" options?

- How quickly can someone who knows exactly what she wants get to the close?

- How do you help someone who knows approximately what he is looking for and quickly wants to find the information that will answer his questions and persuade him toward the close?

- How does your search function handle misspellings?

- Can your search function handle broad category terms?

- What possible actions does your site offer the visitor (in the active window) when the search produces no results?

- Do you provide suggestions to keep the process going if no results are found?

- Can visitors refine their search queries or the parameters of the search?

- Do you offer explanations of how the visitor should word the query or explain the use of helpful elements such as quotation marks and hyphens (if these help in the search)?

- Does your search function return relevant results?
- Does the presentation of these results help the visitor quickly identify what he's looking for?

NEED TO LEARN MORE?

You can learn more at the following locations:

"Qualifying Your Visitors." The Grok. GrokDotCom by FutureNow.
www.grokdotcom.com/index11-01-2002.htm

"Make a Good Investment in In-Site Search Engines" by Bryan Eisenberg. ROI Marketing, ClickZ. April 9, 2004.
www.clickz.com/showPage.html?page=3337221

Search Tools from In-Site Search Engine expert Avi Rappaport.
www.searchtools.com

What to Test

Here are different ideas on what you can test when thinking about product selection and categorization:

- Test offering different ways for visitors to refine and narrow the product selections on a category page.
- Test different size thumbnails to show additional details of the products.
- Test adding different features to the details shown on your category page.
- Test adding an add-to-cart button for each product in the category page.
- Test adding a link to view all the products within a category so that people don't have to click multiple pages to look at all the products.
- Test adding a descriptive headline and/or a sentence to different groups of products.
- Test adding a gallery header to your product pages that offer featured products, or most popular products, before displaying the full category product selection.
- Test adding an offer to the top of your category/search results page.
- Test adding ratings to your products on your category/search results page.
- Test the order of the products listed on your category/search results page.

Apply This to Your Site

You may find different categories require different amounts of information and possibly different product features to help visitors find the product they want.

Go through your top-25 products by sales and come up with all the possible misspellings. Enter these misspellings in your internal search and in Google, and see what happens. Does the search results page offer enough context for users to select the correct product?

Also, make sure to map all the misspellings to the correct product.

CHAPTER 30

Navigation/Use of Links

Keep visitors focused within the active window with navigation features that prevent them from clicking the Back button. If they use the browser's Back button to retrace their steps, they are much more likely to leave the site.

Include keyword-driven clickable links to encourage visitors deeper into the site. Visitors associate blue, underlined text with hyperlinks. If you look at all the top-selling websites, you will find they all have blue links (albeit different shades of blue), and most of the links are underlined.

Avoid making your text hyperlinks red; this color communicates warning and can make the visitor think that clicking the link could generate a cautionary message. Also make sure you don't have any "hidden" links; these are links that visitors aren't sure are clickable. Hidden links can include images that aren't obviously clickable or hyperlink text rendered in colors that are indistinguishable from the surrounding copy.

Mountain Equipment Co-op (Figure 30.1) provides excellent copy on choosing climbing rope but doesn't link any of the copy to help persuade visitors deeper into the site.

Conversely, Cableorganizer.com provides hyperlink-rich copy that helps the visitor identify a need quickly and move forward without having to disengage from the active window.

Link persuasive text (keywords and trigger words), and offer a sense of what the visitor can expect on the other side of the click.

Questions to Ask

Ask yourself the following questions about your site:

- Are there dead ends, with no clear indication in the active window where the visitor can go or what she is supposed to do next?
- Does your site make good use of embedded text links?
- Is it obvious what the visitor can click?
- Does the navigation speak in terms the visitor would use and understand (customer-centered navigation)?
- Are the links embedded in the copy so the visitor does not have to disengage from the active window to complete the conversion process?

Figure 30.1

Mountain Equipment Co-op explains climbing ropes.

Figure 30.2

Cableorganizer.com hyperlinks category descriptions.

Exercise

Try the following exercises:

1. Make two columns. In the first column, list the current order of navigation from top to bottom.

   Next, decide the percent of revenue from each.

   In the second column, reorder the list in the first column based on revenue.

2. Go to your site and take a screen shot (both in color and grayscale).

   • Color or white out all the top and side navigation.

   • Is the primary action you want your visitor to take obvious, and does it stand out in the center section/active window?

   • Do this for all key functional pages (home page, landing pages, category pages, product pages, and so on).

NEED TO LEARN MORE?

You can learn more about navigation at the following locations:

"Fix Navigation to Improve Conversions, Part 1" by Bryan Eisenberg. ROI Marketing, ClickZ. April 16, 2004.
www.clickz.com/showPage.html?page=3340391

"Fix Navigation to Improve Conversions, Part 2" by Bryan Eisenberg. ROI Marketing, ClickZ. April 23, 2004.
www.clickz.com/showPage.html?page=3343301

"Fix Navigation to Improve Conversions, Part 3" by Bryan Eisenberg. ROI Marketing, ClickZ. April 30, 2004.
www.clickz.com/showPage.html?page=3346531

"Hyperlink to Persuasion" by Bryan Eisenberg. ROI Marketing, ClickZ. October 31, 2003.
www.clickz.com/showPage.html?page=3101271

What to Test

Here are different ideas on what you can test when thinking about navigation:

• Test the length of your links (how many words are hyperlinked).

• Test writing your links to include a verb.

• Test moving the order of your hyperlinks.

• Test creating a second link to go to the same target as one of your original links, just worded differently.

• Test the color of your hyperlinks. Test underlining them, especially if your site does not already use blue underlining for hyperlinks.

• Test adding icons next to links that lead to PDFs or other file types.

• Test using a left navigation that changes for the section of the site a person is in.

• Test using or removing breadcrumb trails.

• Test making headlines and headings links to relate to the hyperlink in the block of text that the headline is being used for.

• Test taking out unnecessary categories or adding categories that might be helpful to visitors.

Apply This to Your Site

Often when people create landing pages, they don't offer any links to additional information. This tends to work well when you are dealing with a product or service your visitors are familiar with and they are later in the purchase process. It is worth adding links if your product is more complex and your visitors are earlier in the buying process.

CHAPTER 31

Up-Sell/Cross-Sell

Key up-sell and cross-sell opportunities exist within the following:

- Product pages
- The shopping cart
- "Thank you" pages

Your visitor may already have a new LCD flat-screen monitor in her cart, but does she have a webcam? How about cables that will connect it to both Mac and PC?

Although iPod users are already accessory-conscious, nevertheless, Apple takes advantage of up-sell opportunities when a visitor adds an item to her cart (Figure 31.1). Wal-Mart serves up a more understated up-sell opportunity directly on the product page (Figure 31.2).

Figure 31.1

Apple's up-sell after the add-to-cart click

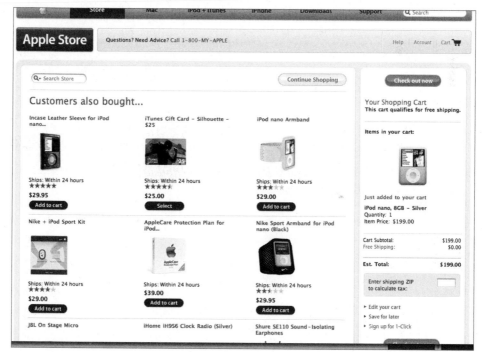

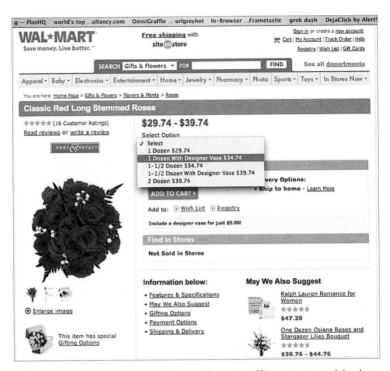

Where you put your up-selling and cross-selling opportunities in your sales process matters. Apple's placement suits a cross-sell that encourages the visitor to consider items related to the item she has already added to her cart. The Wal-Mart placement better suits an up-sell (although it offers a mixed bag of suggested products). There's greater potential in the Wal-Mart opportunity for the visitor to abandon the primary product selection. Be careful not to derail the visitor in her buying mission.

It amazes us how many sites neglect the up-sell opportunity: When visitors select items within a budget range, many businesses show items only from that price range. For example, if you ask someone his budget for the earrings he is planning to buy for an anniversary present, he might tell you he is planning to spend $300–$400. However, in an offline retail environment, he might well spend up to $600. Make sure to include these items as a way to show people that, for a little more money, they can also get other, better products.

Don't overlook your cross-sell opportunities on null-result in-site searches. Depending on your visitor's query, you can often present a bundled offering.

Questions to Ask

Ask yourself the following questions:

- Does the site offer add-ons, accessories, or upgrades?
- Does it provide an "other people who bought this item also bought _____" suggestion?

- Are up-sells presented at the appropriate stages of the buying process?
- Are the cross-sell and up-sell offerings appropriate?
- Does your product lend itself to up-selling?

Exercise

Take a look at your top-20 products to see what products you are cross-selling and up-selling with those:

1. Using analytics and sales data, determine how often they are sold together.
2. Are they the most effective combinations? Look at the possibility of higher- /lower-priced combinations.

> **NEED TO LEARN MORE?**
>
> Learn more about up-selling and cross-selling here:
>
> "If You're So Good, Sell Me" by Bryan Eisenberg. ROI Marketing, ClickZ. July 16, 2001.
>
> www.clickz.com/experts/design/traffic/article.php/843851

What to Test

Here are different ideas on what you can test when thinking about up-selling/cross-selling:

- Test the visibility of the up-sell/cross-sell.
- Test up-sells/cross-sells on "thank you" or confirmation pages.
- Test the location on the page of the up-sell/cross-sell.
- Test the items offered in the up-sell/cross-sell.
- Test how many products you offer in your up-sell/cross-sell.
- Test the price points of your up-sell/cross-sell.
- Test the heading on the up-sell/cross-sell. ("People like you also bought. . . .")
- Test putting an Add-to-Cart button on the up-sell/cross-sell.
- Test how people have to add the item being up-sold (check box, link to other page, and so on).
- Test using different cross-sell options (similar items, best sellers).

Apply This to Your Site

Carefully consider where you place up-sell and cross-sell strategies in your sales process; you don't want to undermine your visitor's progress in making the primary purchase. Also, make sure your up-selling/cross-selling doesn't come off as though you are a pushy salesperson, but as an assistant offering useful and relevant recommendations.

CHAPTER 32

Calls to Action

Any action a visitor can take on a page to move forward in the selling process is a *call to action*. Create calls to action by pairing an imperative verb with an implied benefit. The most obvious calls to action are ones that say "Add to Shopping Cart" or "Buy Now" or "Subscribe"; each is a straightforward "Do this!" At the most basic level, they tell the visitor what she can accomplish on that page and encourage her forward in the conversion process. Every page should have at least one clear call to action.

It's OK to ask your visitors to take action. In fact, you *must* ask them. If you don't, all you can do is hope they'll figure out what they are supposed to do next and then hope they actually do it. Without well-considered, well-placed calls to action, you leave a lot more to chance.

Additional examples of calls to action include the following:

- "Click here to save on shipping!"
- "Sign up to start saving now!"
- "Download free software!"

In Figure 32.1, you can see how the site uses the "Get It Now!" button right in the active window to make sure you click.

Questions to Ask

Ask yourself the following questions about your site:

- Are you asking your visitors to take action?
- Is the call to action placed within the active window?
- Do you use linked text as well as add-to-cart buttons to promote action?

Figure 32.1

Call-to-Action button to get your credit report now

Exercise

Try the following exercise:

1. Look at your product page in grayscale.

2. Look at it again in color.

3. Does the call to action look clickable?

4. Test the wording of the call to action. You might find some key verbs seem to work well in your business space; on other sites, it might be the implied benefit that is semistandard in that space, and there's room for imperative verb tweaking.

NEED TO LEARN MORE?

Learn more about calls to action here:

"So What Exactly Is a Call to Action?" The Grok. GrokDotCom by FutureNow. June 15, 2003.

http://www.grokdotcom.com/calls-to-action.htm

"Push Your Customers' Buttons" by Bryan Eisenberg. GrokDotCom by FutureNow. May 24, 2007.

http://www.grokdotcom.com/2007/05/24/push-your-customers-buttons/

"Large Red Buttons? Oh My!" by Joshua Hay. GrokDotCom by FutureNow. February 15, 2007.

http://www.grokdotcom.com/2007/02/15/large-red-buttons-oh-my/

Evaluate the calls to action on your key pages in the following way:

(IMPLIED BENEFIT)	YES	NO

1. Imperative verb
2. Visible
3. Shape
4. Clickable (shadow)
5. Benefit statement

What to Test

Here are different ideas on what you can test when thinking about calls to action:

- Test the wording on the button or link.

- Test using text or graphics for your call to action.

- Test the shape of your call to action.

- Test the location of your call to action.

- Test adding benefit language near your call to action to remind visitors what they will get when they click.

- Test the style of your call to action. For example, is it flat or 3D?

- Test making your main action on the page larger and a different color than the rest of your call-to-action buttons.

- Test making different combinations of imperative verbs and implied benefits to see what verb and nouns act as "sweet spots" in your business space.

- Test the color of your call to action to make it higher contrast than the rest of the page.

- Test adding an icon to your call to action.

Apply This to Your Site

Try to make sure you keep your calls to action relatively consistent from page to page. Make sure there are links to your cart, checkout, or contact form on every page.

CHAPTER 33

Point-of-Action Assurances

When calls to action are paired with point-of-action assurances (for example, "We Value Your Privacy" and "You can always remove the item later"), you motivate action and build confidence.

You should place these to the right of the field or at the exact place where the visitor will be taking the action. Lands' End (Figure 33.1) provides a thorough point-of-action assurance that addresses guarantees, privacy, and security right next to the places where customers are deciding to purchase and filling in personal information.

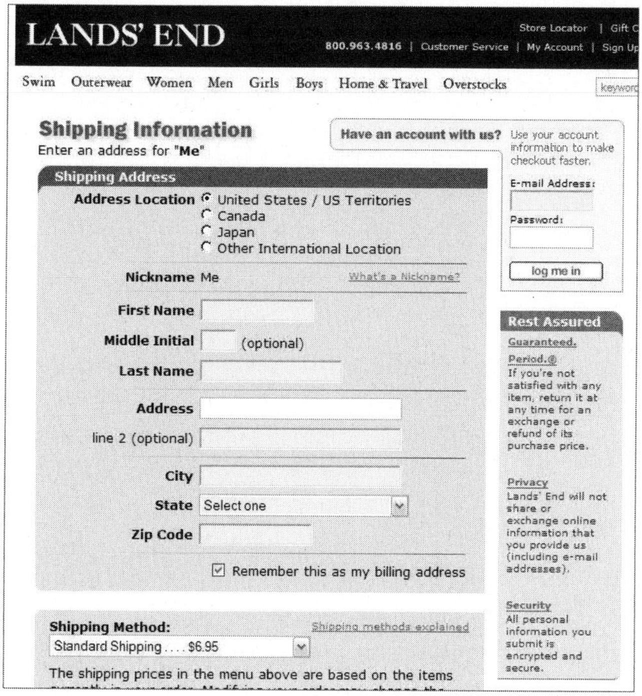

Figure 33.1

Lands' End point-of-action assurances

Take a look at how Sheetmusicplus.com (Figure 33.2) lets visitors know when they should expect their order to arrive. This enhances the buyer's confidence.

Figure 33.2

Sheetmusicplus.com provides delivery expectations.

Questions to Ask

Ask yourself the following questions about your site:

- Do you address privacy issues at the point you ask the visitor to reveal personal information?

- If you ask a visitor to use a tool, do you explain the benefit of using that tool at the point you ask them to use it?

- If there are places where visitors might want to undo an action, do you let them know this is possible?

Exercise

Try the following exercise:

1. Take screen shots of your entire checkout/registration process from the shopping cart to the "thank you" page.

2. Check for any point-of-action assurances that would help a visitor's level of confidence. Examples include policies on returns, privacy, and security; guarantees; price; shipping; gift boxes/options; questions; an easy-to-edit shopping cart; and the ability to compute an actual or estimated total shipping cost.

What to Test

Here are different ideas on what you can test when think-ing about point-of-action assurances:

NEED TO LEARN MORE?

Learn more about point-of-action assurances here:

"So What Exactly Is a Point of Action Assurance?" The Grok. GrokDotCom by FutureNow. October 1, 2003.

www.grokdotcom.com/poaassurance.htm

- Test adding point-of-action assurances on or around your call-to-action buttons.

- Test the location of your point-of-action assurances.

- Test the wording in your point-of-action assurances.

- Test having a graphic explaining your return or satisfaction guarantee vs. having it in text.

- Test adding different point-of-action assurances such as logos for Hacker Safe, VeriSign, and so on.

- Test what pages have assurances. Should you place them on all pages?

- Test how you have your point-of-action assurances displayed. Do you have them in a different color cell than the rest of the page to stand out?

- Test adding a gift-buyer policy during the holidays.

- Test letting people know when they will hear from you if they are submitting a contact form or when they will receive their order if you are an e-commerce site.

- Test having your point-of-action assurances behind links or written out right on the page.

Apply This to Your Site

Point-of-action assurances tend to address the intuitive layer of the hierarchy of optimi-zation. They usually don't require a lot of effort, but when executed well, they often provide a great return.

CHAPTER 34

Persuasive Copywriting

Every website visit is a conversation. Each time visitors click, they are asking a question and hoping that click will lead to the answer. The copy on your site anticipates the questions your visitors will ask and upholds your side of the conversation.

Think about the voice or personality of your site. Is it friendly and less formal? Is it caring and helpful? Is it authoritative and more formal? Whichever is appropriate for you, make sure you keep the voice consistent throughout the site.

Use your copy to answer your visitors' questions, resolve objections, explain the benefits and value of what you have to offer, and provide security and confidence.

Use the words your visitors use to describe their needs or problems and the solutions they are seeking.

Use Active Voice

As much as possible, write using the active-verb voice. Active voice emphasizes the subject of the action; passive voice shifts the focus to what is happening. "Birds build nests" is written in active voice and emphasizes the subject—birds. "Nests are built by birds" is written in the passive voice and emphasizes the action—building nests.

Active voice uses strong verbs and involves the reader in the action; thus, active voice is far more persuasive in driving action.

Passive "These fishing rods have been used to catch everything from bass to bluefish."

"These fishing rods have been used by Molly to catch everything from bass to bluefish."

Active "Molly uses these fishing rods to catch everything from bass to bluefish."

The passive voice tends to be wordier, often sounds pompous, and is sometimes confusing—it often is not clear, especially to those for whom English is not a first language, who is responsible for the action.

The active voice is far more direct, communicates a sense of confidence and trust, and specifies who is taking responsibility for the action.

Avoid Jargon

Avoid techno-jargon. Even if you have a technical product, still provide simple, clear copy everyone can understand. You may think you're impressing people, but if you don't communicate clearly, you can't persuade.

Edit your copy to take out all clichés. More often than not, they are useless phrases. Think about what you are trying to say, and replace clichés with different language that better expresses what you are trying to say. Look for techno-speak clichés like "taking it to the next level" or "think outside of the box," and replace them with more specific explanations. Specifics are more persuasive than generalities.

Be Specific

Back up any broad claims with evidence. If you say "We are the best in our field," back it up with a specific source or statistic. If you say "We are the favorite choice of small-business owners," back it up with a specific reason why.

Speak to the Four Buying Modalities

Use hyperlinks to target the different temperaments, calling them to take action in the particular language that appeals to them, all the while staying in the active window. This is where an effective use of embedded hyperlinks pays off.

Also, write copy that speaks to each of the four buying modalities. The order in which you should address these types, from top to bottom of a web page, is Spontaneous, Competitive, Humanistic, and Methodical. This way, the more fast-paced visitors get their information first, and your more deliberate, patient visitors get their information further down.

If you have a long page, consider using bullet points for all the items on the page at the top (with anchor text links) and then providing a deeper explanation of each point further down the page.

At the very least, incorporate language that addresses where visitors are in the process of their buying decision (early, middle, or late). Pay special attention to the needs of visitors who are not quite sure how to accomplish their goals. Links like "Help me choose" or "See which option is right for you" can take visitors to a page with copy that helps them understand and narrow down their choices.

Benefits/Features

When you want to capture your customer's interest and speak to their felt need (the thing that makes them want to buy), you sell the benefits, not the features of your product or service. A classic example? Take the electric drill. Nobody is going to buy one just so they can have an electric drill. They buy one because they want holes: clean holes, deep holes, accurate holes, fast holes, holes of many sizes, holes in different materials. Most people don't care what the drill is made from or how the circuitry is toggled—they care that it makes holes. They might also care that the drill is lightweight (but spare them a discussion of the space-age aluminum alloy casing), is maneuverable, is UL approved, has a super-long cord, and comes in its own carrying case. But they care about those things only because they add to performance, convenience, or safety—benefits, not features.

- List everything the product does. Include standard, technical, supportive, and abstract features.
- For each feature, list a relative advantage.
- List each advantage's benefits from the customer's perspective.
- List the motives: the benefits, features, and advantages that satisfy the customer.
- When linking your benefits to your features, use the phrase "which means" after each feature to introduce the benefit. Do this until you clearly identify the essential benefit.

Methodical customers do value product specifications, and if you have these, it's important to communicate the specifications. However, these customers will look for the information, so you needn't place it front and center. Your first appeal should always be to the emotional aspects of your products and services (the benefits), and you should never sacrifice these for the logical aspects (the features).

Identify Other Opportunities to Write Persuasively

Incorporate attention-grabbing headlines, and build interest through the use of benefit-oriented language. Headlines should focus on the needs and problems different visitors are experiencing and the solutions they are looking for, as well as any key point that differentiates your product or service.

Make sure your copy is formatted well for reading on a computer screen. Use headers, subheaders, bullet points, and bold formatting so readers can skim and scan the page. Avoid long sentences and long paragraphs.

Include more customer-oriented copy, focusing your language more on the customer and less on you or your business (think "you" instead of "we") (see Chapter 40).

By adding persuasive copy on your website, you can greatly improve your website sales.

Questions to Ask

Ask yourself the following questions:

- Is there a consistent voice throughout the site?
- Does the copy reflect the needs of different personality types (in other words, Competitive, Spontaneous, Humanistic, and Methodical)? Does it fully address their concerns and motivations?

- Does the copy reassure the visitor they're in the right place?

- Is the copy benefit-oriented? Does it speak to the emotional needs and desires of the visitor?

- Do your call-to-action links pair an imperative verb with an implied benefit (as in "View our model comparison chart")?

- Do your embedded point-of-resolution links direct different visitor types to the information they need to answer their buying process questions (as in "Which diamond shape would she most prefer?")?

- Does the site simply list product features, or does it talk about how those features benefit the visitor?

- Ask yourself, "What makes this product different or better than similar products?"

- Where it is appropriate to include features/specifications, does your site list them after focusing on the benefits?

- Is your use of the active voice strong, without being overpowering or full of hype?

Exercises

Try these exercises:

1. Pick your top-10 products, and copy/paste the copy for these 10 products into a Word document. Go to two or three of your competitors' sites and do the same thing. Ask 10 people to compare the copy.

   - Can they tell the difference between yours and your competitors'?

   - Could you buy the product from the description (is there enough information)?

2. Go to your key products. At the end of each line of a product description, say to yourself "which means…." Do this until the answer is very clear and you fully understand the benefit.

3. Rewrite the following sentences in the active voice:

   - "Once the button has been clicked, the order is immediately generated."

   - "Stains are blocked and repelled by our fabric's patented nanotechnology stain blockers."

   - "You will be assisted by the next live-chat operator."

   - "Your information is kept safe over our encrypted HTTPS connection and hacker-safe servers."

   - "Our courses are conducted by highly qualified instructors."

NEED TO LEARN MORE?

Learn more about copy at the following locations:

Persuasive Online Copywriting Seminar, FutureNow workshop. Check dates and availability here:
www.futurenowinc.com/writingforweb.htm

Persuasive Online Copywriting: How to Take Your Words to the Bank by Bryan Eisenberg, Jeffrey Eisenberg, and Lisa T. Davis (Wizard Academy Press, 2002).

"Persuasive Online Copywriting for Beginners (and Dummies!)" by Robert Gorell. GrokDotCom by FutureNow. May 1, 2006.
www.grokdotcom.com/topics/copywritingforbeginners.htm

"Top 10 Ideas for Testing Your Headlines" by Joshua Hay. GrokDotCom by FutureNow. February 13, 2007.
www.grokdotcom.com/2007/02/page/3/

"Headlines + Hyperlinks = Conversion + Cash" by The Grok. GrokDotCom by FutureNow. February 16, 2007.
www.grokdotcom.com/2007/02/16/headlines-hyperlinks-conversion-cash-grok/

"GR8 Web 2.0 Copy" by Bryan Eisenberg. ROI Marketing, ClickZ. June 8, 2007.
www.clickz.com/showPage.html?page=3626079

"2 Simple Steps to Finding Your Website's Voice" by Holly Buchanon. GrokDotCom by FutureNow. February 14, 2007.
www.grokdotcom.com/2007/02/14/2-simple-steps-to-finding-your-websites-voice/

"Increase Sales with Relevant Benefits" by Bryan Eisenberg. ROI Marketing, ClickZ. July 30, 2004.
www.clickz.com/showPage.html?page=3387771

"Appeal to Emotion" by The Grok. GrokDotCom by FutureNow. March 15, 2001.
www.grokdotcom.com/featuresvsbenefits.htm

"You Want Them to Buy? Sell Benefits" by Bryan Eisenberg. ROI Marketing, ClickZ. April 9, 2001.
www.clickz.com/showPage.html?page=840121

"Think Active" by The Grok. GrokDotCom by FutureNow.
www.grokdotcom.com/thinkactive.htm

"How Verbs Help You Convert" by The Grok. GrokDotCom by FutureNow.
www.grokdotcom.com/topics/verbsforconversion.htm

"Activate Your Verbs" by The Grok. GrokDotCom by FutureNow. May 9, 2007.
www.grokdotcom.com/2007/05/09/activate-your-verbs/

What to Test

Here are different ideas on what you can test when thinking about persuasive copywriting:

- Test the offer itself.

- Test the length of your copy (long vs. short) as well as the formatting (bullets vs. block text, amount of white space around text blocks).

- Test long vs. short sentences and paragraphs.

- Test punctuation: Do dashes work better than commas or ellipses?

- Test using bulleting to help you order copy with charts, copy with pictures, and block copy. Which should come first?

- Test placement of copy on the page: Do you need to go with a two- or three-column layout in the active window in order to bring the copy up above the fold? Do you need to use pull quotes to bring readers into the copy?

- Test the emotional connotations of words (everyone wants to be normal, but no one wants to be average).

- Test the voice of the copy: formal vs. informal, plain vs. richly textured, "attitude," and so on. Will your visitors feel better "speaking with a customer service representative" or "talking to Chuck"?

- Test removing all the words that are not absolutely necessary to your copy (the black words); also try testing the use of an uncommon phrase in place of run-of-the-mill language to see whether this keeps your visitor more engaged with your copy ("when the sun goes to sleep" for "sunset").

- Test passive and active voice in your copy.

Apply This to Your Site

Go back to Chapter 12 and look at the 20 phrases you said would describe your products or services for each of the buying personalities. How many of these phrases are in your copy?

Review some of your site's copy for passive-voice content. Rewrite this content using active voice.

CHAPTER 35

Content

If your visitors need to leave your site to find relevant product information, they are far less likely to return and buy from you. So, it's important to keep them engaged with a variety of content that includes (as appropriate) benefit-oriented copy, product images, comparative charts and checklists, customer reviews, testimonials, specifications, and recommendations. Depending on what you sell, the types of content and where it is placed will vary.

Many people now use content on blogs to drive traffic and to sell products or services. We do this with our own blog, GrokDotCom. Figure 35.1 is a retail example.

Figure 35.1

A retail jewelry blog evokes a celebrity's jewelry style to promote sales.

Other sites create content aimed at helping customers buy their products (Figure 35.2). If this content doesn't relate to the customer's buying process, visitors usually don't use the content to purchase. Instead, they abandon the website. Content that includes the search terms and trigger words your visitors use can help your ranking in the search engines; often, what is good for the customer is good for the ranking. However, it doesn't always work in reverse. Not all content designed to help ranking in the search engines will help visitors buy. Remember, search engines don't carry credit cards.

Questions to Ask

Ask yourself the following questions about your site:

- Do you offer enough information to help a visitor make the decision to act?
- Are visitors directed to content that would appeal to different personality types?
- Does the content speak in the visitor's language, addressing their needs, wants, and desires?
- Does your content identify the motivations behind the desire to buy?
- Does your use of graphics help or hinder the persuasion process?
- Are your images engaging?

Exercise

Write down 20 problems your customers might have when ordering from you. (Optional: Ask real customers or your customer service department for 20 more.)

Here are some examples:

- "I need a surround-sound system that will work with my game system, TV, stereo, and so on."
- "I want to buy outdoor hiking equipment for the first time."

How well does your site help solve the problems you have identified?

What to Test

Here are different ideas on what you can test when thinking about content:

- Test writing about the same topic from multiple points of view or focused on a different person's needs.
- Test adding open-ended questions at the end to encourage dialogue.
- Test adding supporting images to your content.
- Test adding hyperlinks to related products in your content.
- Test the length of your content.
- Test where you place hyperlinks to your content from your products.
- Test how you ask for feedback or comments.
- Test the headlines of your content.

Figure 35.2

Mountain Equipment Co-op provides an excellent, keyword-rich explanation of climbing ropes.

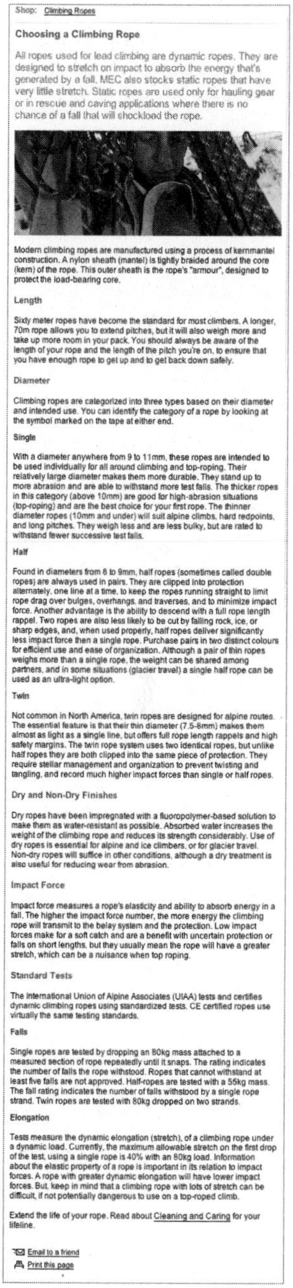

- Test how simply you explain things. Are you assuming too much or not enough knowledge on the part of the visitor?

- Test breaking up your content with headlines, subheadlines, bullets, and so on.

NEED TO LEARN MORE?

Learn more about content at the following locations:

"Online Merchandising Tips from TigerDirect" by Bryan Eisenberg. ROI Marketing, ClickZ. July 16, 2004.

www.clickz.com/showPage.html?page=3381101

"Content, Copy, Language and Prepurchase Behavior" by Bryan Eisenberg. ROI Marketing, ClickZ. February 13, 2004.

www.clickz.com/showPage.html?page=3312141

"3 Tips for Great Web Content" by The Grok. GrokDotCom by FutureNow. June 1, 2005.

www.grokdotcom.com/topics/3contenttips.htm

"Bazaar Blog" by Bazaarvoice.

www.bazaarblog.com

"How Much of My $1000 Rock Climbing Budget Do You Want?" by Melissa Burden. GrokDotCom by FutureNow. August 15, 2006.

www.grokdotcom.com/2006/08/15/how-much-of-my-1000-rock-climbing-gear-budget-do-you-want/

Apply This to Your Site

Create content that helps visitors with the problems you identified in this section's exercise, and find places where you can integrate it into your website.

CHAPTER 36

Headlines

Writing good headlines is an art. It takes time, practice, and patience. This is one reason why we love Website Optimizer. It lets marketers write many versions of a headline and test to see which one is most effective. However, testing alone won't produce a good headline for you; it also takes knowing what works best for your audience (which is not always what you think will work best for them). When you test your headlines, you'll be able to add knowledge of your audience to your copywriting equation. And that's when your headlines will be at their persuasive best! Keep in mind that your headline does not need to sell your product or service; it only needs to grab the attention of your visitor and draw them into the first line of body copy.

Most headlines (and copy, for that matter) suffer from what Chip and Dan Heath refer to in *Made to Stick* (Random House, 2007) as a Curse of Knowledge: Once you know something, it's difficult to imagine what it is like to not know it. So, here are some tips:

- Make sure everyone understands what your headline is about, even if they have no context in which to understand it.

- The headline should set expectations about the content that follows.

- Invest as much time as possible testing your headlines' abilities to attract attention and to motivate visitors to invest the next 30 seconds on your page by explaining what's in it for them—in language they can understand!

Questions to Ask

Ask yourself the following questions about your site:

- Do your headlines stand out on your page?

- Are your headlines "made to stick"?

- Does your headline match the ad scent that drove the visitors?

- Do you use subheadlines to break up the content of your page?

- If visitors read only your headlines, would the headlines give them a meaningful synopsis or abstract of your content?

Exercise

Try this exercise:

1. Take your top-20 visited pages, and evaluate your headlines for the scent from your ads.

2. Determine whether the headlines are more logically based or emotionally based.

3. How well do the headlines describe what the visitor will read on the page?

What to Test

Here are different ideas on what you can test when thinking about testing headlines:

- Test comparing your product or service with something your visitors are familiar with.

- Test engaging people's senses in your headlines, such as "Soft as a baby's bottom."

- Test making a claim by using a remarkable example. "At 60 miles an hour, the loudest noise in this Rolls Royce is the electric clock!"

- Test the formatting of your headlines, including the color, size, capitalization (all caps, all lowercase, and mixed case), and so on.

- Test the length of your headlines.

- Test writing your headline as a before-and-after claim.

- Test using a headline that warns visitors of the problem of not acting on your product or service offering.

- Test limiting who should be considering your product. "If you've already tested all your headlines, don't read this."

- Test accusing your claim of being too good to be true. "Persuasion Architecture Results Are Often Hard to Believe!"

- Test adding an image that reinforces your headline.

NEED TO LEARN MORE?

Learn more about headline writing from the following:

Persuasive Online Copywriting Seminar, FutureNow workshop. Check dates and availability here:

www.futurenowinc.com/writingforweb.htm

Persuasive Online Copywriting: How to Take Your Words to the Bank by Bryan Eisenberg, Jeffrey Eisenberg, and Lisa T. Davis (Wizard Academy Press, 2002).

"Top 10 Ideas for Testing Your Headlines" by Joshua Hay. GrokDotCom by FutureNow. February 13, 2007.

www.grokdotcom.com/2007/02/page/3/

"GR8 Web 2.0 Copy" by Bryan Eisenberg. ROI Marketing, ClickZ. June 8, 2007.

www.clickz.com/showPage.html?page=3626079

Apply This to Your Site

Headlines are among the most important communication elements on your site. They offer the visitor the critical invitation to engage with your content. Spend plenty of your resources on writing and testing headlines. Create headlines that synopsize your material and create manageable, readable chunks of text; if you simply read your headlines, will you have a good idea what the page's content is about?

CHAPTER 37

Readability

If they can't read it, they can't buy it—it's as simple as that. Consider the language you're using to describe your products and services. You may have an international audience on your site that has difficulty understanding certain nuances, so be sure to be plain-spoken and action-oriented. You can't control your audience's reading level, so don't condescend to them (and offend them) with high-falutin' language. Keep in mind that even top-selling business books are written at the sixth- to eighth-grade level. Don't believe us? Just ask Donald Trump!

We've discussed many of these factors in relation to other conversion issues and testing opportunities in Part II, "What You Should Test" (factors rarely exist in isolation!), but these also affect how you help a visitor apprehend and comprehend your content:

- Write using the active-verb voice.
- Keep your sentences direct and uncomplicated.
- Keep your paragraphs on the short side.
- Make use of white space and headers to differentiate sections and facilitate visual identification of information.
- Avoid using jargon, and when you must use it to promote your credibility with certain segments of your audience, treat it as you would features and specifications (in other words, you can put it much lower on a page or in a tabbed presentation or provide access through a link).
- In general, write to a fourth- or fifth-grade reading level, because the average American reads at a fifth- to eighth-grade level.

You need to be aware of whether your font choice is clear and whether the text is large enough for your audience. Readability is an area where sweating the small stuff pays off. (And, no, we don't mean literally "sweating," which is why your copy should avoid colloquialisms unless they're genuinely appropriate.)

Scanning and Skimming

You take the time to write correctly. Your text is persuasive. How do you ensure a reader engages with the text on your web pages?

This goes beyond copywriting. It's also a usability issue. Usability professionals use two easily confusable terms to describe how visitors engage with text: skimming and scanning.

"There's a difference? And I need to understand it?" you're wondering. You bet! If visitors can't scan and skim your web pages quickly and efficiently as soon as they arrive, they won't stick around to dig deeper. Not good. Although skimming and scanning are related, they're distinct experiences in the usability equation and require separate treatment. Lump scanning and skimming together, and chances are you'll miss the lessons to be learned from the serious usability research that's been conducted.

How do you keep visitors merrily scanning and skimming toward taking the action you want?

Before we go further, let's look at the dictionary. The *American Heritage Dictionary* defines the terms as follows:

Scan To look over quickly and systematically; to look over or leaf through hastily

Skim To give a quick and superficial reading, scrutiny, or consideration; glance

Can you see that although the two are similar, they're not quite the same? Both scanning and skimming are information-gathering activities. People perform them quickly, usually without much thinking. But they don't work the same way, and they don't serve the same purpose.

Think of it this way: You're on the wild and woolly Western frontier. Your trusty horse crests the hill. Before you is a vast expanse. You don't know whether there's danger out there. You look around. A thicket to the left...a lake in the distance...a tendril of smoke drifting above a small rise...a wooden fence near you on the right. Your "scan" suggests things look pretty safe. So, you spur your horse to a trot. Passing the fence, you notice a piece of paper nailed to a post. It's a "Wanted Dead or Alive" poster. You dismount, get closer, and "skim" the text for the most salient facts to help decide whether you'll bother with the fine print.

See the difference between scanning and skimming? Let's apply it to your website.

A visitor arrives and her eyes immediately begin scoping out the situation to determine whether she's in the right place. First, she'll scan the visible screen for prominent elements, determining whether they mesh with her mental image of her mission. As she scans, in addition to collecting top-level clues such as headlines, she'll evaluate larger-scale issues, such as legibility, arrangement, and accessibility. This is where more prominent features, including type size, page layout, and color use come into play. You want to help her minimize the time she spends finding, sorting, and selecting information, as well as engage her in the conversion process. If she doesn't find top-level clues that she's in the right place or if she finds the page hard to deal with, she's back on her horse, galloping to another site.

Skimming is the second, but equally important, activity. It's reading based, a refinement of the information-gathering process. When a visitor has a fairly good idea of the lay of the land, she's going to start engaging with the copy. She's not ready to stop and read anything thoroughly—yet. She's not sure if it's worth her while. She'll start with a superficial skim, looking for highlights and important keywords that help direct further involvement. This is where bold keywords, bullets, short text blocks, strong first and last sentences in each paragraph, legible fonts, and even effective hyperlink use make a difference.

This critical distinction helps our clients understand as we guide them in improving their sites and their persuasive copy. It's a subtle distinction, but it's one that makes a big difference.

Figure 37.1 and Figure 37.2 show how Amazon.com made formatting changes in their product descriptions to improve readability. Notice how changes to type sizes and colors (you'll have to take our word on this) increased white space, and the inclusion of a product thumbnail has contributed to making the description much easier to read.

Figure 37.1

Amazon.com's original product description template

Figure 37.2

Amazon.com's product description template after reformatting

Questions to Ask

Ask yourself the following questions:

- Is your copy overly technical?
- Does your copy use active voice?
- Is the page laid out so it is easily skimmable and scannable?
- Do you make good use of headers, bold text, and bullet points?

Exercise

Try the following:

1. Take your top-20 visited pages and run them through a readability tester.
2. Increase and decrease the font size. Try reading your site at these different font sizes.
3. Could you make sense of your page if you read only the headlines and the bold and/ or hyperlinked words?

What to Test

Here are different ideas on what you can test when thinking about readability:

- Test the font size you use for your body copy and headlines.
- Test changing the color of different copy elements to make them stand out more.
- Test making your paragraphs shorter.
- Test making your sentences shorter.
- Test the length of your headlines.
- Test bolding key phrases throughout your copy to highlight the main points.
- Test using pull quotes to highlight key points on your page.
- Test the length of your page. Do you have one long page or multiple pages that are interconnected through hyperlinks or tabs?
- Test the reading grade level of your copy and try it at different levels.
- Test the amount of white space used around the text.

NEED TO LEARN MORE?

Learn more about readability at the following locations:

"Can Your Customers Read What You Write?" The Grok. GrokDotCom by FutureNow. September 15, 2006.

www.grokdotcom.com/topics/readability.htm

"Customer-Focused Excellence" by Bryan Eisenberg. ROI Marketing, ClickZ. December 19, 2003.

www.clickz.com/showPage.html?page=3290721

Tool: Readability.info provides a quick online tool to evaluate the reading level of web pages and Word documents.

www.readability.info

Microsoft Word will also calculate your reading level if you have the option checked in your spelling and grammar checking.

Apply This to Your Site

It's sad how often you can find decent content that is impenetrable because of its formatting. Reformat all the content and copy on your site so that it is more readable.

CHAPTER 38

Use of Color and Images

Choosing site colors is often an afterthought when businesses create websites, but the final color palette does affect customers and could cost you money.

Color doesn't simply look nice. It speaks to the subconscious, evoking meanings, feelings, and moods. It persuades or discourages. It influences buying behavior. Different people actually have different physiologic responses to different colors. Forty-six percent of visitors judge a site's credibility based on the visual design's overall appeal.

Evaluate each of your pages, first in grayscale. Make sure the site's design and layout hold up under the absence of color; it's important that you give the structure of your conversion process priority before introducing the emotional element of color. Looking at the design in full color, you should be able to identify whether the color palette reinforces or undermines the emotional experience you want to impart to your visitors. Color should always *enhance* the site's experience.

However, people perceive color in different ways, so color alone cannot define or carry your online experience.

Be careful which colors you choose for background and text, and make sure they correspond with what you learn from the following resources.

NEED TO LEARN MORE?

Learn more about color at the following locations:

"The Color of Money" by Bryan Eisenberg. ROI Marketing, ClickZ. December 12, 2003.

www.clickz.com/showPage.html?page=3286651

"Color Me Calm?" The Grok. GrokDotCom by FutureNow. January 1, 2003.

www.grokdotcom.com/colorandpersonality.htm

"Color and Usability." The Grok. GrokDotCom by FutureNow.

www.grokdotcom.com/usability-of-color.htm

Vischeck shows you how things appear to those who are color-blind:

www.vischeck.com

Questions to Ask

Ask yourself the following questions about your site:

- Are the colors soothing?
- Do they echo the image you think the business is trying to present?
- Do they promote the function of the site?
- Are they harmonious or glaring?
- Are colors consistent throughout the site?

- Do you rely on colors with negative connotations (such as red or black) or use colors that are difficult on the eyes (such as bright yellows)?

- Are you using red text to your advantage? Be aware that red text carries with it a cautionary quality—it's the color people associate with error messages and big red flags that could impede progress.

Exercise

Try this exercise:

1. Look at your whole site, or at least your key pages, in grayscale.

2. Using the Vischeck tool, evaluate how your pages and images look to a person who is color-blind.

3. Look at your page with your browser images turned off. Do you provide descriptive alt tags to reinforce your message if images are not viewed?

What to Test

Here are different ideas on what you can test when thinking about color and images:

- Test the color of your page background.

- Test the color of your copy and headlines.

- Test adding pictures of real people in your testimonials. Don't use stock images.

- Test using stock photos vs. clip art.

- Test the background color of your images to see what helps draw more attention.

- Test the color of the background of your main call to action, forms, or ready-to-buy area.

- Test using male vs. female models in your images.

- If your site uses a style sheet for its color scheme or layout, test different style sheets to see which is most effective.

- Test the color of the words you may have embedded on top of any images to make sure they are clearly visible.

- Test the placement of elements with strong contrasting colors to see where they will be most effective.

Apply This to Your Site

Use color and imagery not only to promote your brand, but also to improve the perception of trust, reinforce your categorization schemes, and call attention to key elements in the buying and selling processes.

Color is a language that speaks to the subconscious of your visitors. Use color and imagery to reinforce the structure and persuasiveness of your site's conversion system rather than treating it as so much decorative trimming. Always be sensitive to the fact that images consume valuable screen real estate; testing will help you determine whether that tenancy is merited.

CHAPTER 39

Terminology/Jargon

Often the person visiting your site is not the ultimate decision-maker but is investigating solutions for someone else. When you speak in industry terminology, jargon, and acronyms, you can't assume your visitor finds this language engaging, understands what you are saying, or, more important, shares your information accurately with the ultimate decision-maker. Your content needs to be as accessible to the novice as it is to the expert.

For the primary presentation of your product, do the following:

- Use descriptive language to explain product features.

- Don't rely on the vocabulary of your industry to sell the benefits of your service.

- Be concise, accurate, and direction-oriented without assuming any advanced or preexisting knowledge of the product or service.

- Avoid jargon wherever possible.

Selling a complicated product, such as a medical imaging machine or a military tracking system, requires balancing the language associated with the industry without sacrificing copy that must speak to the benefits. This is true even when it comes to selling a laptop or a digital camera. You will have customers who will not—or don't want to—understand the "insider-speak," and you will have customers who demand, for credibility's sake, that you demonstrate you do understand the insider-speak.

An effective way to handle these conflicting customer needs is to separate your technical information from your general product descriptions and benefit-focused copy. All your customers require these at varying levels to actually make a decision to buy.

Place your descriptions and benefits high on the page. Then devise a way to provide the technical information. This may simply mean placing this copy lower on the page. Many sites use an effective "tabbed" format to separate descriptions from specifications from testimonials.

Cnet (Figure 39.1) has created a product page that first addresses the nontechnical, benefit-oriented qualities of the product, including a Cnet-authored review that details the product's performance from both a nontechnical and technical point of view. Visitors can access customer reviews (excellent elements to persuade Humanistic visitors) and technical features (the information Methodicals look for) via a product menu. When the visitor clicks Specifications, Cnet serves up a comprehensive technical explanation of the product (Figure 39.2).

Figure 39.1

Cnet's product page provides a menu link to technical information.

Figure 39.2

Cnet's specifications information

Questions to Ask

Ask yourself the following questions about your site:

- Does your site depend on a lot of technical terms and jargon?
- Are you talking about "quality staffing augmentation," or do you say "We help you hire the best people"?

Exercise

Take screen shots of your top-20 key pages, and ask five people who are totally unfamiliar with your business to highlight any words they don't understand, whether they're industry terms or even uncommon English terms.

What to Test

Here are different ideas on what you can test when thinking about jargon:

- Test adding links to words that define them in a pop-up.

- Test rewriting words that seem like jargon.

- Test adding graphics or illustrations next to copy that is complex to understand.

- Test adding video to help explain complex terms.

- Test adding content that helps explain complex terms and ideas for visitors.

Apply This to Your Site

Find ways to present even the most complex information in language the uninitiated will understand. (It's OK to assume the uninitiated are reasonably intelligent.) There will be those among your audience who will require your technical information, either because they simply need to know or because they need to be convinced of your credibility. Be sensitive to why they require that information, and find a way to present that information so it meets the needs of how these customers buy. Avoid making this the primary way you explain your product or service, because this is exactly the sort of information that will leave others among your audience feeling discouraged, misunderstood, and lost.

NEED TO LEARN MORE?

Learn more about jargon at the following locations:

"Can Your Customers Read What You Write?" The Grok. GrokDotCom by FutureNow. September 15, 2006.

www.grokdotcom.com/topics/readability.htm

"Power Persuasive Copy to Punch Up Sales" by Bryan Eisenberg. ROI Marketing, ClickZ. September 24, 2004.

www.clickz.com/showPage.html?page=3412131

Persuasive Online Copywriting Seminar, FutureNow workshop. Check dates and availability here:

www.futurenowinc.com/writingforweb.htm

Made to Stick: Why Some Ideas Survive and Others Die by Chip Heath and Dan Heath (Random House, 2007).

CHAPTER 40

"We We": Customer-Focused Language

Phony & Plastic! Are you that company? The one that claims they are the #1!, leading!, premiere!, fastest!, greatest!, smartest!, most dynamic!…blah, blah, blah. All that chest pounding translates into pretty anemic, saccharine copy. The tone is at odds with today's customer demands for greater transparency and authenticity.

Customers want the real deal. Your customers want to know "what's in it for me?" How does your copy measure up? Care to find out?

Let's take a look at the words on your website. Are you talking about all the wonderful ways your visitors can benefit from your products or services, or are you talking about all the great features of your products, services, or company? In other words, are you speaking the language of "you," or are you caught up in the language of "we"? As our friend Roy Williams asks, "Are you 'we we'-ing all over yourself?"

Our free Customer Focus Calculator (http://futurenowinc.com/wewe.htm) parses your page for self-focused words such as "I," "we," "our," and your company name (which functions much like "we"), as well as for customer-focused words such as "you" and "your." Then we calculate the ratio of customer-focused words to self-focused words. (See Figures 40.1 and 40.2 for a sample site and results page.) Run the tool to check your site; then run it to check a variety of competitors' sites. Seeing your site through your customers' eyes can be an eye-opening experience. This should be part of every audit process in your copywriting. A score between 60 percent and 70 percent seems to have the most natural tone. We have two versions of the calculator—one that works on web pages and one you can copy and paste your text into.

Figure 40.1
ACS extols the "we."

Figure 40.2

Sample results from FutureNow's Customer Focus Calculator

These are the Customer Focus Calculator results:

For the url: http://www.futurenowinc.com/aboutus.htm

Your Customer Focus Rate: **36.49%**
You have **27** instances of customer-focused words.

Your Self Focus Rate: **63.51%**
You have **31** instances of self-focused words.
You have **16** instances of the Company Name.

You speak about yourself approximately 0,002 times as often as you speak about your customers.
Might that have an impact on your effectiveness?

Original length of Page (including all HTML)= 25,094 bytes
Content length after stripping HTML = 11,647 bytes
Total word count: **1,372**

Return to Customer Focus Calculator

Your customer-focus ratio is not a perfect predictor of success (there are lots of variables, of course), but it has already helped a lot of people improve their conversion rates.

Consider these tactics for extracting yourself from the tendency to overdo the self-congratulations:

- Speak to the customer's needs directly.
- Using words such as "you" or "your" helps customers relate to a product or service.
- Let the products and services speak for themselves as much as possible without resorting to "We provide such-and-such" or "Our nonstick pans are the best."
- It's easy to say that "we" do anything and everything better than the competition, but don't just tell your visitors—show them!
- A customer-focus rate of 60 percent or just greater than that is ideal.
- You can cut yourself some slack on your About Us pages, which are by their very nature about you. That said, keep in mind that most people find overinflated self-congratulation of questionable taste. Focus on credible statements, and offer evidence to confirm your right to crow.

Questions to Ask

Ask yourself the following questions about your site:

- Is your company name mentioned unnecessarily?
- Have you combed through your copy to make sure it is customer focused throughout?
- Does your copy instill trust in the visitor, or does it exist to make you feel better about your own business?

Exercise

Try this exercise:

1. Use the "we we" calculator on your home/landing page and your About Us pages.
2. Use the "we we" calculator on three of your competitors' home pages and About Us pages.

Which one seems to be the most customer focused?

What to Test

Here are different ideas on what you can test when thinking about customer-focused language:

- Test using "we" vs. "you" in your headlines.
- Test making your copy more "you" focused vs. "we" focused.
- Test the copy of your About Us page.

> **NEED TO LEARN MORE?**
> You can find the "we we" calculator here:
> www.futurenowinc.com/wewe.html

Apply This to Your Site

Imagine what your customer really needs to know about your products and services based on their needs and not your business goals. Rewrite your copy and campaigns to be more customer focused. Consider treating what you have to say about you as a benefit-feature exercise (see Chapter 34): If you are "top of your industry," how can you phrase that in What's In It For Me language for your visitor (see Chapter 12)? If you "empower," how does that *really* translate to the ways your visitors would describe their needs?

CHAPTER 41

Using Reviews

If you recently purchased something online, did a review influence your purchase decision?

Don't assume negative reviews hurt sales. In fact, a negative review surrounded by glowing reviews can inspire confidence by demonstrating you stand by the products you sell. Furthermore, if a customer doesn't buy a certain product because it's poorly reviewed, they're more likely to search your site for a similar product that is well reviewed—and buy it! (An additional benefit of reviews is that you don't have to pay visitors to write copy.)

Over the past few years, customer reviews on e-commerce sites have become more important. New research illustrates their value:

- Seventy-seven percent of online shoppers use reviews and ratings when purchasing (Jupiter Research, August 2006).

- Reviews drive 21 percent greater purchase satisfaction and 18 percent greater loyalty (Foresee Results Study, January 2007).

- In a study of 2,000 shoppers, 92 percent deemed customer reviews as "extremely" or "very" helpful. (eTailing Group).

- Fifty-nine percent of users considered customer reviews to be more valuable than expert reviews (Bizrate).

- Sixty-three percent of consumers indicate they are more likely to purchase from a site if it has product ratings and reviews (CompUSA and iPerceptions study).

- Approximately 86.9 percent of respondents said they would trust a friend's recommendation over a review by a critic, while 83.8 percent said they would trust user reviews over a critic (MarketSherpa).

- According to the survey, 92.5 percent of adults said they regularly or occasionally research products online before buying them in a store (BIGresearch).

- Sixty-three percent of all word of mouth is positive. Across all of Bazaarvoice clients, 80 percent of product ratings are 4 or 5 stars out of 5 (Keller Fay).

Figure 41.1 shows an example of text, photo, and video review in one.

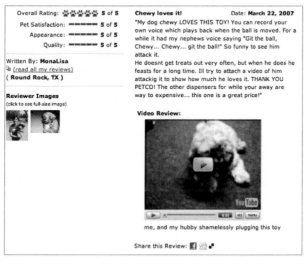

Figure 41.1

A media-rich for-mat for customer reviews from Petco

Whether you enable review functionality from your e-commerce platform or from a third-party hosted solution such as Power Reviews and Bazaarvoice, it's important to test and optimize for conversion and persuasion by focusing on the following areas:

Placement for visibility

- Above the fold
- Size
- Stars or other graphic
- Near point of attention or action

Review interaction

- Ease of reading
- Sorting
- Rating distribution
- Use across the site

Single-dimension vs. multidimension reviews

- What are the key attributes across different categories?
- Can review content influence purchase decision?

Credibility factors

- Negative and positive reviews
- Review approval policy
- Reviewer characteristics

What does a review mean?

- Number of reviews
- What questions are you asking?
- Qualitative vs. quantitative

Questions to Ask

Ask yourself the following questions about your site:

- Do you offer credible, quality reviews?
- Are they fresh? Specific?
- Are there sufficient numbers of reviews?
- How do the negative reviews compare to the positive reviews?
- Are you encouraging reviews that transcend the "nice," "worked fine," and "great product" responses that really don't contribute to elaborating on your product descriptions?
- Do you offer multiple or appropriate ways for customers to provide review information?

- Do you screen your reviews or have a procedure for removing blatantly inappropriate reviews?

- Do you manipulate your reviews to skew feedback in a way that could backfire on you?

- Do you make the effort to communicate intelligent reviews to product manufacturers so that they might work to improve their product?

Exercise

Go to Apple.com and look for an iPod nano. Read the product information on Apple.com for the product. Now go to the same product on Amazon.com and read the reviews for the iPod nano.

Think about the benefits and possible limitations to your sales process if potential customers read these reviews.

What to Test

Here are different ideas on what you can test when thinking about features such as reviews:

- Test the placement of the rating on the page. Should it be above the fold, near the price, near the image, and so on?

- Test the graphic icons you use for your ratings. You can use stars, check marks, or other icons.

- Test using multiple dimensions on your reviews.

- Test expert reviews vs. consumer reviews.

- Test the format of your reviews (text, photo, and video).

- Test having the reviews on the same page as your product or on a separate page.

- Test different ways to present the summary of review scores.

- Test the options available for sorting reviews.

- Test what level of identification you give to a reviewer (skill level, full name vs. anonymous, and so on).

- Test adding a score for how many people would recommend this product to someone else.

NEED TO LEARN MORE?

Learn more about using reviews at the following locations:

Bazaarvoice and its blog offer social communication technology solutions to employing customer reviews as part of a website's conversion process.

www.bazaarvoice.com and www.bazaarblog.com

PowerReviews provides customer reviews solutions for e-businesses.

www.powerreviews.com

IPerceptions and 4Q (voice of customer surveys). 4Q is a collaboration between Avinash Kaushik and iPerceptions.

www.iperceptions.com and http://4q.iperceptions.com

Apply This to Your Site

Just because you have reviews on your site does not mean you are using them optimally. It takes an effort on many levels to encourage customers to add reviews to your website, but it is a great way to leverage other people's content to help you sell; after all, Amazon built its business on this model.

Consider the ability of reviews to persuade your customers. Work reviews into your product descriptions in ways that feel seamless to the site visitor. Present them in a manner that will make people want to read them. By all means, make sure the reviews come across as representative of customer reactions; don't shy away from honest negative appraisals, and if at all possible, use those appraisals to reevaluate what you are doing on your website and whether you are offering products that meet your business standards.

PART III

Diving Deep for the Technically Challenged

This final part *of the book gives you the information you need to feel confident speaking with your technology team so you can make informed and intelligent decisions that intimately affect your business.*

We aren't trying to turn you into a techie, but we would like you to understand enough to plan, implement, and optimize in conjunction with your marketing and IT staff so everyone can operate effectively as a team. Understanding the general principles and challenges benefits everyone involved in measuring success!

The topics we'll be covering in this part include the following:

- *Explaining some basic math concepts useful when working with Website Optimizer*

- *Understanding how Website Optimizer's scripts actually work their magic*

- *Understanding static and dynamic sites, and how Website Optimizer works with them*

- *Using Website Optimizer to measure key user events*

- *Using Website Optimizer with WordPress, a popular blogging platform*

CHAPTER 42

Mathematics, Misperceptions, and Misinformation

You don't need to be a mathematics whiz to reap the benefits of testing with Website Optimizer; in fact, the software does all the math for you and serves up your results in an elegant report package that gives you the basic overview you can use to evaluate the success of your test and plan where you next want to go.

There are, however, some math concepts and concerns with which you should be familiar if you want to optimize the planning phase of testing. It's important that you realize the nature of some of the testing challenges you face. In this chapter, we'll help you understand how each of these relates to the conclusions you might make about your results:

- How to determine the center of your data
- What a "standard deviation" is
- What "statistically significant" means and how to sample
- The local vs. global maximum issue
- The nature of the two-armed bandit
- Degrees of freedom
- Orthogonality

Finding Your Center

Most of us are familiar with the idea of a *mean*, sometimes called the *average*, of some numbers. To calculate the mean, add all your data results, and then divide that answer by the number of data results you have gathered.

For example, let's say Bryan, John, and Lisa are standing in a room. Bryan is 6′1″ tall, John is 6′2″, and Lisa is 5′9″. Their average height (the mean) is 6′0″.

If you're visually oriented, you might like to think of the mean as the balance point in a sample, such that if you subtract every value in the sample from the mean and add all those differences (those "deviation scores") together, the result will be zero.

Continuing our example, the deviation of Bryan from the mean is 6′0″ minus 6′1″, which is –1″; the deviation of John is –2″; and the deviation of Lisa is +3″. Adding those together, (–1) + (–2) + (3) = 0.

Why find a center? Well, you can't carry this data in your tote bag all the time; it gets "heavy" (for lack of a better term). Instead, you want to describe the data in some way that represents all the data. That's what you'll use the mean for. But by itself, knowing the mean is not enough.

The Spread of Your Data

Once you calculate the mean, you can examine how individual results vary from the central value. Are your results clustered around the center, or are they flung far and wide? It helps to have a way to convey how narrowly or how widely the results vary.

Let's return to the earlier example with Bryan, John, and Lisa standing in that room. Bryan is 6′1″ tall, John is 6′2″, and Lisa is 5′9″. Their average height (the mean) is 6′0″.

Now Bryan wanders into the next room and meets Antonio, who is 5′4″, and Shaq, who is 6′7″. The average height of these three is also 6′0″—do the math yourself if you need convincing—but what a spread in the numbers! *Variance* is how you represent this spread numerically. The more varied the range of your data points, the larger the variance.

In fact, when you're considering the spread of your data and deciding how to proceed, you really want to emphasize the "way out there" numbers. To understand what importance to give the mean, you have to keep in mind the outliers often contain many interesting aspects.

If you're a basketball talent scout, you really want to meet that Shaq guy who is 6′7″. If you're a mining company looking for new spelunkers, Antonio is the man who will probably be able to get into smaller spaces. If you're a clothing designer, you want to know the height of your average customer and the *spread* of height data, because your production schedule will be much easier to manage if everyone is within an inch of each other—it's time- and resource-intensive to manufacture the same design for a wide range of super-short or super-tall customers.

The ideas around variance lead directly to other measures you've heard of but perhaps not understood, such as *standard deviation*. Standard deviation is a measurement based on the *average* difference of individual results from the center of the data set. In essence, the standard deviation is much like a mean—average—of these differences. If all the data results had the same value, the standard deviation would be zero. If the data results are far apart, the standard deviation is large.

You're likely to see standard deviation quoted after a mean as the number following the phrase "plus or minus." In the room with Bryan, John, and Lisa, the mean is 6′0″ plus or minus 2″—that is, the standard deviation is 2″. In the room with Bryan, Antonio, and Shaq, the variance is 6′0″ plus or minus 8″; the standard deviation is 8″.

If you prefer a visual interpretation, imagine a bell curve as in Figure 42.1, sometimes called a *normal* distribution. Here, the mean is the highest point on the graph, and the standard deviation describes the width of the curve.

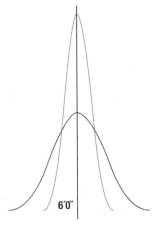

Figure 42.1

Hypothetical normal distribution showing a low standard deviation

If the standard deviation is low, the curve will be sharp and narrow, as in the taller distribution in Figure 42.1. There is more data in the middle near the mean.

If the standard deviation is larger, the curve is correspondingly wider, as in the shorter distribution in Figure 42.1. There is more data spread out over a larger range of values.

Knowing the average value of something is not terribly meaningful if you don't also get a sense of the variance. So when someone tells you the average height of the three people in the first room is 6 feet, you're getting only half the story. "Plus or minus what?" you might ask.

Or "What's the variance?" Or even "Did you calculate the standard deviation?" Be very wary of quoted averages when they don't include the key assessment of the spread of the data that were used to calculate the average.

Quoting only an average is the most common mistake we see among companies performing web analytics testing. Many place significant weight on the reported mean results of testing, without providing a corresponding emphasis on the variance of those results.

Of course, this doesn't mean the results are wrong. If anything, the results have virtually no meaning: They are neither right nor wrong. Being incomplete, there is insufficient information to interpret them in a useful way, so they are of dubious value. If you're planning marketing campaigns based on such results, they may even be dangerous—results that appear "better" on average might in fact be worse if the spread of the data is very wide. That brings us to the notion of significance.

Statistical Significance and Sampling

The *statistical significance* of your results reflects the probability the relationships you observe between variables or variations, or the differences between averages, in your sample are simply due to chance. You could call this the luck of the draw. In nonmathematical jargon, statistical significance tells you something about the degree to which your results are "true" and representative of your testing audience.

Essentially, in any form of online testing, you have an extremely limited opportunity to sample your audience in a way that would constitute a truly valid scientific experiment. You cannot set up any test to secure results that are completely representative of your potential visitors—to do that you'd have to test the entire population of people who might buy from you, given the desire, impetus, and opportunity. Instead, please keep in mind that your online tests simply reflect what works or doesn't work for those visitors who choose to come to your site, which is only a sample of the total population of humans. On top of this, you run your tests for a limited amount of time, which gives you a subsample of the sample.

In other words, your tests are fundamentally a best guess, and you need to be aware of this in any test you design and launch.

The ramifications affect what you can say about your results in relation to the results of your competitors and others completely outside your business. At the end of the day, *your* sample is yours. Their sample is theirs. This is the root of the problem in assuming best practices have any value to your website.

You can certainly incorporate a best practice in your site, but don't be surprised if it doesn't work as well for you as it might for others. Be equally wary of absolutes. "Red buttons always convert better!" Really? Be skeptical and test to see whether this is really the case in your industry and with your unique set of products or services presented in the context of your site's color palette.

Best practices do, however, provide a great starting point for testing. If you had no idea what to test—and this book should solve that problem for you—it may be worth your effort to begin testing ideas that are considered best practices.

Local vs. Global Maximum

In the process of planning your test, you define the criterion that will allow you to determine which among your variations is the winner. In Chapter 7, we called this, simply, a *metric*. You might hear it sometimes referred to as a *fitness function*. We'll use both terms interchangeably in this book, although we tend to consider a "metric" as a literal number and a "fitness function" as some sort of graph.

Recall our hypothetical A/B test in Chapter 7 to choose the better baseball player between Nolan Ryan and Homer Simpson? You'll probably look at any number of metrics for distinguishing their talents: pitching speed, number of strikeouts, runs batted in, even weirdo stuff like ratio of length of arm to size of waist. Sorry, Homer! By all those metrics, we have to pick Nolan.

But take Nolan and Homer, change the job to official donut taster, and suddenly Homer seems a leading candidate. You, the arbiter, get to decide what constitutes the fitness function for "donut tastiness." Is it sweetness, mouth feel, or dough density? If you are the donut seller, you want to know what contributes to the tastiest donuts so you can decide whether Nolan or Homer is the better donut taste tester. Based on your cultural awareness, please welcome Homer to your team.

You typically don't want your test subjects (online, your visitors) to be aware of the fitness function you've defined for your test, but it's deadly if you, the experimenter, are unclear about it. If you don't know the fitness function, then you have no reason to believe the testing and optimizing you're doing can give you anything more than a local maximum. That's why we put such emphasis on defining *both* your goals *and* your key performance indicators for all tests.

In other words, without knowledge of the fitness function, you might as well call split testing *A/B Feng Shui*.

We also need to revisit the discussion (in Chapter 7) of testing that brings you closer and closer to the maximum conversion rate possible for the element you are testing—optimization nirvana. Figure 42.2 shows a theoretical conversion fitness function for a single page with a hypothetical maximum of 4.5 percent.

Figure 42.2

Hypothetical conversion rate curve

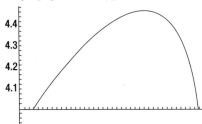

The brave of heart probably realize that how you plan to get to the maximum is the real art. From what direction do you approach the maximum? Does it make a difference? How can you be sure you're there until you "overshoot" a bit and the conversion begins to drop off?

If you look at Figure 42.2 again, you'll notice that approaching the maximum from the left side of the graph constitutes a longer series of steps on a gradual incline than you would have if you approached the maximum from the right. The direction of approach is significant: The nature of the fitness function will determine your ability to make any positive improvements with A/B testing.

Let's look at another fitness function in Figure 42.3. Ask yourself two questions:

- Is the goal you're shooting for affected by the shape of the graph—that is, does it have at least one peak?

- Does the direction you start in affect your ability to reach that peak?

Figure 42.3

Example of local and global maxima

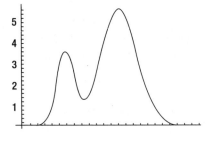

In this example, you have two maxima: a "local" maximum on the left and a "global" maximum on the right. If you were trying to maximize your conversion rate from web analytics, your CEO would really appreciate reaching that global maximum. But there are pitfalls.

If you start on the left of the graph, you increase conversion nicely with A/B testing. You will overshoot slightly, correct a bit, and reach what seems to be a promising solution at a local maximum near 3.5 percent. If the standard for your industry is 3 percent, you might feel justified in performing the "marketer's strut." But without the fitness function visually presented in front of you for this example, you'd be unaware of the unrealized potential.

If you start on the right, you get to the 5 percent global maximum. Could you use another free 1.5 points of conversion?

You can't pat yourself on the back yet just because you reached a global peak; you still don't know the fitness function.

What happens if you start at the valley near the middle? Depending on the direction you take, you may get to the global maximum, or you may get to the local maximum. Again, the topology of the fitness function, not the A/B test, determines your eventual success.

In fact, without knowing the fitness function, you might suffer a midlife A/B testing crisis of "Is this all there is? Are we at a local maximum and missing some big upside? Are we at a global maximum, and further testing is now wasted resources? What if our competitors know how to get to a maximum and we don't?"

Now let us throw an epistemological wrench in the process: If you don't know the topology of the fitness function, how do you even know there is a maximum (global, local, or otherwise)?

Quite simply, you don't.

How do you know the fitness function isn't discontinuous so that when you overshoot, you end up in an entirely different topology?

Nope, not a clue.

Of course, in a perfect world, our conversion fitness function is continuous and has a single global maximum—if we're lucky. But if your conversion improvements with split testing are merely based on luck, what's the point of calling it "testing"? It would be more honest to call it the "lottery."

In essence, split testing, as companies usually conduct it, ignores variance and statistical confidence. Without answers to the previous questions, you're operating in a bit of a vacuum. That's why statistical confidence is so important; it gives you an idea of how dependable the data is and how much faith to put in it. It answers questions such as "What is the likelihood that the improvement we just saw in our testing is due to more than just random chance?" When you're working with real money, that's the critical question to answer.

The Heart of the Problem: The Two-Armed Bandit

Let's take this concept of variance and apply it to the field of game theory. We'll use a classical thought problem called the *two-armed bandit*.

Imagine a machine similar to a Vegas slot machine, but with two arms instead of one. Let's call these Arm A and Arm B. You'll be given a certain amount of money—a million bucks—to play this machine over a series of "pulls" of one arm or the other. How do you decide which arm to play?

The two arms have different payouts—Payout A and Payout B—but the casino is not going to tell you whether Arm A or Arm B has the higher payout. Your job is to decide how to apportion your money after each bet so that as your testing continues, you will maximize the amount of money you win (or, perhaps more realistically, to minimize the amount of money you lose).

Clearly, you want to minimize the amount of money it takes for you to determine which arm is better in order to dedicate the maximum amount of remaining money toward playing only the better arm. After all, if you knew for sure which arm was better, you'd put all your money on that arm. But you don't know that. Before reading on, think for a moment: What would *you* do?

Most people, or at least those who do split testing, would dedicate some portion of their bankroll to test each arm for a certain number of pulls. After this test, whichever one pays off better will be judged the winner, and then they'll commit the rest of their bankroll to it.

The problem is, it turns out this solution is nonoptimal and carries significant cost and risk. H.L. Mencken once famously quipped, "For every complex problem, there is a solution that is simple, neat, and wrong." That's exactly the solution A/B testing would lead you to here.

What's wrong with such an approach? Well, answer this: What does it mean to pay off "better"? Doesn't that entail examining the actual results of each arm to determine, say, their average calculated payoff, AvgA and AvgB, and then go with the higher? Yes, and that's what the A/B test on the arms did for you.

But we discussed earlier that quoting an average has useful meaning only if you also measure the standard deviation for the measured payoff of each arm. How would you know whether the average payout results from your A/B test is anywhere near the true payouts, Payoff A and Payoff B?

A better testing method must correctly determine both the mean and the variance. Remember, you don't get to do an infinite amount of free testing to determine which arm has the best payoff; you have to bet in real time with real dollars. You must carefully conserve your resources while some sense of confidence emerges as to which arm is better.

The essence of the bandit problem is that you cannot know the reward distributions for your variables and variations. In testing, you face a fundamental trade-off between gathering information about the reward distributions you don't know and choosing the arm you currently think is the best.

When you consider the two-armed bandit problem in the context of split testing (as people typically practice it), you realize that simple testing cannot provide you with enough information to make absolute rational choices. Fortunately, it can help you make a bunch of good relative rational choices, which is why any type of testing is better than none as long as you sprinkle some human gray matter into the process.

Degrees of Freedom

Have you ever wondered when you should do univariate A/B testing and when you should do multivariate? Or, have you considered why you shouldn't always do multivariate, since A/B testing is just multivariate using only one variable?

A "degree of freedom" is a single aspect of a complex system that is allowed to vary in some significant way. You can think of this as similar to earning an allowance for doing your chores—you earn one dollar for each chore you complete (for our purposes, "each piece of data you collect"), and you spend one dollar for each candy you eat (for our purposes, "each parameter you estimate"). Since you're earning \$2 for collecting data-piece A and data-piece B and spending \$1 to see how they compare, you have \$2 − \$1 = 1 degree of freedom.

Suppose you wanted to measure both the efficacy of a red vs. blue buy-it-now button and whether this element should be presented as a round button or a square button. Univariate testing would give you no information, since your "income" is the same (you're collecting data A and data B, which equals 2 data points) but your "spending" has increased to 2 (you want to estimate a parameter for "best color" and "best shape" and 2 − 2 = 0 information).

How could you deal with that? One solution is to perform one A/B test for the colors and another A/B test for the shape. This brings up its own set of issues, such as the order in which you test your variables. You might assume the order does not matter (the fancy word for this is *commutative*), but you have no particular proof on which to base this assumption: An astute web analyst may have already divined that "blue" plus "round" carried more impact combined than either separately. You'll also be forced into doing some cross-testing because someone is going to ask the really interesting question, "Red round button or blue square button?" So even if colors and methods of testing were commutative, there's a good chance you'll end up having to test that assumption anyway.

Another solution is to perform what you might call *ABCD testing*, which is entirely legitimate because the degrees of freedom will be higher. But this leads to testing a larger number of candidate solutions spread over an exponentially larger search space. You can imagine how much more complex this will get after you start adding other variations such as "green," "purple," "aligned center," "font = Sans Serif," and so on. Where does it end? You will quickly run out of letters in the alphabet, and long before that, you'll have left the realm of A/B testing.

What you're really looking for here is multivariate testing, which allows you to collect those two data points for each dimension, so now your earned "income" is $2 \times 2 = 4$, and you're "spending" 2 on estimated parameters "best color" and "best shape," leaving you with 4 − 2 degrees of freedom. How do you know you have the right dimensions? This brings us to the next math concept, orthogonality.

Orthogonality

To discuss orthogonality, we'll need to introduce a few $10 words. These sorts of problems and solutions have cropped up in many other fields, and a specific vocabulary has developed to support those discussions. It benefits us if we stick to some conventional, known definitions. But we'll try to keep things on a vocabulary budget, since we'd prefer you come away with some new ideas, not just new words.

With A/B testing, you change only one thing at a time; even if there are multiple variations on that one thing, you're still testing between two or more variations of one variable. Which converts better, the red button or the blue button? (Or the red button, the blue button, or the green button—button is your element, button color is your variable, and each specific hue is your variation.) Which gets you more sales, "Buy It Now" or "Add to Cart"? (Here, the call to action is the element, the actual copy of the call to action is your variable, and the different wordings are your variations.) This is directly related to the degrees of freedom we just discussed.

Yet, the most interesting and meaningful tests take place across a spectrum of variation. A/B testing has no mechanism for handling such cases. What happens to poor yellow and green and purple and "Get My Stuff"? You can't just leave these out of testing simply because they're inconvenient to test in tandem. You actually require a multivariate approach, using something we call *conversion calculus*.

Simple testing in an earlier example examined a single degree of freedom as you varied two variations of one variable, A and B. You measured that against the actual conversion result (your metric) and produced a two-dimensional graph (one degree of freedom plotted against the metric).

When you add a second variable, you have two degrees of freedom, so you'll expect a three-dimensional plot (two degrees of freedom plotted against the metric). So, in the hypothetical fitness function shown in Figure 42.4, we've added only one additional way to vary the testing, and now we have a 3D plot.

Figure 42.4

Hypothetical 3D plot of two degrees of freedom

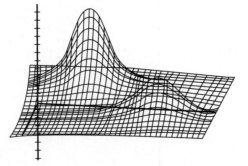

You'll recall that when we discussed Figure 42.3, we risked finding only a local minimum and getting stuck there. Now we must find the correct path in two directions to successfully find the global maximum—will you be able to do this if you don't have the fitness function in front of you? Try to imagine where you will be in N-dimensions (which you can't even visualize) and a correspondingly more complex fitness function (to which we don't even have access). Now you'll understand why a conversion calculus is required. This is as complex a problem as Mencken envisioned, and quite frankly, A/B testing as a solution truly is "simple, neat, and wrong."

To address multivariate testing, you'll need to examine the issue of (sorry, big word alert!) *heterogeneity*—or whether the candidate solutions you are testing may be diverse and not comparable in kind. The layperson's term for this is "comparing apples and oranges." Have you ever noticed that whenever a discussion gets to that point, people often stop comparing altogether? They just shut down. That's a sure sign that the comparison technique is insufficient to handle the job.

But even that doesn't get at the heart of the matter since the diversity may span a much larger gap. What if you're actually comparing apples and carburetors? Will it even make sense to A/B test a red button "Buy It Now" with a blue button "Add to Cart"? Or what about more complex and subtle testing, such as the conversion efficacy of "Buy One Ticket, Your Companion Flies Free" vs. "Frequent Flyers Get Seat Upgrades and Free Booze"? Do we even have a method to classify this sort of diversity?

For this, we introduce the concept of *orthogonality*. One way to think of orthogonality is to consider ways of measuring along an axis. The typical xy-axis uses an x-axis that is independent or orthogonal of the y-axis, allowing you to measure along one axis independent of the other.

You could do solid multivariate testing if you could express the variables you want to test in terms of orthogonal axes. Determining what those axes are is, of course, the nub of the problem.

In a closed system (such as your website), an object in the system is orthogonal to other objects in the system if it serves one specific function in the system and no other object serves that same specific function. Do you have this in web analytics? No, because a given page (or an element within a page) may serve multiple uses: An element could be part of several pages, and a page it's part of may be part of multiple scenarios. Or, that same page may act as a point of resolution for one type of visitor coming to the site, whereas for another visitor, the page is an absolutely essential call-to-action point for her to buy from you.

Don't lose any sleep over orthogonality—there isn't much you can do to prevent it anyway—but do realize that designing tests is a very complex problem.

CHAPTER 43

How Website Optimizer's Scripts Work

In this chapter, we'll give you an overview of how Website Optimizer scripts work their magic. This isn't about installing the scripts that determine what goes where and how to name your elements. Instead, we'll explain what the scripts do once you've installed them successfully and launched your test. We're grateful to Ophir Prusak, who had many insightful tips and comments during our various talks about testing with Website Optimizer and how Website Optimizer's scripts work.

Three Vital Script Functions

To perform split testing, A/B (univariate), or multivariate testing, the testing platform must perform three essential functions. This applies whether you're dealing with Website Optimizer or any other platform. These essential functions are as follows:

- Dealing with what content will be displayed to each visitor
- Tracking and recording who saw the testing page
- Tracking and recording who reached the conversion page

What a Visitor Will See

When dealing with what content each visitor will see (the Control script in Website Optimizer parlance), you need a way to present different visitors with different content. When you first view a test page, Website Optimizer has to determine whether you've been to that page before. If so, it should show you the same content it presented to you on the previous visit. If not, it should randomly present one of the variations being tested.

For example, suppose you're doing a test that has three variations: A, B, and C. The first time you arrive on the page, the script goes to Google's web server, has it flip a coin (metaphorically), and randomly assigns you, say, Variation B. Variation B (which you specified when you set up your test) is then called up from Google's server and replaces the default content on the page with Variation B's content.

It's also the Control script's responsibility to set the appropriate cookies to ensure that when you come back, you see the same content, Variation B in this case. If you were presented with a different version of the content on your next visit, how could anyone know which version actually caused you to convert? Even if we as humans knew, how would the script gain and record that knowledge?

And, apart from this, displaying differing versions of the same page on each subsequent visit would be confusing and could cause an unintended drop in conversion just by the cognitive dissonance of seeing inconsistent content. Smart visitors might even infer, correctly, that they were the subjects of a test, and such knowledge itself may change how they act—a sort of Heisenberg Uncertainty Principle applied to split testing.

Website Optimizer solves this by showing the same content each time. So if you see Variation B once, you'll always see Variation B no matter how many times you go to that page. The Control script does this by putting a simple cookie on your browser. In effect, it's saying, "For this test, this visitor saw Variation B." The next time you visit the site, the script will read that cookie, pass its value to the Google servers, and show you Variation B again.

Another important note is that the Control script is placed at the top of the testing page(s) and performs a vital role in this position. By passing the value of any existing test-specific cookie to the Google servers, the servers determine whether this is a new or a repeat visit by you. They also determine which version of the page you should be shown before anything else is displayed. This means your browser is not generating some default content and then overwriting that content in the browser (which may manifest itself as a "flicker" as the page is displayed). Rather, the Control script makes this determination before any content is served up. In essence, the default content is always there; the call to the Google server simply causes the appropriate variation to be shown to you and suppresses the display of the default content.

You want to improve. You want to optimize. You're concerned that doing any sort of testing will goof up your customers. Never fear. If all the Google servers are down for any reason and the call by the Control script fails, it will gracefully and elegantly degrade to the default behavior, which is simply to show the original content that existed before you began the test. In other words, if Website Optimizer is ever momentarily nonoperational, your worst-case scenario is that your visitors will see the same stuff they were seeing before your test.

Tracking a Visitor on the Testing Page

The next component of Website Optimizer's scripts is tracking and recording the test page. When a visitor has viewed the test page, the script records it as an event—Website Optimizer calls this a *visitor view*. It will increment by one the number of *impressions* (or visitors) to the test page, and when it does so, it will be primed to track a later conversion. So, the important part of the testing script is a simple snippet of code that records the viewing event.

Here, too, location plays an important role. Whereas the Control script is placed at the beginning of the page so that what will be displayed is determined before anything at all is displayed, the Testing script is placed at the end of the page so that recording the viewing of the test page is done after all the content is presented.

Tracking a Visitor on the Conversion Page

The third component of Website Optimizer's scripts is the tracking and recording of the conversion page. As with the Testing script, it's a small bit of code at the end of the conversion page that says the following: For this experiment, bundle up all the cookie data for this test, pass it to the Google servers, and determine whether the visitor saw the test page and then encountered this conversion page (by definition, that's a conversion); then record that conversion as part of this test by incrementing the conversion count by one. Obviously, if the visitor comes to the conversion page without having seen the test page, then no conversion or visit is recorded (at least in the context of *this* experiment). This component also makes sure the cookie is up-to-date so that both test- and conversion-page tracking have been recorded.

How long do these testing cookies last? Website Optimizer now uses a two-year cookie (previously it was 30 minutes!). As long as you return to the site within that time, you'll see the same content on the test page, and if you convert, you'll also credit that content as having been involved in your conversion.

By the way, you might ask, "Can the cookies be deleted to stop tracking the test variations?" The answer is twofold. First, if you want to stop tracking the test variations, simply turn off the test. The Tracking and Conversion scripts do their recording only when a test is active. Second, although you cannot automatically delete a visitor's cookie via the scripts, you can, of course, write your own JavaScript functionality that kills off the cookie—and the visitor can simply delete all the cookies at any time. If a visitor has deleted all her cookies and returns to your test page, it will appear to the Control script that she hasn't been there before, and content will be randomly assigned to her as if it were her very first visit.

This is a concern only if you have reason to believe your visitors delete their cookies frequently, which would mean your impressions count would be artificially high and your conversion rate would be artificially low. You might try some workarounds to factor in such visitor behavior; however, if the incidence of cookie deletion is constant (or at least approximately so), then you're probably better off measuring conversion rates relatively rather than absolutely.

Marco Polo's Cookie

Did you ever play the swimming pool game called Marco Polo? One player, eyes closed, is "it" and tries to tag any other player. He calls out "Marco!" If any other players are above water and hear the call, they must answer "Polo!" If a player is below water, she needn't respond. Thus, the player who is "it" can hear where people are and gropingly reach out to try to tag them. (Note to self: Never play this game with a family member who is a ventriloquist.)

Marco Polo is analogous to how Website Optimizer's cookies work. The Testing script sets a cookie that confirms the test page has been viewed, effectively calling out "Marco!" If the Conversion script then metaphorically responds with "Polo!"—thus confirming the visitor has been there—a conversion is recorded.

The cookie is also used to make sure the visitor count is not incremented if you've already visited it once; otherwise, if you saw the test page three times before you converted, you'd have incremented the impressions count by three but the conversion count by only one, when really there's only one impression and one conversion going on. You want the cookie to record the number of visitors who saw the test page, not the number of visits to the test page.

You also want the cookie to ensure that only someone who saw the test page can be considered for conversion—if you convert for some other reason and you never saw the test page, the business should happily accept your money, but not count it as a conversion for that particular test.

You might have many scenarios that end at the conversion page, but only those tests that involve both the Testing and Conversion scripts for the same experiment will record a conversion. Otherwise, the conversion page will send a page track back to Website Optimizer, it will see you don't have a cookie that says you viewed the test page, and it will just ignore the conversion (at least from the point of view of that test).

Multiple Tests, One Conversion Page

You can have multiple tests going on at the same time whose pages (or steps in a scenario) overlap. Multiple tests can have the same conversion page. However, you need to have the Conversion script for *each* test on the conversion page. You might have one, two, three, or more different conversion codes on the conversion page, each with its own test ID, unique to each test.

Is it possible to have more than one test going on a given test page? No, that's not something Website Optimizer currently allows, at least not without some major hacking. And if you know how to do that, you don't need to be reading this chapter. If you had two different Testing scripts on the same page, Website Optimizer wouldn't know to whom to attribute what (mainly because it uses some global variables that aren't test-specific, and two multiple tests on the same page would overwrite each other's variables). You can, of course, do a multivariate test on that test page, but that's still one test, just with multiple independent variables.

Multiple Tests Running on the Same Site

What about running multiple tests on the same site? Of course, that is possible and even encouraged, albeit with some cautious restraint. The technical aspect of running multiple tests on the same site, as explained earlier, makes it clear there's not a problem as long as you account for each test's Conversion script on the appropriate conversion page, even if that conversion page is shared across multiple tests.

But imagine you were testing a headline on your home page while also trying to improve conversion along the checkout process. It's important from the business and statistical aspect that the two tests you're running not interfere much with each other.

For example, suppose you were testing the product of the month on the home page but also testing the checkout page. The product of the month test is between a high-priced $500 item and a low-priced $10 item. Your checkout test compares a short checkout process vs. a medium-length checkout process. A visitor might consider the high-ticket item and may even add it to the cart, but in the end choose not to buy because of the sticker price, whereas a visitor who adds the low-price product of the month to the cart might be less inclined to abandon the cart.

You can see how the nature of the product on the home page could influence the test you're running on the checkout process. This may not affect the conversion rate of the high-priced item or of the low-priced item, but it could affect the total traffic numbers of the checkout process you are testing. Because the amount of traffic you get to your site often strongly influences how long you have to run tests in order to be confident in the results, there is too much potential overlap of these two tests; there'd be some question as to whether, say, the medium-length checkout process was unduly affected by the caution visitors sometimes exhibit when buying high-priced items.

Be careful when running multiple tests alongside each other on the same site; they can affect each other in ways you did not intend, polluting the results. And all too often, they do so in an unobvious way that you're unlikely to notice.

Now, you could turn these two separate tests into one blended multivariate test that involved four combinations. In our example, you could specify two "variables": product of the month and checkout process. Then you could specify two "variations" for each:

Product of the month: $500 item and $10 item

Checkout process: Short checkout and medium-length checkout

But that's quite advanced, and Website Optimizer doesn't easily do that type of multi-step, multivariate testing for you (nor do we know any widespread commercial software that does, although we know several that claim to do so). The best you can do with Website Optimizer is design a multivariate section test on the same test page and the same conversion page.

We don't know any current clients or even practitioners of the testing arts—and certainly no retailers—who are showing such a deep level of sophistication in that level of testing. It will get there someday. But that's another book.

CHAPTER 44

Using Website Optimizer on Static and Dynamic Sites

When you first begin to explore using Website Optimizer, the examples you'll see are almost always for static sites, particularly if you're doing page-based (what Google calls A/B) testing. What exactly is a static site anyway? How is a dynamic site different?

At first glance, you might think a static site is one that is unchanging. But people change their websites all the time. In fact, the whole concept of optimizing obviously implies change.

What Is a Static Site?

On a *static* site, all content—be it pages, images, PDFs, and what have you—has been generated and produced before your visitors ever reach your site. Perhaps you have a welcoming home page that you generated last month. Everyone coming to the site sees that home page; nothing about it changes from visitor request to visitor request. In fact, that home page was created long before the visitor's request.

For small businesses with a modest web footprint, a static site might be sufficient; these sites often have a manageable number of pages, perhaps 10 or 12, that provide basic information about the business. The Web circa 1997 comes to mind, but if that's all your site needs to communicate effectively with your visitors, then that's what you should provide. You don't need flash and a steroid-addled database to tell people your store's physical address or phone number.

Or you might be with a larger company but producing a small, targeted, segmented site for just one new product or service you're launching. There actually may be some good business reasons to limit this microsite to just a handful of simple, static pages.

In short, static sites are based on the concept that the requested content is complete unto itself and already in place by the time the visitor points her browser to your site. We'll return to static sites and Website Optimizer shortly.

What Is a Dynamic Site?

A *dynamic* site generates content on the fly; that is, the content isn't fixed and existing before the visitor request arrives. Typically, a content management system (CMS) on your server and/or a server-side scripting language such as ColdFusion, PHP, Microsoft's ASP, or others generate the content the visitor will see.

One benefit of dynamically generated content is maintainability. If your site uses a common visual theme—which most sites do these days—it is essential to be able to maintain, say, the header and footer in a single place so you don't have to alter each and every existing page when you make a change to the header and footer. If you dynamically render your pages by including the header and footer at the time of the request, you can make a single change that will affect many pages on your site. If you're a larger company with hundreds or thousands of products and each product has a page, imagine the time it would take to make one change to one common element hundreds of times. Making changes by hand puts you at greater risk for Murphy's Law. There's every chance someone updating the site will forget something somewhere if they have to do the same thing more than once.

Another advantage of a dynamic site is scalability. Making changes to a site is a maintenance as well as a scalability issue—but consider the matter of *merchandizing*, that is, presenting your goods to the buying public. Your marketing team will love the idea that the presentation is done in a regularized fashion, and if you have 10,000 SKUs of products, all of which you want on the Web, you need a process for standardizing how you present that information. You want templates you can follow, and rather than creating 10,000 instances of one template, you'd really like to have the single template and populate it, perhaps on the fly, with data on that product pulled from a database. In fact, if you're big enough, you probably want a database of the templates since a template for selling baseball bats may differ from a template for selling bras. You never know.

A third way to take advantage of managing your site dynamically is personalization. Even if a given page doesn't change, your business may find real value in greeting a returning customer by name, asking how a previously purchased product worked out, or presenting her with customized offers. If you have many branch brick-and-mortar locations, you might use visitor location information to help guide a visitor to your nearest office. And while we're on the topic of geography, you can offer your site in various languages and dynamically change the content to a visitor's native tongue.

If you're using a server-side scripting language, as mentioned earlier, you might even dynamically change the content on a page based on user-supplied information, perhaps from a submitted form.

Yet another advantage to dynamic sites is the temporal aspect it allows you to bring to the site. It's one thing to change all your site's pages by hand in time for the Christmas rush, but that's just once a year. What if you need to change information on your site every week? Every day? Every hour?

These are just a few of the good, solid reasons to dynamically generate content on your site.

Mixed Static and Dynamic Sites

In fact, most sites today are mixed-use, static, and dynamic. Some pages are unchanging. Others take full advantage of dynamically generated content. But to manage all that requires some systemization, which often lends itself more easily to treating all pages as dynamic for the simple ease of manageability. Obviously, you don't need a dynamic site to change your privacy policy, but if the rest of your site is dynamic, you also don't need a second system for managing just the privacy-policy page—let's make believe that particular page is dynamic so you need only one system.

In other words, sometimes it's easier to take something that's static and redefine it as dynamic, just with a really long time frame. It's sort of like continental drift—we're pretty sure Paris is in the same place on the maps since the last time we visited, even if it's nudged a half centimeter north in the interim.

Applying Website Optimizer to a Static Site

When you consider the relative merits of a static site vs. a dynamic site, you might think, "Well, I would have a lot more options if I created a dynamic site." And that can be true if your goal is to ensure flexibility. But if your business has a relatively stable site or if your business lends itself more to "microsites," you may find testing with Website Optimizer easier if you have a static site rather than a dynamic one.

When you want to do some A/B testing (which, as we mentioned earlier, is the term Google uses for page-based testing), your static site has individual pages that you can easily modify into A and B (and C and D and...) pages. Testing in this situation is almost textbook, straight out of Website Optimizer user's manual.

In fact, if you're new to testing with Website Optimizer, we advise setting up some static pages to test on, even if your main site is dynamic. Understanding how to test static sites is a prerequisite for understanding how to test dynamic sites.

If you have a static site and want to do some multivariate testing, this, too, is textbook. You will have no problems setting up section tests across one or more variables in a manner similar to our explanation in Chapter 2. We'd encourage you, even with a dynamic site, to explore multivariate testing with several static pages and then migrate to testing your dynamic site soon thereafter.

Applying Website Optimizer to a Dynamic Site

If you have a dynamic site, you will have to do some planning to get your testing campaign up and running. Let's outline some of the challenges you may face.

If your company has a large number of product pages generated by calls to a database and then rendered using a common template, you can probably guess your first challenge: "What if I just want to test one product?" If you change the template—the very thing that kept you sane maintaining 10,000 SKUs—you change it for all products that use that template.

Fortunately, those with very large inventories apply the template at the category or subcategory level, so you're unlikely to have a single template. But that doesn't reduce the choices you'll soon have to make.

Do you create a new template? Will the new template simply apply to those products you want to test? What if you want to test those products in different ways or across multiple testing campaigns? Do you reorganize your products and templates to make testing easier, even though when you put your products together originally you based your templates on the type of product or how customers shop for it? What's the point of having a system if you keep breaking its organizing rules?

In other words, if you're going to test product descriptions for umbrellas and for soy milk, should you be using the same template? Remember two of the advantages of a dynamic site are scalability and organization—will you suddenly throw them away for just the few products you're testing?

And what sort of testing are you doing? You might hypothesize (based on what you learned in Part II, "What You Should Test," of this book) that the umbrella product description would be a fine element to test, and that probably makes sense for umbrellas. But when it comes to soy milk, it's more likely that customer reviews and recommendations play a bigger part.

You might take another approach and keep the original template but add what programmers call *conditional code*, something like "Use this template for products 1 through 9,999 except for product 654—treat that one differently." This works exactly once; the second time you do it, you'll have to remind yourself what the first conditional referred to, and every time you add a layer, the complexity will grow, and pretty soon you'll forget what meant what. This is organizing by exception, not by intent. It also means you're weaving business logic into the presentation layer of your website, and that's almost always a bad idea, too.

One approach you could take—and we'll cover this concept in a different way in Chapter 45 when we discuss testing for key user events—would be to have your developers add fields or tables to the database, using these to "mark" products that are part of a testing campaign and that should be tested in a certain way. The template could then be modified to include the appropriate Website Optimizer testing code only when the mark is present. So now you've loosened the tie between the change in the template and the product itself by marking the product as part of a group and picking a rendering template based on that product's membership in a special "testing" group. It's subtle, but it makes a huge organizing difference.

If you're doing A/B testing on your dynamic site, you'll definitely find it effective to inject testing code into the template. Just pay careful attention to using the correct testing experiment ID as provided by Website Optimizer. The A/B testing will actually encourage the use of multiple templates where the variation of what you are testing is exactly what's in each template.

If you're interested in multivariate testing, you will find it useful to isolate parts of the dynamic template that will be section-tested and then to ensure your page is coded to be as XHTML compliant as possible. This will help your developers wrap key sections of the page for testing into separate divisions of content (*divs*). It will also make it easier to mark each section for Website Optimizer so it knows what to serve up when rendering each combination.

The complication you'll be up against with multivariate testing and dynamic sites is this: Each section you want to test needs to have code inserted to mark the beginning and end of each section, as well as the variations for content inside. This works fine for multivariate testing one product or even a product category, but can present some confusion if many products sharing a template are involved. Again, one solution is the previously mentioned technique of building additional tables into your product database so your site can deliver the testing variations dynamically.

Choose the Approach Appropriate to Your Site

Here's an easy way to remember the relationships between testing and static vs. dynamic sites. If you're working on a static site, you need a static approach to testing. The two mesh well together because both come from the same philosophy of prerendering content.

If you're testing on a dynamic site, then you want to also use a dynamic approach to testing. Using templates to render content dynamically, consider how to "templatize" the rendering of the key portions of content that contain Website Optimizer's testing and conversion scripts.

We'll finish by restating something that can be easily overlooked: Website Optimizer's scripts work their magic by running on the client browser. As such, the scripts themselves don't really "know" whether you have a static or dynamic site. And by running on the client side, Google achieves a much broader reach for testing because it tests against the client browser rather than your company's web server configuration. But your approach to testing—your testing framework—should contain a plan that effectively marries your testing campaigns to the static or dynamic nature of your website.

CHAPTER 45

Tracking Key Events and Other Advanced Topics

In this chapter, you'll explore some fascinating topics such as testing only a certain amount of traffic, testing for important user events such as clicking an item or submitting a form, testing for time spent on a page, and even stacking key events together. Each of these is fascinating by themselves, but we think the truly exciting part will come when you realize you can weave all of these together. Again, we'd like to thank Ophir Prusak for the many conversations we've had on these topics.

Testing Subsets of Your Traffic

When you set up a test in Website Optimizer, you can define what percentage of your traffic you want to expose to the test. The balance is shown only the original content as if the test never even took place.

For example, if you want 40 percent of your traffic to participate in the test (randomly assigned original content and variant combinations), then the remaining 60 percent will see the original content and will not be considered in the results. Thus, in a test containing the original content plus three variants—a total of four variations a visitor could see—each variation will get about 25 percent of the traffic exposed to the test (40 percent × 25 percent = 10 percent of the total traffic to the site).

The 60 percent of visitors not exposed to the test won't be counted as impressions to the testing script. The testing script will set a cookie that tells the Google server not to include this visitor in the test, now or on a future visit. When and if any of those 60 percent reach the conversion page, the conversion script will not find an appropriately set cookie and thus won't count such conversions in the conversion totals.

Testing Less Than 100 Percent of Traffic

Testing against less than 100 percent of your traffic is helpful if you have a lot of traffic and you're testing something that might cause a decrease in conversion. So, only part of the traffic is exposed to the change, thus "shielding" the base conversion rate of the remaining traffic until the test is complete and you have your results.

In our experience, though, your best default plan is to test 100 percent of your traffic, because you'll accumulate enough traffic sooner to see statistically valid results, if any. If you expose only half your traffic to testing, it will take twice as long to get the same amount of tested traffic before you can call the experiment complete.

Having just advised you to use 100 percent traffic tests for normal testing, let's diverge a bit so you can understand a case in which you would prefer to dedicate less than 100 percent of your traffic.

Suppose your current conversion rate is significantly better than your industry average and you have enough traffic volume to allow a shorter testing period. You have an innovative idea you'd like to test but not a lot of evidentiary support—yet. You also don't want to risk a dramatic drop in conversion. That's the nice thing about being "in the lead" (that is, having a great relative conversion rate and being a market share leader): You get to play defense by exposing less of your core money-generating traffic to as yet unproven improvements.

In such a case, you might consider "staging" your way into a significant test: Perhaps test 10 percent of the traffic using the new, innovative idea; run the test for some short, minimum amount of time (a week or two), just to get enough traffic for a sense of overall direction; and then report those results to your team so you can come up with a plan for testing the idea across more of your traffic. This is the same reasoning large food chains adopt when they introduce new products into smaller test markets first; it allows them to judge how well the product might do in a wider release.

How Long Should Testing Last?

Often people who come to your site on the weekend act differently from those who come during the week. Perhaps some folks prefer to do their browsing on the weekend but their buying during the week. Or it's vice versa if they can get away with spending lots of time online while at the office.

As such, the minimum time you should ever run a test is a week, even if your site gets enough traffic for statistically valid results within days. Two weeks would be even better. That's another argument for testing less than 100 percent of your traffic, so as to spread it out over a slightly longer period. You're looking for a fair balance between rushing to complete the test vs. enough time over which the test occurs to factor out the effects of traffic spikes and weekly cycles.

What's "too long" to run a test? So much of the correct answer has to do with what you're testing, how much traffic your test will get, and the impact it will have on your visitors. But it is worth noting that if you've run the test for a while and have gotten enough traffic—we'll go out on a limb here and give a rough figure of "six weeks" and "at least several thousand impressions"—darn, we can already envision the email feedback we're about to be blasted with for suggesting such numbers—then maybe it's fair to remind yourself of what your goals are.

If you still aren't seeing any statistically significant impact from the test, positive *or* negative, then for goodness sake, consider rethinking your test. Now, positive impact is a wonderful thing, especially for your wallet. Negative impact isn't bad either—it proves you're influencing visitors, and it will confirm your approach is not all wrong (maybe you have the variables right about what to test but goofed a little on which variations to test), and it will most definitely suggest inspiration for future testing. But no impact? It begs the question, "Do I really need to be testing something that has no impact? Isn't that the same as just leaving stuff the way it was?" In other words, what's your return on testing?

Your goal is to improve. If you're not doing that, ask yourself what assumptions you made in the test that might be factored out by running an improved test. Or leave the test running but also fire up the next most important test on your campaign (on a different part of your website) and use this time effectively. You're not trying to experimentally measure the value of pi to 800 digits; you're looking to improve conversion, add to your company's top line, and learn what works. If you're not doing that with the current test, consider moving on to another test.

Think of it this way. Suppose your next test gives you a 10 percent lift to conversion, and that lift translates into $10,000 more sales per week for your company. Then running the first nonimpact test for 10, 12, 16 extra weeks, when clearly it was going nowhere after 6, means your opportunity cost is $100,000. You have sacrificed more in lost revenues than you otherwise would have enjoyed by moving on earlier. That sure is an expensive "nonimpact"!

And, please, don't use this as an excuse for not letting the test run long enough. Let it run as long as it needs to achieve impact, but no longer.

Modifying the Weight of Each Combination in the Testing Sample

We've discussed the relative merits of dedicating all or a portion of your traffic to a test. An astute reader might note the previous example discussed four variations for a test and each variation received approximately 1 out of 4 (or 25 percent) of the test traffic. What if the goal were to have some variations receive more traffic than others? Can Website Optimizer do this?

Unfortunately, out of the box, Website Optimizer can't accommodate this. It will randomly assign traffic to variations in approximately equal quantity. There are some hacks floating around the Internet that would let you change that weighting, but these are beyond the scope of this book. (We think everyone should encourage Ophir Prusak to write a book on advanced Website Optimizer hacking!)

In the meantime, if you wanted to experiment with this concept a bit, you could just create more variants that are actually identical to some other variants and thus increase the relative weight of that variant in the test. Suppose, for example, that you want a certain variation—let's say variation B—to receive half the overall test traffic. You could expand the variations from their current count of four (A-B-C-D), wherein each got 25 percent of the traffic, to a count of six (A-B-C-D-E-F), where each received $1/6 =$ 16.7 percent of the traffic. But since you, the experimenter, create the variations, you could easily make E and F look the same as B, effectively creating A-B-C-D-B-B, and now the Bs are getting 3×16.7 percent $= 50$ percent of the traffic.

Of course, Website Optimizer will still report these as separate variations, so this is at best a workaround and at worst a hack, and either way you'll still have to add the results together by hand. Overall, that's inconvenient, but a little ingenuity will go a long way with the versatile Website Optimizer tool.

Testing for Key User Events (Clicks and Submits)

When Website Optimizer launched, Google realized it was a fairly new concept and it would take a while for the public to become accustomed to testing. Usually we talk about a test page and a conversion page, but in reality, we can consider these more generally as a "test event" (such as "visitor viewed the test page") and a "conversion event" ("visitor viewed the conversion page"). This lines up nicely with Persuasion Architecture's concept of persuasion events and conversion events, and we thank Ophir Prusak for the use of the term *test event* to describe a persuasive event undergoing testing. And, happily, Website Optimizer is technically capable of testing for events as easily as it tests for pages and sections of content.

Since it's a very simple JavaScript that describes and records a test view and a conversion view, it is extremely easy to attach this script so Website Optimizer can call upon it when the event, such as a click or a submit (from a form), occurs in the browser. Basically, any event JavaScript can capture is immediately available to be tested, either as the test event or as the conversion event.

So, there's really no difference between an "on click" event compared to an "on submit" event. JavaScript can capture any of these events, which can be mapped to call the test script or the conversion script.

Using a Timer to Fire Off a Conversion

You could use a timer to see whether visitors stay on a page for a certain amount of time. Suppose your definition of a conversion (really, a "mini-conversion") is "visitors who stay on my page for at least 30 seconds." The test script would be set up to fire as soon as the page loads, much as it does for any standard testing with Website Optimizer. The conversion script would be called on the same page as soon as a JavaScript timer function has counted off 30 seconds. And suddenly, you can experiment with key events in the persuasive process intrapage.

You can look in Google's advanced documentation for Website Optimizer for tips on how to slightly modify the existing testing and conversion scripts so they can be called by

JavaScript functions. This is one of those things your IT department will know how to do right away, as soon as they read up on it.

Testing Flash Video Events

Suppose you were testing some Flash video you had embedded in your pages and you wanted to run some tests only for those visitors who watched the video all the way through. You could set the testing script to be called only at the end of the Flash movie (which fires off an event that JavaScript can capture), and thus the test would be running only for visitors who watched the entire video. Some interesting ideas for segmentation testing come up: What's the conversion rate among visitors who started watching the movie vs. those who saw the movie all the way through? Who skipped the movie altogether?

Stacking Events

It's also possible to stack events together, that is, to make the calling of the testing or conversion scripts dependent on multiple key events you determine should occur. Suppose you want to test not only how many visitors make a purchase, but also how many visitors bought a shopping cart up-sell item. You just bought a dozen roses for your sweetheart, and now we offer you a crystal vase to put them in.

On low-traffic sites, if you measure conversion only by actual purchases, it may take a long time to build up enough testing traffic if the only criterion is that a single product was sold. But if you were optimizing the scenario that leads up to the visitor putting the item in the cart and then responding to the up-sell, you'd want to record both those events to count it as a "full" conversion. By having the add-to-cart event record a variable (say, a session cookie), which later, during checkout, could be used by yet another JavaScript function to determine whether the up-sell occurred, you could begin to run tests on things such as "What was the conversion rate of those who bought roses versus those who bought roses and the vase?" The variations are endless.

Explore the Bleeding Edge (If You Dare)

A number of hacks to Website Optimizer's scripts are available on the Internet that let you interface and share data between Website Optimizer and Google Analytics. A treatment of this topic is beyond the scope of this book and really is for a more technical audience. But we are mentioning they're available because this opens up a world of possibilities for melding Google Analytics' goals functionality with Website Optimizer's ability to test. The best way to learn is to experiment, so set up a sandbox site with an extra domain name you have hanging around and see what Website Optimizer can let you do. The great thing about a sandbox is that you can explore new ideas and learn something, armed with nothing more than the willingness to be wrong.

Nothing Takes the Place of Planning

What we would like you to do is think. When you consider doing a test, spend time truly thinking about the test. If you've done an A/B test of button colors red/green/lime (OK, that's really an A/B/C test, but you know what we mean), do you really know how to interpret the difference between the red results vs. the green and lime results? Aren't green and lime a little too closely related to really know how one differs from the other, at least vis-à-vis red? Might it not be better to test red vs. green and then test forest green vs. lime green?

In the context of multivariate testing, it might make sense to run a test of button colors and button shapes to determine what combination of color and shape is most effective, but what about adding a third variable such as 3D shading? Would you be better off testing the major factors affecting the button (color, shape) first and then considering the expected minor effect of shading? We would be suspicious of reported results that showed 3D shading had a huge impact on one combination of color and shape but little impact on its component pieces, especially if a smaller test of color vs. shape showed a different combination winner.

Again, make your tests worthy of testing by valuing your own resources and your own ability to know what's right for your business. Don't just throw everything up against the testing wall and see what sticks. Use your own knowledge of your business to inform your testing.

CHAPTER 46

Website Optimizer's Plug-in for WordPress

Individuals and businesses incorporating WordPress blogs and pages in their online initiatives can now use a third-party plug-in to insert the tracking codes required to test headlines, copy, images, and forms to determine which content drives the best conversion rates. We (FutureNow) developed this plug-in in coordination with Content Robot; the plug-in is in no way affiliated with Google.

Blogging, originally the arena of personal journalists and social networking, is becoming an important activity in promoting business goals, especially through word-of-mouth marketing. But how do you really know whether the content you include on your blog is persuading people to do what you want them to do on your site? This plug-in for WordPress lets you test your blog sections exactly as Website Optimizer lets you test your website:

- The plug-in allows users to insert Google experiment code into the header and body of any blog post or page.
- The plug-in uses WordPress custom fields to add the code correctly.

Will It Work on Your WordPress Blog?

To use the WordPress plug-in, you must have a Website Optimizer account. The current version at the time of this writing—version 0.2—works with WordPress 2.*x* and later. If you are running WordPress version 2.0.*x*, you must patch `/wp-includes/functions-formatting.php` to fix this WordPress bug. If you do not apply the patch, any parentheses will be converted to the HTML equivalent (`#8221;`) and will cause Website Optimizer's section scripts to fail. This bug has been fixed in WordPress 2.1.*x*.

Installing the Plug-in

To install the plug-in, follow these steps:

1. Download Website Optimizer's plug-in `.zip` file from `http://websiteoptimizer.contentrobot.com`.

2. Extract the `google-website-optimizer-for-wordpress` directory, and upload the entire directory and its contents to your server's `wp-content/plugins` directory.

3. Go to your WordPress administration area, click Plugins, and activate the plug-in called "Google Website Optimizer for WordPress."

What to Do Before Using the Plug-in

Before you begin using Website Optimizer's plug-in for WordPress, you'll want to run through this checklist:

- Make sure you have a Google account. (This is the same account you use for other Google services, such as Gmail.)

- Determine which sections you will test—these can include a headline, image, or paragraphs of text.

- Prepare alternate content for each test section.

- Make sure you disable the WYSIWYG editor in WordPress. In the administration area, under My Account, uncheck Use the Visual Editor When Writing. Switching between the Visual and Code tabs in 2.1.*x* (and greater) WYSIWYG editor will not work—you need to disable this function.

- If you are running WordPress 2.0.*x*, make sure you've applied the patch mentioned earlier.

Detailed Setup Instructions for Website Optimizer

In the following sections, we'll go through the step-by-step procedure for setting up and launching a Website Optimizer experiment through WordPress. Please note that at the time of the printing of this book, Website Optimizer only recently left beta status, so you may see a slightly different Website Optimizer interface when you visit the site. All the steps, however, are the same, and Website Optimizer continues to work seamlessly with other Google business-solution platforms.

To access Website Optimizer, log in with the email and password you use for all other Google services that require basic registration (such as Gmail).

Create Your First Experiment

To create your first experiment, follow these steps:

1. Click the Create a New Experiment link. (It may also say Create Another Experiment if you already have created other experiments.)

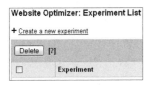

2. When prompted to select the type of experiment, select the multivariate experiment.

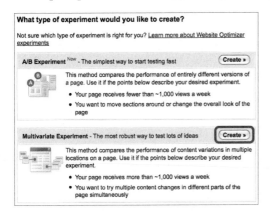

3. Click the Go button to identify the experiment pages.

Step 1: Set Up Test and Goals Pages

To set up your test and goals pages, follow these steps:

1. Give your experiment a name.

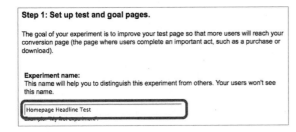

2. Enter the URL of your test page.

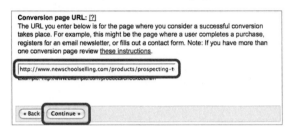

3. Enter the URL of your conversion page and then click the Continue button.

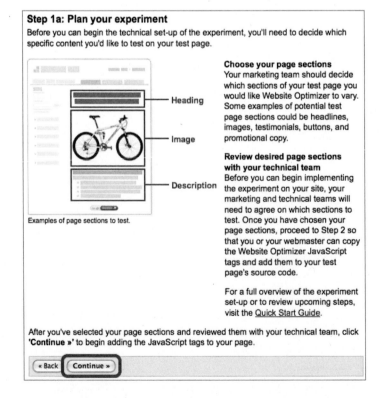

Step 1a: Plan Your Experiment

In this section, you decide which page sections you'd like to experiment with on your test page. You will not be entering data here; just click the Continue button to proceed to the next step.

Step 2: Add JavaScript Tags to Experiment Pages

To add JavaScript tags to experiment pages, follow these steps:

1. Select the "I will be installing the tags on my website" option.

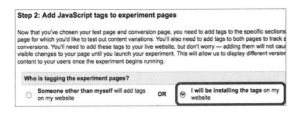

2. Copy the JavaScript Control script for the test page.

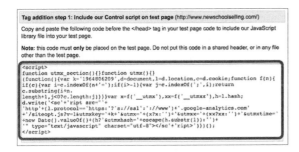

Step 2a: Switch to Your Blog's WordPress Administration Area

To switch to your blog's WordPress administration area, follow these steps:

1. Navigate to the page you want to test by clicking Manage → Pages (or Posts).

2. Locate the post/page in the list, and click its Edit link under the Action area.

3. Within the test page post, scroll down to the Custom Fields area (if necessary, press the + key to open).

   a. Type **go_control_script** in the Key field.

   b. Paste the JavaScript Control script you copied earlier into the Value field.

c. Click the Add Custom Field button.

4. Scroll up to the Page Content area, and add the Section script around the test copy.

a. Before the test copy, add the following code:

```
<script>utmx_section("Headline")</script>
```

Note: In our example, the text `"Headline"` is the section descriptor. You should change this to something appropriate for your test section.

b. After the test copy, add the code </noscript>.

Step 2b: Return to Website Optimizer

Copy the JavaScript Tracking script for the test page.

Tag addition step 3: Install Tracking script on test page (http://www.newschoolselling.com/)

You need to add these specific tags in order for the experiment to track visits to the test page correctly.

Click to select the Tracking script below, then copy and paste it before the </body> tag on the test page.

```
<script>
if(typeof(urchinTracker)!='function')document.write('<sc'+'ript src="'+
'http'+(document.location.protocol=='https:'?'s://ssl':'://www')+
'.google-analytics.com/urchin.js'+'"></sc'+'ript>')
</script>
<script>
_uacct = 'UA-420387-3';
urchinTracker("/1964806209/test");
</script>
```

Step 2c: Return to the Test Post You Are Editing in WordPress

1. Scroll down to the Custom Fields area again.

a. Type **go_tracking_script_test** in the Key field.

b. Paste the JavaScript Tracking script you copied earlier into the Value field.

c. Click the Add Custom Field button.

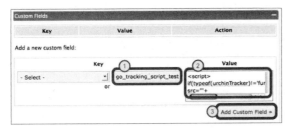

2. Scroll up, and click the Save button to save your changes.

Step 2d: Return to Website Optimizer

Copy the JavaScript Tracking script for the conversion page.

Step 2e: Return to Your Blog's WordPress Administration Area

Follow these steps:

1. Navigate to your conversion page by clicking Manage → Pages (or Posts).

2. Locate the page in the list, and click its Edit link under Action.

3. Within the conversion page post, scroll down to Custom Field area.

a. Type **go_tracking_script_conversion** in the Key field.

b. Paste the JavaScript you copied earlier into the Value field.

    c. Click the Add Custom Field button.

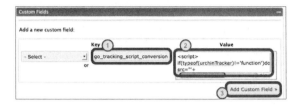

4. Scroll up, and click the Save button to save your changes.

Step 2f: Return to Website Optimizer to Validate Your Code

Follow these steps:

1. Click the Check Tags on Pages button.

2. If you have errors, retrace your steps. If there are no errors, click the Save and Continue button.

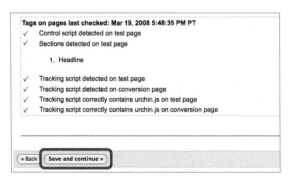

Step 3: Create Variations

To create variations, follow these steps:

1. You will see that the original text has been added automatically. To add a variation, click the Add New Variation link.

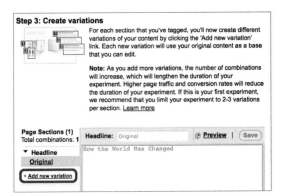

2. Enter the variation name, and click the Add button.

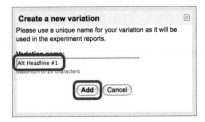

3. Enter the new variation text, and then click the Save and Continue button to proceed to the next step. (Note: If you want to create more than one variation, you can click the Save button instead of the Save and Continue button; then repeat the earlier steps for each variation.)

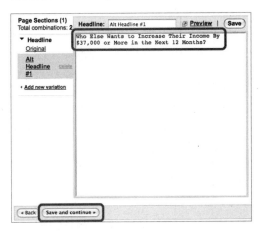

Step 4: Review Experiment Settings and Launch

To review the experiment settings and launch the test, follow these steps:

1. Review the settings. You can view a preview by clicking the Preview link. If everything looks good, click the Launch Now button to activate the experiment.

Your test is now running.

2. You are ready to track the experiment via the Report area. (Note: It may take some time for the first data to appear.)

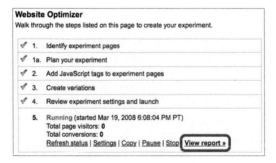

Creating Additional Experiments

When you create subsequent experiments, you do not need to reenter the WordPress keys (go_control_script, go_tracking_script_test, go_tracking_script_conversion)—just use the drop-down menu to select the appropriate fields and to paste the appropriate JavaScript code in the Value area.

Useful Resources

This appendix contains useful resources to further your study of the topics covered in this book.

Analytics and Testing

Testing Toolbox (www.testingtoolbox.com) The official website of *Always Be Testing* contains additional resources and services to help you manage and improve your testing efforts.

MarketingSherpa (www.marketingsherpa.com) MarketingSherpa is a research firm specializing in tracking what works in all aspects of marketing (and what does not). It conducts and publishes case studies and surveys, and undertakes exclusive lab as well as partnered research. In addition to being a valuable resource for conversion rate marking, MarketingSherpa offers information on what to test from the perspective that you should never accept the results of others as gospel.

Blogs

GrokDotCom by FutureNow (www.grokdotcom.com) GrokDotCom is FutureNow's (www.futurenowinc.com) slightly irreverent online conversion rate blog and newsletter for managers, entrepreneurs, and investors, and it covers topics including web design, optimization, sales, marketing, copywriting, usability, SEO, relationship marketing, consumer psychology, and much more. The original newsletter, written by Lisa T. Davis and published by Bryan Eisenberg, began in 2000, and five years later was transformed into a comprehensive blog of articles, posts, and announcements written by the Future-Now team. It is also a monitoring resource for thousands of other blogs related to the industry.

Prusak.com: Online Since 1996 (www.prusak.com) Ophir Prusak writes about hacking Website Optimizer and Google Analytics so they can handle more complicated and interesting aspects of testing, measuring, and optimizing.

Occam's Razor by Avinash Kaushik (www.kaushik.net/avinash/) Avinash writes as a Google Web Analytics Evangelist about testing and web analytics.

Website Optimizer (http://websiteoptimizer.blogspot.com) The official Google Website Optimizer blog.

Books

Call to Action **by Bryan Eisenberg, Jeffrey Eisenberg, and Lisa T. Davis; hardcover edition (Wizard Academy Press, 2005), paperback edition (Thomas Nelson, 2006)** *Call to Action* is a primer for conversion tactics FutureNow has developed in the course of 10 years. It also offers conversion tips from specialists in the field of conversion rate marketing.

Web Analytics: An Hour a Day **by Avinash Kaushik (Sybex/Wiley, 2007)** Avinash offers a step-by-step guide to implementing a successful web analytics strategy, debunks leading myths, and leads you on a path to gaining actionable insights from your analytics efforts.

Landing Page Optimization: The Definitive Guide to Testing and Tuning for Conversions **by Tim Ash (Sybex/Wiley, 2008)** Tim's book focuses on optimizing your landing pages and teaches you the skills necessary to identify mission-critical parts of your website and their true economic value, define important visitor classes and key conversion tasks, gain insight on customer decision-making, uncover problems with your page and decide which elements to test, develop an action plan, and avoid common pitfalls.

Advanced Web Metrics with Google Analytics **by Brian Clifton (Sybex/Wiley, 2008)** Google insider and web metrics expert Brian Clifton reveals how to get a true picture of your site's impact and stay competitive using Google Analytics and the latest web metrics methodologies.

General Links to Key Topics

As you well know, there's so much information on the Web that finding the right information, even among a stack of almost-right web search results, can be time-consuming. The following are several links to material we've found to be particularly helpful with respect to testing:

Wikipedia: mean and standard deviation (http://en.wikipedia.org/wiki/Mean and http://en.wikipedia.org/wiki/Standard_deviation/)

Wikipedia: confidence intervals and margin of error (http://en.wikipedia.org/wiki/Margin_of_error/)

Wikipedia: binomial distribution (http://en.wikipedia.org/wiki/Binomial_distribution/)

Google Documentation and Support

Google offers a wide range of support should be for Website Optimizer, including videos, webinars, documentation, a user forum, and a certified consultants program (in which capacity FutureNow is honored to participate). The following are several links to material we've found to be particularly helpful:

Website Optimizer Forum (http://groups.google.com/group/websiteoptimizer/)

Website Optimizer Help Center (www.google.com/support/websiteoptimizer/)

Website Optimizer Technical Overview (www.google.com/support/websiteoptimizer/bin/answer.py?hl=en&answer=61146)

Other Publications by the FutureNow Team

Discovering Fusebox **by John Quarto-vonTivadar, et al. (Techspedition Press, 2005;** www.techspedition.com) Sometimes the simple act of having a regularized approach to a problem gives you a platform for testing and experimentation, including architecting your website. Fusebox is a lightweight framework for website development originally evangelized by Hal Helms, John Quarto-vonTivadar, and others for ColdFusion that found wide adoption in other languages. What we find useful about this book is that even a passing knowledge of key development concepts can help you "talk the talk" with your IT staff and thereby bring your technology team into your emerging culture of testing. It also means you can do more independent experiments, perhaps on microsites, to gain insight for more substantial tests on your main business site.

Persuasive Online Copywriting **by Bryan Eisenberg, Jeffrey Eisenberg, and Lisa T. Davis (Wizard Academy Press, 2002, out of print)** Written early in the life of FutureNow, this exposition on creating writing that supports the critical persuasion mission of e-business continues to provide an important perspective on developing copy in an online environment.

The Soccer Mom Myth **by Michele Miller and Holly Buchanan (Wizard Academy Press, 2008)** Michele and Holly give marketers a wake-up call about who today's female consumer really is, how she really thinks, and why she really buys both online and offline. In their pointed, humorous, on-target way, they kick the Soccer Mom myth to the sidelines and help businesses learn how to market to women in a way that translates into more customers and bigger profits.

Waiting for Your Cat to Bark? **by Bryan Eisenberg, Jeffrey Eisenberg, and Lisa T. Davis (Thomas Nelson, 2006)** *Waiting for Your Cat to Bark?* examines the implications for the field of marketing in our evolving "experience economy." It discusses in depth the valuable role of persuasion in designing websites that take conversion rate marketing beyond the tactical techniques addressed in *Call to Action.*

Index

Note to Reader: **Bold** page numbers indicate definitions and main discussions of a topic. *Italic* page numbers indicate illustrations.

Q